Cassell's Colloquial German

A HANDBOOK OF IDIOMATIC USAGE

Completely revised by
Beatrix Anderson and Maurice North

Formerly *Beyond the Dictionary in German*

CASSELL

Cassell Publishers Ltd
Villiers House, 41/47 Strand
London WC2N 5JE

First edition 1968
Revised edition 1980
Reprinted 1982, 1987, 1989, 1991
This edition 1993

ISBN 0 304 07941 3

Printed and bound in Finland

Contents

Preface

The present volume has been kept to the basic pattern of the other books in the series and the German–English section forms the main portion. In the Miscellaneous Notes an attempt has been made to deal with some important points of grammar and usage within the limited space. To save space most of the words in the Special Vocabularies have not been repeated in the main German–English section. A knowledge of the fundamental grammar and a fairly advanced vocabulary have been assumed to be already in the reader's possession.

There is no bad slang in the book; the words and phrases are standard colloquial German and although some may be a little racy they can all be safely used save where there is an indication to take care. Hackneyed proverbs and *Redensarten* have been excluded. Readers will note with relief the absence of a section on 'Disconcerting Genders', there is only one important example of such in German (v. *Weib*).

Literal translations have been avoided except where really necessary and an attempt has been made to find an English equivalent in meaning and tone; where this has not been possible, an explanation has been given as no useful purpose is served by a misleading or inexact translation and this is the main reason why no English–German has been provided for the 'Food and Dishes' section.

It is hoped that the book will prove useful to those who travel in Germany on business or pleasure and those who study the language for its own sake; if it helps to guard against misinterpretations and gives some information on current usage it will have served its purpose.

The authors wish to acknowledge their debt to Brigitte Kämmer for her invaluable help and to Nina North for her constant encouragement.

Preston Polytechnic
March, 1980

BEATRIX ANDERSON
MAURICE NORTH

Miscellaneous Notes

Pronunciation. German, in spite of the popular views on it, is, when spoken properly, an elegant, expressive and forceful language with a cadence all of its own and a sound that few would dare to describe as displeasing. Regional accents are numerous and while there is little social pressure to eliminate them, they are usually unobtrusive when present in the speech of educated Germans; education weakens the regional accent in Germany as elsewhere. There is a kind of neutral 'standard' German, comparable with 'BBC English' and used mainly in the theatre and on radio and television, called *Bühnensprache* but the man in the street does not usually imitate it.

The Bavarian accent seems to cause non-Bavarian Germans the same sort of amusement as broad Lancashire gives to southern Englishmen. The hard *-ch* after *e* and *i*, which characterizes the Austrian and the Swiss, sounds foreign to most Germans, which is rather unfortunate as it is the accent that many English people learn because it seems easier for them; it is, of course, no more 'incorrect' than any other regional accent.

Contemporary Trends. Because of its complexities of grammar, German is not easy for the native speaker and grammatical mistakes are quite common in everyday speech. Many of these have become so much part of the language that they are no longer condemned as mistakes but are referred to as 'colloquialisms' or 'modern usage', as it is expected that sooner or later they will replace the original forms. Typical of the above is the use of the dative instead of the genitive after prepositions such as *wegen*, and the use of indicative or conditional forms

5

where the present or past subjunctives are required. These 'colloquialisms' are still frowned upon by purists, but a good example of one that has become completely accepted is the use of *sich* instead of *einander* as long as no misunderstanding can arise; what used to be *sie schrieben einander* is now *sie schrieben sich* 'they wrote to one another'.

Another modern tendency, which is also accepted even by purists but creates some confusion, is the elimination of various rules regarding capital letters; for example, nouns are nowadays mostly spelt with a small letter when they are used in a stock combination: *in bezug auf* 'with reference to'; *jemandem angst machen* 'to frighten somebody'; *etwas außer acht lassen* 'to disregard something'; the same applies to adjectival nouns in such combinations, e.g. *den kürzeren ziehen* 'to lose', 'to be at a disadvantage'; *im reinen sein mit* 'to be in the clear with'. Confusion arises when one is forced to decide whether the phrase in question is an accepted standard combination or not, and as opinions may vary so the use of a small or capital letter may vary considerably from one person to another. In time, new rules will probably be formulated and bring order into what at the moment is often not a question of grammar but a matter of personal taste.

Special Use of Comparative Forms. There are a number of comparative forms which assume a new meaning when not used as such, and Germans are rather fond of this construction. Adjectives which are commonly used in this way are *nahe* (near, close), *gut* (good), *lang* (long), *kurz* (short), *groß* (large), *klein* (small), *jung* (young), *alt* (old), *stark* (strong, corpulent), *schwach* (weak), and the meaning of the comparative form approximates that of '-ish' or '-ly': *ein jüngerer Mann* 'a youngish man', *ein älterer Mann* 'an elderly man'.

Transitive and Intransitive Verbs. There are a number of

German verbs which may be used transitively and intransitively, and it is important to differentiate between the two uses as only the transitive verb has a regular past tense and past participle. One of these verbs is *hängen* 'to hang'; 'I hung my coat in the cupboard' is *ich hängte meinen Mantel in den Schrank* or *ich habe meinen Mantel in den Schrank gehängt* whereas the intransitive 'the coat was hanging (hung) in the cupboard' is *der Mantel hing in dem Schrank* or *hat in dem Schrank gehangen*. Another verb of this type is *erschrecken* which is *erschreckte, erschreckt* when it means 'to frighten' someone else and *erschrak, erschrocken* in the sense of 'to be frightened' oneself; *stecken* 'to stick' is *steckte, gesteckt* transitively e.g. *ich steckte es in meine Tasche* 'I stuck (put) it in my pocket' and *stak, gesteckt* when it means 'to be' e.g. *es stak in seiner Tasche* 'it was in his pocket'.

This can also be taken as a general rule in the far commoner case of the transitive and intransitive verbs being derived from the same stem such as *legen* (*legte, gelegt*) 'lay' and *liegen* (*lag, gelegen*) 'lie', *stellen* (*stellte, gestellt*) 'put' and *stehen* (*stand, gestanden*) 'stand', *setzen* (*setzte, gesetzt*) 'put' and *sitzen* (*saß, gesessen*) 'sit' etc.

Separable and Inseparable Verbs. It is easy to distinguish between the purely separable and the purely inseparable verbs: when a prefix has a meaning on its own (e.g. is a preposition: *ab, an, auf*, an adjective: *fest, gleich, voll*, or a noun: *Teil, Not, Acht*) it is separable; a mere prefixed syllable (e.g. *be-, er-, ent-, ge-, miß-, ver-, zer-*) is inseparable.

As the separable prefix qualifies the meaning of the verb it is accorded the main accent in speaking; the inseparable prefix helps create a completely new word often far removed in significance from the original so there is no stress on the prefix.

Difficulties arise from the fact that some prefixes are

used separably as well as inseparably. They are: *durch* 'through', *um* 'round' 'about', *unter* 'under', *über* 'over' 'across', *voll* 'full', *wieder* 'again' and, though rare, *wider* 'against' 'counter' and *hinter* 'behind'. A guiding rule for these is: when used in their literal significance they are separable (and have the main accent in speaking); when used figuratively they are inseparable (and not stressed). Some examples:

Separable		Inseparable	
durch-	'to look through'	*durch-*	'to see through'
schauen	(a book, window)	**schauen**	(a pretence)
wieder-		*wieder-*	
holen	'to get back'	**holen**	'to repeat'
um*reißen*	'to pull down'	*um***reißen**	'to outline'
über*setzen*	'to ferry over'	*über***setzen**	'to translate'
über*stehen*	'to stick out'	*über***stehen**	'to survive'

Verbal Nouns. In English there is only one verbal noun, e.g. 'the singing' and the corresponding German form is *das Singen*. German has, however, two other verbal noun forms and they are extremely common in everyday speech. One is obtained by prefixing *Ge-* and leaving out the *-n* of the infinitive: *das Gesinge*; the other by leaving out the *-n* and adding *-rei* or, if the stem ends in a consonant, *-ei*: *die Singerei, die Quengelei* (*quengeln* 'to whine', 'to wrangle'). Both forms contain a slight note of condescension or annoyance 'all that singing' or 'that silly singing' so that care should be taken when using them.

Compound Nouns. A compound usually consists of two or three components and always acquires the gender of its last component. But as it can be formed at will and Germans are so fond of coining new compounds at a moment's notice that it might well be described as a national sport, you may easily encounter words consisting of five parts or more; to understand such creations you will have to consider each individual element: the compound *Fernsehgerät* (n *-e*) is made up of *fern* 'far', *sehen* 'to see', and *Gerät* 'instrument', 'apparatus'. An exhibition of television sets would become *eine Fernsehgeräteschau* and if they happened to be colour TV sets the word *Farbfernsehgeräteschau* would not strike a German ear as long or clumsy; even referring to the manager of the exhibition as the *Farbfernsehgeräteschauleiter* would raise no frown or comment.

There is only one difficulty about forming compound nouns and even Germans do not master this completely as there is no specific rule. In some cases, an *-s* is added to one of the component nouns; usually with nouns ending in *-tum, -ing, -ling, -heit, -keit, -schaft, -ung, -ion,* and *-tät;* also with the words *die Armut* 'poverty' (*Armuts—*), *die Liebe* 'love' (*Liebes—*), *die Hilfe* 'help' (*Hilfs—*), *die Geschichte* 'story' or 'history' (*Geschichts—*) and with infinitives used as nouns, e.g. *lesenswert* 'worth reading' (derived from *des Lesens wert*), *Schlafenszeit* 'bedtime' etc.

When by coupling words a consonant is tripled, one of the consonants is omitted (except when the word is carried over from one line to the next and hyphenated): *das Bett-tuch* becomes *das Bettuch* 'sheet'.

German–English

A

ab. 'Off', 'away from'. In colloquial German the verb conjugated with the prefix *ab* is often omitted and only the *ab* remains: *Der Knopf ist ab* (*abgegangen, abgerissen*), 'The button has come off' or 'is missing'; *ich bin ab* (*abgespannt, abgearbeitet*), 'I'm worn out'. Note the 'from' and 'after' meanings in *Ich bin ab sechs zu erreichen,* 'You can get me from six onwards' and *Der Zug führt einen Speisewagen ab Frankfurt,* 'After Frankfurt the train has a dining car'.

abhängen. In colloquial usage it can mean 'to outdistance'. The intransitive form with *von* is frequent and like the English 'hinge on': *alles hing von seiner Entscheidung ab,* 'everything hinged on his decision'; *es hängt davon ab, ob* . . ., 'it depends on whether or not . . . .'.

Abhörgerat (n -e). A (hidden) microphone, a 'bug'.

abnehmen. Colloquially often means 'to believe': *das nehme ich Ihnen nicht ab,* 'I don't buy that'.

abreagieren. *Seinen Ärger abreagieren,* 'to let off steam', 'give vent to anger' and origin of the psycho-analytical 'abreact'.

abregen, sich. Opposite of *sich aufregen,* 'to become excited', thus 'to calm down'.

abschneiden. 'To cut off' but colloquially 'to do', 'to fare': *Wie hat er in der Prüfung abgeschnitten?* 'How did he do in the exam?'; *er hat ganz gut abgeschnitten,* 'he did quite well'. It can also mean 'to short-cut': *Zum Bahnhof sind es eigentlich zwanzig Minuten, aber wir können abschneiden,* 'It's actually twenty minutes to the station, but we can take a short cut'.

abschrammen. To 'scram', flee.

Absicht (f -en). 'Intention' and often heard in apologies: *Entschuldigung, das war keine Absicht!* 'Sorry, I didn't mean to . . .' (in the German phrase the actual discourtesy is not mentioned). *Mit Absicht* and *absichtlich,* 'on purpose'.

abspecken. Popular for 'to lose weight' by means of a diet. *Sie hat durch eine strenge Diät 20 kg abgespeckt,* 'She lost 20 kg by keeping to a strict diet'.

Accessoires (n -) (mostly in plural). Accessories, i.e. handbag, gloves,

11

shoes, belt, etc., to go with a woman's dress or coat.

Accrochage (f -n).   Strange importation from the French and meaning: 1. unexpected attack on an outpost (mil.), 2. clash between police and demonstrators, 3. an art exhibition composed of the work of more than one artist.

ach.   The meaning often depends on the tone of voice. It expresses surprise: *Ach, was Sie nicht sagen!* 'Really? You don't say!', *ach was! ach nein! ach nee!* 'is that so!'. Shock at something that has gone wrong or is unbelievable: *ach du liebe Zeit! ach du lieber Himmel! ach du grüne Neune!* 'good heavens!'. Compassion: *ach, wie schade!* 'oh, what a pity!', *ach je!* 'oh dear!'. Disappointed or belittling: *ach, du bist's,* 'oh, it's only you', *ach, gehen Sie weg,* 'oh, come off it' ('don't tell me that'), *ach was! ach wo!* 'of course not' and with a shrug 'why worry'. Emphasizing: *ach ja!* 'yes please', *ach, wie schön!* 'how very nice'. An introductory noise: *ach, sagen Sie mal . . .* 'I say, could you tell me . . .'. Finally *ach so* ('I see') which is very frequently used but the *-ch* is slurred as the stress is on the *so* and it sounds like 'ah-so'.

Achse (f -n).   *Auf Achse sein,* 'to be on the move'.

acht.   'Eight' but illogically indicates a week: *in acht Tagen,* 'in a week', *Sonntag in acht Tagen,* 'Sunday week' or 'next Sunday'.

achtkantig.   *Jemand achtkantig or hochkantig rauswerfen* is very emphatic for 'to throw somebody out'.

Advent (m -e).   The four weeks before Christmas. Families with children usually make a fuss about *Adventszeit* and almost every home has an *Adventskranz* (m ¨-e), a small wreath of fir branches with four coloured candles on it, one of which is lit ceremoniously on each of the four Sundays before Christmas. The family gathers round, sings *Adventslieder* and *Weihnachtslieder,* 'Christmas carols', eats homemade biscuits, *Plätzchen* (n.pl.) and the children are frightened by stories of the *Weihnachtsmann* (Father Christmas) who will carry them off in a sack if they are naughty. On 1 December, children are given an *Adventskalender* (m -) with twenty-four little numbered windows and they open these one a day; under each window is a little picture of some Christmassy event or object.

Ahnung (f -en).   Hardly ever used in its original sense of presentiment or misgiving (nowadays rendered by *Vorahnung*) but as 'idea' or 'notion': *ich habe keine blasse Ahnung . . .,* 'I haven't the faintest idea . . .'; *Er hat von Tuten und Blasen keine Ahnung,* 'He hasn't a clue about anything'. The verb *ahnen* can translate the English 'know' when there is foreboding or misgiving present: *ich hab's ja geahnt, daß etwas schiefgehen würde,* 'I just knew that something would go wrong'.

Akademiker (m -).   A person of university education; the word is used in the English sense of a 'don' and indicates some considerable degree of prestige. Professors are said to keep their students waiting at lectures for a quarter of an hour and *das akademische Viertel* is the time that an *Akademiker* can legitimately be late for an appointment. It is said that some professors even wait the required minutes outside their lecture rooms lest they be on time. *Die Vorstellung beginnt mit dem akademischen Viertel,* 'The performance begins a quarter of an hour late'.

Aktie (f -n). *Eine Aktie* is 'a share' in the capital of a business firm; *Aktionär* (m -e) or *Aktieninhaber* (m -) is a 'shareholder'. *Die Aktiengesellschaft* is the generic name for the many varieties of public and private 'joint-stock company', of which there are more types in Germany than Britain. The type is indicated by the standard abbreviation following the name, e.g. *AG, GmbH, oHG.* The nearest approach to the British 'Limited Company' is the *GmbH: Gesellschaft mit beschränkter Haftung. Das Aktienkapital* is 'the share capital' and *das Grundkapital* is 'the nominal capital', both can be reviewed at the annual general meeting of the shareholders, i.e. *die Hauptversammlung. Der Vorstand* is 'the board of directors' and *der Vorsitzende* 'the chairman', *der Geschäftsleiter* is 'the managing director'; *der Aufsichtsrat* is a special body without an English equivalent, composed of members elected partly by the shareholders and partly by the employees, which supervises and advises the *Vorstand.* The question *Wie stehen die Aktien?* only means 'How are things (going)?'

Aktion Sorgenkind. A nationwide drive that started about the time of the Thalidomide (Contergan) scandal, 'help for the disabled child'.

Aktualneurose (f -n). Neurosis brought about by real experience.

Alcotestverfahren (n -). Shortened to *Alcotest* (m -s), 'breathalyzer test', colloquially described as *ins Röhrchen pusten.*

alle. 'All' but its idiomatic uses are difficult; *alle sein* means 'to be finished', 'used up' and *alle werden,* 'to be coming to an end' (speaking of supplies). *Die Dummen werden nicht alle,* 'There is a sucker born every minute' literally 'the supply of fools never comes to an end'. *Er hat sie nicht mehr alle,* 'He isn't all there' ('he has a screw loose'). In some dialects *alls* is used to mean 'always'.

Alleingang (m). Used in the phrase *im Alleingang,* i.e. 'unilateral action'.

Allerwertester (adjectival noun). This used to be a form of address: *allerwertester Herr,* 'most worthy sir' but its contemporary use is a non-vulgar name for the human behind: *Er rutschte aus und setzte sich auf seinen Allerwertesten,* 'He slipped and landed on his behind'.

Alleskleber (m -). General colloquial name for 'glue'.

Allgemeinheiten (f.pl.). 'Platitudes' but in the singular 'general public'.

Alloplastik (f -en). Substitute for a part of the body but made from synthetic substances; 'bionic'.

Allrounder (m -). Never used in the English sense; it means a garment that can be worn on any occasion.

also. Does not mean 'also' but 'so'. There are many idiomatic uses: *Also ich fand es schön,* 'If you ask me (for my part) I found it beautiful'; *Also das war was!* 'That was something, I tell you'; *also gut,* 'well, all right' (hesitantly); *na also,* 'I told you so' (in self-satisfaction); *Also doch,* 'So I was right after all'.

Alwegbahn (f -en). Elevated mono-rail, named after its inventor Axel Wenner-Gren.

an. Not 'on' but usually 'at'. Colloquially it is used to form something approximating the English progressive tense: *ich bin am Nachdenken,* 'I am thinking'. This usage is popular but considered bad German; it is slightly more acceptable when the verb refers to a physical action: *ich bin am Lesen (Schreiben, Arbeiten usw.).*

anders. 'Different' and 'else'. Some useful and often heard phrases are: *Es ist nun mal nicht anders,* 'That's the way things are'; *am anderen Tag,* 'the next day'; *er ist alles andere als zuverlässig,* 'He is anything but reliable'; *es geht nicht anders,* 'there is no other way'; *anders rum* (coll.) or *anders herum* (High German), 'the other way about'. When meaning 'else' the modern form is *anders* except with *etwas*: *etwas anderes,* 'something else' but *etwas anders,* 'slightly different'. *Woanders* (coll.), 'somewhere else' is in High German *anderswo.*

Anhieb, auf. 'At the first shot', 'right off the bat'.

ankommen. *Gut (schlecht) ankommen bei . . .* is 'to go down well (badly) with . . .', e.g. *der Film wird bei dem Publikum gut ankommen,* 'The film will go down well with the public'.
   Es kommt darauf an is like *es hängt davon ab,* 'it depends', but whereas the latter can only be used in complete sentences, the phrase *es kommt darauf an* can be a non-committal answer.

Anlage (f -n). Numerous meanings depending on the context: *die Anlagen, Grünanlagen,* 'public parks and gardens' in a town; *Fabrikanlagen,* 'factory' or 'plant'; *militärische Anlagen,* 'military installations'; *der Junge hat gute Anlagen,* 'the boy is talented'; *Anlagen* are 'enclosures' with a letter; *VW-Aktien sind eine gute Anlage,* 'Volkswagen shares are a good investment'.

anlegen. The verb *anlegen* has an idiomatic use when a shop assistant asks *wieviel wollen Sie anlegen?* 'How much are you thinking of spending?' Note the idiomatic *er hat es darauf angelegt, mich zu betrügen,* 'He is out to cheat me'.

Annonce (f -n). An 'advertisement' in a newspaper; the verb is *annoncieren* or *eine Annonce aufgeben*; *ein Inserat* and *eine*

Anzeige are other words for *Annonce* and the verbs are *inserieren, ein Inserat aufgeben, eine Anzeige aufgeben* (but not *anzeigen*).

Anschaffungsdarlehen (n -).   A loan made by a commercial bank to a customer to enable him to buy equipment, a house, a car, replace equipment, or build additions to a house, shop etc.

Anschluß (m ˝-(ss)e).   'Connection'. It can also mean 'company': *er sucht Anschluß,* 'he is looking for company'; and 'electric socket' or 'point': *Das Zimmer hat zwei Anschlüsse,* 'The room has two points'. *Im Anschluß daran* is 'after that', 'following that'.

ansehen.   'To look at'. *Ich werde es mir ansehen,* 'I'll have a look at it'. It can mean 'to tell by looking at': *Man sieht (es) ihm nicht an, daß er ein Polizist ist,* 'You couldn't tell by just looking at him that he's a policeman'. It expresses surprise in *Nun sieh mal einer an* (or just *sieh mal an*), *du bist also doch nicht in Köln,* 'So you're not in Cologne after all', or disbelief in *Sieh mal an, das hätte ich nicht gedacht!* 'You don't say, I shouldn't have thought so'.

Anstand (m).   'Good manners'; *Er hat keinen Anstand,* 'He has no manners' and the same is expressed by the colloquial *er hat keinen Benimm* (m) from *sich benehmen,* 'to behave'. *Anstandswauwau* (m -s) is colloquial for 'chaperone' and comes from *Anstandsdame* (f -n). *Anstandslos,* however, means 'without a word of protest or complaint': *Ich sagte dem Kellner, daß das Fleisch zäh sei, und er nahm es anstandslos zurück,* 'I told the waiter that the meat was tough and he took it away without a word'.

anstellen.   It has a colloquial meaning when used reflexively 'to behave' or 'go about' something: *Er stellt sich bei der Sache geschickt an,* 'He goes about this thing skilfully'; *Ach, stell dich nicht so an!* 'Don't make such a fuss', and it also means 'to queue up' in the reflexive form. The basic meaning of *anstellen* is 'to employ' or 'to give work to' and from it we have *ein Angestellter,* 'an employee' or 'clerk'.

anstoßen.   'To nudge' or 'knock against' and it is also 'to clink' or 'touch glasses in a toast', a very popular practice in Germany and obligatory on most social drinking occasions; it indicates bad manners, however, to touch glasses when they contain different drinks. The 'clinking' is usually accompanied by ritual phrases such as *Prost! Prosit! Zum Wohl! Auf Ihr Wohl!* all of which are about equivalent to 'cheers'. *Darauf wollen wir anstoßen!* 'Let's drink to that'.

antizyklische Wirtschaftspolitik (f -en).   Economic measures to mitigate the effects of cyclical booms and recessions.

antun.   Bad but colloquial to use this to mean 'to put on' clothes: *ich muß (mir) noch mein Kleid antun,* 'I still have to put my dress on'. *Sich etwas antun* is a common euphemism for 'to commit suicide' or 'try to commit suicide'.

Apartment, Appartement (n -s).   Small flat.

Appetitzügler (m -), **Appetithemmer** (m -).   A drug to diminish the desire for food.

April (m -s).   'April'; *jemand in den April schicken* means 'to make an April Fool of somebody' and is accompanied by cries of *April! April!* In recent years the custom has been much abused and has ceased to be funny when ambulances and fire-engines are unavailable because they are on fools' errands, and firemen have been known to go on strike as a protest against this stupidity. The newspapers contain extraordinary statements on 1 April and readers have to wait until the next day to know the true from the *Aprilscherz* (m -e) 'April joke'.

Arbeitgeberzeit, Arbeitnehmerzeit (f).   If a person's watch is slow one says *er hat Arbeitgeberzeit,* if it is fast, . . . *Arbeitnehmerzeit* (as the employer, *Arbeitgeber,* likes employees to stay late, and the employees, *Arbeitnehmer,* like to leave early).

arriviert.   Successful, experienced, capable.

Art (f -en).   Not 'art' but 'kind' or 'sort': *Es war eine Art Wohn-Schlafzimmer* 'It was a sort of bed-sitting-room'. It can also mean 'species' and the user must be careful in the plural: *Menschen aller Art,* 'all sorts of people' but *Menschen aller Arten,* 'people of all races'. Colloquially it means a way of doing something or behaving: *Das ist doch keine Art!* 'That's no way to behave'; *Er hat eine Art an sich, die mir nicht gefällt,* 'He has a way of doing things that I don't like'. *Aus der Art schlagen* is an idiom meaning 'to diverge from the expected' but not necessarily 'to degenerate' as some dictionaries say, e.g. in a family of fair heads a dark-haired boy could be described as being *aus der Art geschlagen* (and degeneracy is not implied).

Arzt (m ¨-e).   'Physician', 'doctor'; on name-plates G.P.s usually put *praktischer Arzt* and often add *Geburtshelfer* 'obstetrician'. Most name-plates also bear the words *alle Kassen,* short for *alle Krankenkassen,* which means that the doctor has been accepted by all the state-recognized health insurance schemes and can treat their patients besides his own private patients. *Facharzt* is a 'specialist' or 'consultant'. *Vertrauensarzt* or *Amtsarzt* is recognized by and responsible to the *Ortskrankenkasse* (local health insurance office); a patient is sent to him if there is an official query concerning his claim for sickness benefit. To get oneself certified unfit for work, the person *läßt sich krank schreiben* or *wird krank geschrieben.* The newspapers are full of stories of patients *gesund geschrieben* by *Amtsärzte* and then dying at work. This is probably much exaggerated as is the equally widespread belief that many people go to their *Hausarzt* 'family doctor' in order to get themselves certified unfit when they are quite well; the expression often heard in office and factory *krankfeiern* derives from this belief; *er feiert krank* has no English equivalent, it implies that the person may be taking a holiday pretending sickness. *Frauenarzt* is a 'gynaecologist'.

Atommüll (m -). Atomic waste.

Atomsperrvertrag (m -e). Nuclear non-proliferation treaty.

Aufenthaltsgenehmigung (f -en). Also *Aufenthaltserlaubnis* (f -se): residence permit for a foreigner.

aufgeben. 'To give up'; also 'to hand in' a letter, telegram etc., at the post office. (*v.* ANNONCE)

aufgekratzt. Colloquial when used as an adjective and describes a person who has come 'out of his shell' and is 'lively'.

aufgeschmissen. This is derived from *schmeißen* which is colloquial for *werfen* 'to throw' and indicates that the subject is 'thrown open to misfortune', thus *ich bin aufgeschmissen, wenn er nicht kommt,* 'I'm done for if he does not come'; it really means to be in a predicament if something does not happen as expected and always translates into an 'if not . . . then I'm . . .'.

Aufhänger (m -). 'Loop' on inside of collar for suspending clothes; colloquially a 'pretext' (for talking about a subject).

aufheben. 'To pick' or 'lift up' but in colloquial usage 'to keep'; *Heben Sie den Abschnitt gut auf,* 'Keep the counterfoil carefully'; *Dein Geheimnis ist bei mir gut aufgehoben,* 'Your secret is safe with me'. *Aufhebens* (n) is also common but means a 'fuss': *Machen Sie doch nicht so viel Aufhebens um die Sache,* 'Don't make such a fuss over the matter'.

Aufklärungsquote (f -n). The number of crimes solved annually by the police; *v.* also DUNKELZIFFER.

aufmüpfig. 'Rebellious', especially of young people.

Aufnahme (f -n). 'Reception'. *Herzlichen Dank für die freundliche Aufnahme,* is a way of saying 'thank you so much for your kind hospitality' as *Gastfreundlichkeit* (f -en), 'hospitality', is rarely used when speaking directly to your host but only to a third party. It also means 'photographic exposure' and 'snapshot' and is even an alternative to *Photographie* (f -n), and *Photo* (n -s) (these last two are often spelt with *f* instead of *ph* in modern German); *Großaufnahme,* 'close-up'.

aufpäppeln. Also *jemanden hochpäppeln,* 'to feed up (a sick person or animal)'.

aufpassen. 'To pay attention' or 'be careful'. So *passen Sie doch auf!* 'Watch where you're going' (when one is pushed in the street); also an introductory phrase preceding an explanation: *Passen Sie mal auf,* . . . 'Look here, . . .'.

aufputschen. To stimulate artificially, i.e. by drugs.

aufrappeln, sich. Also *sich hochrappeln,* 'to pick oneself up (slowly and with difficulty) after a fall', literal and figurative.

aufreißen. A vulgar common colloquialism for 'to find by luck or skill'. Used often about women (by men) but also for objects: *Wo hast Du denn das aufgerissen?* 'How did you manage to get hold of that?' A kind of serendipity.

aufsitzen. 'To mount (a horse)'; *jemandem* or *etwas* (dat.) *aufsitzen,* 'to be deceived by someone or something', e.g. *Sie ist ihm aufgesessen,* 'She's let herself be deceived by him'; but *Er hat sie aufsitzen lassen,* 'He's left her in the lurch'.

auftragen. *Er hat mir etwas für Sie aufgetragen,* 'He's given me a message for you'. The verb also refers to clothing particularly underwear 'making itself known' as in *dicke Schlüpfer tragen unter einem engen Rock zu sehr auf,* 'Thick panties show too much under a tight skirt'.

auftreiben. Nothing to do with 'drive' but is colloquial in the meaning of 'to get hold of' or 'find with difficulty': *Wo hast du das Buch aufgetrieben?* 'Where did you manage to get hold of that book?'

aufziehen. 'To wind up' (a watch) or 'draw' a curtain and colloquially 'to make fun of somebody' or 'pull someone's leg'. *Aufzug* (m ¨-e) is a lift and there are two main varieties: the push-button stop-and-start kind and the *Paternoster* (m -) which is often found in office blocks and large public buildings and has a doorway but no door; it travels very slowly from floor to floor and never stops, passengers just step in and out as it reaches the required floor. *Aufzug* also means 'get-up' or 'inappropriate clothes': *In dem Aufzug kannst du doch nicht auf die Straße gehen,* 'You certainly can't go out in the street in that get-up'.

Auge (n -n). 'Eye' but there are some common idioms: *haben Sie etwas Bestimmtes im Auge?* a salesgirl might ask, meaning 'have you anything special in mind?' and implying that it is something that you have seen in the shop or window. *Eine Person im Auge behalten* is 'to keep an eye on someone' but *eine Möglichkeit im Auge behalten* is 'to keep a possibility in mind'. *Das ging beinahe ins Auge!* 'That was a close shave!'

ausbooten. Colloquial for 'to get rid of . . .' or 'to ditch', usually referring to an associate in a joint undertaking.

ausgefallen. 'Far out', 'unusual'.

ausgesprochen. Much used as an adverb in the sense of 'most', 'really'.

Aushängeschild (n -er). A 'front' for criminal activities. *Die Agentur ist nur ein Aushängeschild,* 'The agency is only a front'.

ausknocken. To knock out or down.

auskommen. Not 'to come out' but 'to make do with', 'manage', 'get on with': *ich komme nie mit meinem Geld aus,* 'I can never manage on my income (salary)'; *damit mußt du auskommen,* 'you must make do with this'; *er kam gut mit dem Freund aus,* 'he got on well with his friend'. The noun *Auskommen* has three meanings: *mit ihm ist kein Auskommen,* 'one can't get on with him'; *er hat sein Auskommen,* 'he can just manage (get by)'; *er hat ein gutes Auskommen,* 'he makes a good living'.

ausmachen. 'To make out' or 'distinguish'; but more important is its use as 'to matter' or 'mind': *Würde es Ihnen etwas ausmachen, wenn ich rauche?* 'Would you mind if I smoked?' A frequent use is 'agreed': *Es war ausgemacht, daß wir alle das gleiche sagen,* 'It had been agreed that we'd all say the same thing'. The participle *ausgemacht* used as an adjective means something like 'hapless': *ein ausgemachter Dummkopf,* 'an absolute fool', 'stupid as they come'; *ausgemachter Unsinn,* 'downright nonsense'.

ausnehmen. 'To fleece' a person.

auspacken. 'To unpack'; colloquially 'to tell all one knows', 'to spill the beans'.

ausrechnen. 'To calculate' but the adjective *ausgerechnet* can have a different meaning: *ausgerechnet jetzt,* 'now of all times'; *ausgerechnet er (sie),* 'he (she) of all people'.

ausrichten. 'To convey a message': *ich werde es gern ausrichten,* 'I shall be happy to convey the message', but *bestellen* (q.v.) is as common.

ausschellen. *Schellen* is colloquial or regional for *klingeln,* 'to ring'; on doors may be seen the notice *2 mal schellen* or *2 × schellen,* 'ring twice'. *Ausschellen* is a custom in some very small villages and means that the bellringer (town crier) goes round the streets, ringing a handbell and giving out official notices.

aussehen. 'To have the appearance of': *Er sieht müde aus,* 'He looks tired'. When shopping, you often hear customers say *es soll nach etwas aussehen,* 'It mustn't look too cheap' or *es sieht nach nichts aus,* 'It doesn't look much', 'It looks cheap'. In Southern Germany *schauen* is often substituted for *sehen* in compound verbs and with prepositions, thus *es soll nach etwas ausschauen.* Note the phrase *so sehen Sie aus!* or *so schauen Sie aus!* 'That's what you think!'

außer. 'Except', 'out of' but there are some idiomatic phrases that cannot be readily understood: a sign outside some cafés and restaurants *auch außer Haus* or *Verkauf auch außer Haus* or *auch über die Straße* means that food and drink can be bought for consumption off the premises. *Außer Betrieb* on telephones etc., 'Out of order'; *außer der Zeit,* 'outside normal working (or consultation) hours'; *außer der Reihe,* 'out of one's turn in the queue'.

auswärts. This rarely means 'outward', which is rendered by *nach außen,* but 'out of town', 'not from this (my, your etc.) town'. When making an out-of-town call you might say to a switchboard operator who is being slow, *ich rufe von auswärts an,* so that she knows it's costing you money. *Auswärts essen,* 'to eat out'.

Ausweis (m -e). 'Means of identification'. After the age of sixteen, people in Germany are expected to carry some means of identification such as a *Personalausweis* or *Kennkarte* (f -n) 'identity card', a *Paß* (m ¨-(ss)e), *Reisepaß* 'passport' or a *Führerschein* (m -e) 'driving licence'. A policeman or other authorized official might ask you *können Sie sich ausweisen?* 'Can you identify yourself?' or more curtly *Ihren Ausweis, bitte!* 'Your papers, please!'

Automatenrestaurant (n -s). These are found off the *Autobahnen* or in big towns and are nothing more than large shop-like rooms full of automatic vending machines selling food and drinks.

B

Bahnhof (m ¨-e). 'Railway station'. *Mit großem Bahnhof empfangen,* 'to receive with great pomp' or 'to welcome like a V.I.P.', something which nowadays usually occurs at airports. A frequently heard colloquialism *ich verstehe nur Bahnhof* means 'I don't understand a word of what is being said' and may indicate an honest lack of comprehension or stand for a rebuff.

Band. *Der Band* (¨-e) refers to the volume of a book; *das Band* (¨-er) is a 'tape' or 'ribbon' and *die Bandaufnahme* (-n) is the 'tape-recording'; *das Tonband(gerät)* is a 'tape-recorder'. Figuratively *das Band* means a 'link' or 'tie'. *Die Bande* (-n) is 'the gang'. Note the colloquial phrase *am laufenden Band* (n), 'without interruption'. *Die Band* (-s) pronounced as in English is the musical 'band'.

Bar (f -s). 'Bar'. Bars of slightly dulled or heavily tarnished reputation are called colloquially *Bums, Bumslokal, Kaschemme, Spelunke* and sometimes *Kneipe.* When they have striptease or a similar attraction they are usually described as *Bar mit Programm, Nachtbar* or *Kabarett* and a general term describing them all is *Tingeltangel.*

Bart (m ¨-e). 'Beard'; *Der Bart ist ab,* 'You've had it'; 'That's it'.

Beamtensilo (m -s). Contemptuous term for tall building for offices of central or local government: from *Beamte,* civil servant.

bedauern. Note *er ist zu bedauern,* 'One must feel sorry for him'.

bedeutend. 'Important', 'significant', very commonly used as an adverb in the same sense as 'much'.

bedienen. 'To serve', 'attend to'. *Werden Sie schon bedient?* 'Are you being served?'; *Bitte, bedienen Sie sich,* 'Please help yourself' (at table). When no sales staff attends a customer in a shop or restaurant: *Bedienung, bitte,* 'What about some service here'; *Ich bin bedient,* colloquial for 'I've had enough', 'I'm fed up with . . .': *Ich bin von Zahnärzten bedient,* 'I've had enough of dentists'.

begegnen. 'To run across' or 'meet by chance'. *Sich treffen mit* is 'to meet by pre-arrangement'; *treffen* alone can indicate either depending on the context.

Begriff (m -e). 'Concept', 'notion'; *Er ist schwer von Begriff,* 'He is slow on the uptake' but *das ist für meine Begriffe zu schwer für ihn,* 'I think (if you ask me) that is too difficult for him'.

begrüßen. Not 'to greet' which is *grüßen* but 'to welcome', i.e. stop and shake hands and exchange a few words or welcome visitors to your home.

Behandlung (f -en). 'Treatment'. *Ambulante Behandlung* 'out-patient treatment' at a hospital or clinic; *die Ambulanz (-en)* is 'the emergency ward' of a hospital as well as the 'out-patients' department' but 'the ambulance' is *der Krankenwagen* (-) or in hospital jargon *der Sanka (-s)* from *Sanitätskraftwagen. Stationäre Behandlung* is 'in-patient treatment' and *das Behandlungszimmer* (or *Sprechzimmer*) is 'the surgery'.

Beileidsbesuch (m -e). A visit of sympathy and condolence to a bereaved person but also a term used unofficially by the police amongst themselves to refer to the predictably fruitless investigation that has to be made by them into every trivial crime.

Bein (n -e). 'Leg'. Archaic meaning was 'bone' and this is still retained in *es geht mir durch Mark und Bein,* 'It sets my teeth on edge' when used of sounds and 'it shakes me' when used of events (*Mark* is 'marrow'). A phrase used to minimize an event or calm someone down is *aber das ist doch kein Beinbruch* (m ¨-e). 'Well, that's not the end of the world' or 'it could be worse'.

Beistelltisch (m -e). Occasional table.

bekannt. 'Known'. *Es ist mir bekannt,* 'I know'. The adjective *bekannt* means 'well known'. *Bekanntmachen* 'to announce officially' and *die Bekanntmachung* is 'the official announcement'; but *bekannt machen* (often but incorrectly spelt as one word) means 'to introduce' or make two or more people acquainted with one another. The adjectival noun *ein Bekannter* is more widely used than the English 'acquaintance' as *Freund* mostly refers to the relationship between two people; when speaking of a family friend, Germans would not say *er ist ein Freund von uns* but *er ist ein guter Bekannter von uns;* the addition of *gut* or *alt* makes it more than just an acquaintance.

bekommen. A false friend that does not mean 'become' (*werden*) but 'to get' (*v.* KRIEGEN). *Ich bekomme Kopfschmerzen,* 'I'm getting a headache'. *Dabei bekommt man Gänsehaut,* 'that gives you goose pimples' or 'the willies'. You might be asked in a shop or restaurant *bekommen Sie schon?* 'are you being served?' or *was bekommen Sie?* 'what may I bring (or show) you?' which when asked by the customer means 'how much do I owe you?' *Lust bekommen* means 'to feel inclined to . . .'. *Bekommen* also means 'to agree with' when used of foods. Menus offer items as being *bekömmlich* 'light', 'easily digested'; *Tomaten bekommen mir nicht,* 'Tomatoes don't agree with me'; waiters often say *wohl bekomm's!* 'I hope you like (or enjoy) it'.

berappen. To pay up (unwillingly).

Berufsverkehr (m). 'Rush-hour traffic'.

Bescheid (m -e). A useful and frequently heard noun used only with *geben, sagen, wissen: Können Sie mir rechtzeitig Bescheid geben, ob Sie mitkommen?* 'Can you let me know in time if you are coming along?'; *können Sie mir Bescheid sagen, . . .* 'can you tell me . . .'; *ich weiß Bescheid,* 'I know all about it' or 'all there is to know'; *ich weiß hier nicht Bescheid* means 'I don't know my way about in this place' or 'I don't know the details'; *in Steuergeschichten weiß ich nicht Bescheid,* 'I'm at a loss when it comes to tax matters' and finally the idiom *ich habe ihm gehörig Bescheid gesagt,* 'I told him off properly'.

Bescherung (f -en). The giving of presents on Christmas Eve or Morning. Colloquially it means an unpleasant surprise or result: *Da haben wir die Bescherung,* 'That's a fine how d'you do' or 'now we're in a mess'.

beschlagen. 'Misted over' when used of a window, mirror or any glass object.

beschuppsen. (Colloquial), 'to diddle'.

beschwipst. 'Tipsy', 'high', also *einen Schwips haben,* 'to be tipsy'.

Besen (m -). 'Broom'; *ich fresse einen Besen, wenn das stimmt,* 'I'll eat my hat if that's true' (not vulgar). *Sie ist ein Besen* is often said of women who always manage to get their own way; it means that you can't get the better of them or can't win.

besetzt. There is a special meaning in theatre language: *das Stück ist gut besetzt* or *hat eine gute Besetzung,* 'the play has a good cast'.

besorgen. Often used instead of *einkaufen* 'to shop': *etwas besorgen* or *einige Besorgungen machen,* 'to do some shopping'. It often means 'get': *Arbeit besorgen,* 'to get work' but sometimes it indicates a slightly unorthodox way of getting something: *Kaufen* *kann man es nicht, aber ich kann es besorgen,* 'You can't buy it but I can get it'.

best. 'Best'. *Am besten* 'the best thing (to do in a situation)'. *Der erste beste* is the first person or thing that comes along but in colloquial German *der erst beste* is often heard with *erst* treated as an adverb and thus having no terminations: *Du nimmst den erst besten Zug in Richtung Köln,* 'You take the first train bound for Cologne'. A common answer to a query as to how things are is *danke, bestens,* 'thanks, couldn't be better'.

bestellen. 'To order' (goods etc.), 'to arrange', 'to convey a message', and one of the words used in translating the English 'to make an appointment': *Bestellen Sie Frau Braun für sechs Uhr,* 'Arrange an appointment for Frau Braun at six'; *ich war für drei Uhr bestellt,* 'I have an appointment at three' (v. VERABREDUNG). Note the colloquial phrase: *er hat bei mir nichts zu bestellen* which is equivalent to the American 'I'm through with him'. Another often heard phrase is *wie bestellt und nicht abgeholt,* e.g. *wir sitzen wie . . .* 'We're sitting here as if we don't know whether we're coming or going'.

bestimmt. 'Certain' or 'definite' is the usual meaning but it can also mean 'meant for': *das ist für dich bestimmt* (stress on *dich*) 'that's meant for you' whereas *das ist bestimmt für dich* (stress on *bestimmt*) would mean 'I'm certain that's for you'.

Betreff (m -e). The 'subject line' of a business letter; it precedes the salutation and the abbreviation is *Betr.*

Betthase (m -n). Colloquial for a girl who is always ready for sex; she 'jumps into bed' like a hare. Indicates that she is little use for anything else, i.e. good-looking but stupid.

Betthupferl (n -). A sweet or chocolate taken on going to bed, common in Bavaria and Austria.

Bettlerharfe (f -n). Colloquial for a guitar.

Beziehung (f -en). *Beziehungen haben,* 'to know the right people'.

BH. (Pronounced bay-ha) short for *Büstenhalter* (m -) 'brassière', and is the equivalent of 'bra'.

Biedermeier. Name invented by Adolph Kussmaul and Ludwig Eichrodt in 1853 for an imaginary poet. In the 1890s it was used as a derogatory term for the style of the fine and applied arts of the period 1815 to 1848 in the German-speaking lands. In early 1900s under influence of Viennese Art Nouveau and the Secessionists (Joseph Hoffmann and Gustav Klimt) it became a neutral adjective for the art of the 1820s and 1830s. As the years have passed so *Biedermeier* has been increasingly appreciated.

Bienenhaus (n ¨-er). Humorous name for a hostel for single girls.

Bier (n -e). 'Beer'. Beer is drunk in enormous quantities in Germany and it is quite respectable for ladies to drink it too. Although there are many varieties, in practice you find that most of it is a pale lager type and is called *helles Bier* or just *Helles* and is what you get when you order *ein Bier* without being specific. *Pils, Pilsner* is the standard beer and *Export* is slightly better quality. It can be *Flaschenbier* 'bottled', or *Zapfbier* or *vom Faß* 'draught'. It is less bitter than English beers, slightly stronger than ordinary English bitter and much frothier; it is always poured into a glass so that a great head of froth *Schaum* (m) or colloquially *Feldwebel* (m -) (literally 'sergeant-major') results. It is drunk in glasses or mugs *Krug* (m ¨-e) (v. STEIN) and can be obtained almost everywhere, every smart café sells it as well as every pub. Beer is part of the 'German way of life' but is not accompanied by the 'beer cult' which is found in Britain. German beer seems to smell less strongly than English beer and even in the poorest pub is served neatly on a small mat and often with a little paper collar *Manschette* around the stem of the glass. *Dunkles Bier* is dark, contains almost no alcohol and is also called *Malzbier* 'malt beer'; it is supposed to be 'good for you' and is often drunk by women or children and rarely by men; it should not be mistaken for a German version of stout. There is a type of beer similar to stout, *Salvator*, but it is mostly drunk in Bavaria. *Weißbier* is made from wheat instead of barley and as it is a Berlin speciality it is often called *Berliner Weiße* (f), it is very pale and frothy and served in an overgrown champagne glass. *Eine Berliner Weiße mit Schuß* has a dash of raspberry juice in it and is said to be very refreshing in summer and is sold in cafés. *Bockbier* or *Doppelbock* is a very light beer stronger than the other types and sold only in very small bottles.

Biermarke (f -n).   Actually a token given to a customer in a restaurant, café or at a reception indicating that his drinks have been paid for but colloquially a name for the badge carried by a plainclothes policeman.

bieten.   'To offer'; there is another word for 'to offer': *anbieten,* and a subtle difference exists between the two. When you wish to share something with another person you use *anbieten: kann ich Ihnen eine Zigarette anbieten?* 'may I offer you a cigarette?'; *bieten* refers to the advantages inherent in a thing or to a business offer: *Diese Stadt hat einem Fremden nichts zu bieten,* 'This town has nothing to offer a tourist (stranger)'; *Wieviel bietet man dir in deiner neuen Stelle?* 'How much are they offering you in your new job?'. There is an idiom *sich nicht bieten lassen* which means 'not to stand for' or 'not to endure'.

Bild (n -er).   'Picture' and note the German expression so like the colloquial English: *ich bin im Bilde,* 'I'm in the picture' (I know). *Bild Zeitung* is the most popular national daily in Germany and has a multi-million circulation; it sells currently for 30 Pfg. and is tabloid in format; it is right-wing and rather like the old *Daily Sketch. Bild am Sonntag* is the Sunday edition, much bigger and resembling the *News of the World* in content. The Swiss version of *Bild* is *Blick Zeitung*; both papers are rich sources for good colloquial German.

Bilderbuch (in compounds). Means 'excellent': *zu Ostern herrschte Bilderbuchwetter in Deutschland*, 'Germany had lovely weather over Easter'.

billig. A popular saying is *was dem einen recht ist, ist dem anderen billig*, 'What's right for you is right for me too'. The verb *billigen* does not mean 'to cheapen' but 'to approve of'.

bitten. 'To ask for' or 'request'. *Darf ich bitten?* is still the correct formula for asking a girl for a dance, it should be accompanied by a bow. *Ich muß doch sehr bitten!* is a firm but polite request to someone to stop doing whatever he is doing that is annoying such as getting 'fresh' with a girl. *Bitten* can also show polite disbelief: *Aber ich bitte Sie, das kann doch nicht sein*, 'But really, that can't be so'. *Bitten lassen* means 'to have come in'; when you are told that someone wants to see you and is waiting outside, you can say *ich lasse bitten*, 'have him (or her) come in'.

blamieren. This does not mean 'to blame'; the exact translation is very difficult as the basic notion implied by this word is doing something that makes you (*sich blamieren*) or another person (*jemand blamieren*) lose face in front of others, for example: *Das hättest du nicht sagen sollen, damit hast du uns schön blamiert*, 'You shouldn't have said that, you really put us in a spot' or *das hättest du nicht tun sollen, damit hast du dich unsterblich blamiert*, 'You shouldn't have done that, you've made yourself look a hopeless fool'. If one of a group embarrasses the rest, they will often say *du blamierst ja die ganze Innung*, 'You're shaming the lot of us'.

blau. 'Blue'. *Blau sein* does not mean to feel blue, i.e. depressed, but 'to be drunk'. *Blau machen* is to stay away from work without sufficient cause. *Ein blauer Brief* is a warning letter sent by a school to parents preparing them for examination failure on the part of their offspring; it comes from the blue envelope which at one time was the recognized cover for letters of dismissal from the civil or military service. *Blau* is often seen on menus and means 'boiled'.

Blechschaden (m -). In road accidents, damage to the body of a car as distinct from major damage to motor or other important parts of the car.

Blei (n). 'Lead', also a colloquial abbreviation for *Bleistift* (m -e) 'pencil' and then it is masculine and has a plural *Bleis*. *Blei gießen* 'lead pouring' or 'melting' is a widespread New Year's custom: on New Year's Eve (*Sylvester* or *Silvester* (m)) at midnight, people melt a piece of lead in a spoon held over a fire and then throw the liquid lead into a bowl of cold water and the shape that forms as the lead solidifies is supposed to indicate something about the lead thrower's prospects in the coming year.

bleiben. 'To remain', 'stay'. There are a number of useful idioms such as *bleibt's dabei?* which often terminates a discussion and means 'so we'll stick to this?' but in sentences such as *du bleibst zu Hause, und dabei bleibt's* it means 'that's that': 'you stay at home and that's that'. Note also *bei der Wahrheit bleiben,* 'to stick to the truth' and *am Leben bleiben,* 'to survive'. *Wo bleibt er nur?* usually means 'where's he got to?'

blicken. 'To glance' but *er läßt sich gar nicht mehr bei uns blicken* means that 'he never visits us these days' and *lassen Sie sich hier ja nicht mehr blicken* 'never show yourself here again'. Another idiom is *das läßt ja tief blicken!* 'that tells a tale!'

bloß. 'Only' and is equivalent to *nur* in many instances. *Bloß nicht* is a warning: *komm bloß nicht näher,* 'don't you dare come any nearer', but as an exclamation it means 'I hope not' or 'God forbid': *sie wird dich wahrscheinlich anrufen,* 'she'll probably 'phone you', *bloß nicht!* 'God forbid!'

blühen. (Figuratively) 'to be in store for'.

Blüte (f -n). '(Single) bloom or blossom' but in colloquial speech a 'forged banknote'.

Bogen (m ¨-). 'Bow', 'arch', 'curve', 'crescent'. Figuratively used for 'avoid': *ich mache einen großen Bogen um alles, was mit Arbeit zusammenhängt,* 'I shy away from (avoid) anything that is connected with work'. *Jetzt hast du den Bogen überspannt, ich mache nicht mehr mit,* 'Now you've gone too far, I'm getting out', it has nothing to do with the English saying 'to draw the long bow'. *Er hat den Bogen heraus,* 'He knows the trick', 'He knows how it's done'. *Ein Bogen Papier* is a large sheet of paper (Din A4). *Der Fragebogen* 'the questionnaire', particularly the questionnaires of the Allied Military Government in Germany after 1945 which were used in 'de-nazification' procedures and made well known outside Germany by the autobiography of Ernst von Salomon under the title *Der Fragebogen* in 1951 (English translation 'The Answers', 1954).

Bonze (m -n). 'Industrial, political or trade-union boss', also 'V.I.P.'.

Brand (m ¨-e). *Ein Brand* is 'a fire' but colloquially it means the 'thirst' that accompanies most hangovers.

Bratkartoffelverhältnis (n -se). 'Roast potato relationship', a contemptuous term for a relationship between a man and a woman from which he derives some practical advantage such as having his clothes washed or his food cooked or being invited in to meals frequently.

breit. 'Broad' or 'wide' but colloquialisms with *breit* are not always easy to understand: *sich breitschlagen lassen,* 'to let yourself be talked into something', e.g. *ich wollte es ja nicht, aber dann habe ich mich breitschlagen lassen,* 'I actually didn't want to but then I let myself be talked into it'. *Sich breit machen* 'to take up a lot of space for yourself and your belongings'; you could say to someone in a railway carriage who was taking up two or three seats with his luggage etc. *machen Sie sich doch bitte nicht ganz so breit* which is about equivalent to 'could you try not to spread yourself so much?'

Brett (n -er). 'Board'; *das schwarze Brett* is not the school blackboard (*die Wandtafel*) but any kind of notice board. *Er hat heute ein Brett vorm Kopf,* 'He's really stupid today'. *Ich habe bei ihm einen Stein im Brett* means 'I'm in his good books'; it is derived from the boards on which innkeepers used to keep customers' accounts and the *Stein* is short for *Edelstein* ('precious stone') so that not only has the customer no debts but he is also in credit.

Brief (m -e). 'Letter' but there are many kinds such as: *Eilbrief* (*Brief per* (*durch*) *Eilboten*), 'express letter': *Einschreibbrief* (*Einschreiben* (n -)), 'registered letter'; *Wertbrief* (*Brief mit Wertangabe*), 'insured letter containing something of value' such as money; *Luftpostbrief,* 'air letter'; *Aerogramm* (n -e) (prepaid) 'aerogramme'; *Briefsendung mit Nachnahme,* 'C.O.D. letter'. *Büro für unzustellbare Briefe* is the 'dead letter office'.

Brieffach (n ¨-er). 'Pigeon-hole'; but *Postfach* is a 'P.O. Box'.

Briefkasten (m ¨-). 'Letter box', 'pillar box', painted yellow; a red spot on the box indicates that there is a special late collection.

Briefmarke (f -n). 'Postage stamp' but there are other words: *Wertzeichen* (n -) which is the legend above most post-office counters where stamps are sold; *Postwertzeichen, Freimarke* are also common; *Porto* (n -) is the business term for postage although in officialese it is *Frankatur* (f -) and to put stamps on a letter is *einen Brief freimachen* or *einen Brief frankieren*.

Brot (n -e). 'Bread'. Ordinary German bread is made of rye *Roggenbrot, Mischbrot, Bauernbrot* or *Landbrot* and is brown and rough. *Vollkornbrot* is made from unadulterated wheat and is brown and gritty and full of roughage; *Pumpernickel* is 'black' bread made from rye and it is dampish, sweetish and sticky. *Weißbrot* (more rarely *Milchbrot*) is white bread of a delicate texture and quite unlike the rubbery white bread sold in Britain. *Ein Brot* is short for *ein Laib Brot* and is the usual way of asking for a loaf in a shop but in a restaurant it is often used to mean a sandwich (*eine Scheibe Brot*) which unlike an English sandwich has only one slice instead of two. Figuratively *Brot* is used for 'living': *Bergleute haben ein hartes Brot* 'miners have a hard life' and sometimes *Brötchen* (a white roll) is used colloquially for 'money', 'earnings', 'living': *er muß die Brötchen verdienen,* 'he has to earn the lolly'.

Brummer (m -).   'Bluebottle', but colloquially refers to an extra heavy lorry, a juggernaut: *dicke Brummer*.

Buch (n ¨-er).   'Book'. An often heard phrase is one using *wie er* (*sie, es*) *im Buche steht* and it means 'as (typical as) they make them' or 'as they come': *er ist ein Lehrer wie er im Buche steht,* 'he is as typical a teacher as they make them'.

Buchstabe (m -n).   'Letter of the alphabet'. *Die vier Buchstaben* is a euphemism for a person's behind and is not vulgar; a teacher might say to a class *Sie müssen sich zu Hause etwas mehr auf die vier Buchstaben setzen,* 'You must sit down and do a bit more homework'. *Buchstäblich,* 'literally' when used figuratively: *Er war buchstäblich blau vor Kälte,* 'He was literally blue with cold'; but 'don't take this too literally', *nehmen Sie das nicht zu wörtlich.*

Buddel (f -n).   A Northern German dialect word for *Flasche* (f -n) 'bottle' and it has no connection with the colloquial *buddeln,* 'to dig'.

Bude (f -n).   'Stall' such as might be found at a fair and our 'coffee-stall' would be described as a *Kaffeebude. Würstchenbude* is a kind of portable snack-bar found in big towns and they are usually trailers and open at 10 or 11 p.m. although many are open all day as well. When *Bude* is used to describe a permanent non-movable place it is derogatory: *Das Geschäft ist eine richtige Bruchbude,* 'That shop is a proper little hole'; when used by students or teenagers it refers to 'digs' or a room in their parents' home and *eine sturmfreie Bude* is one that has a separate entrance so that parents and landladies cannot enter unexpectedly: 'trouble-free digs'.

bügelarm.   'Almost non-iron', i.e. little ironing is needed; *bügelfrei,* 'non-iron'.

Bürgerinitiative (f -n).   Voluntary action by concerned citizens against government or local authorities or public bodies in defence of individual or collective rights; it usually takes the form of an action at law and is not to be confused with the wild antics of the extreme left.

C

Café (n -s).   'Café'. The German café is usually a smart and elegant place often associated with a *Konditorei,* 'cake-shop'; cafés specialize in *Kuchen* (m -) and *Torte* (f -n), 'cakes' made with fruit and cream and often of unbelievable complexity. Beer, wines, spirits, soft drinks, chocolate, coffee, snacks, light meals, cigarettes and cigars are obtainable as well. Cafés always serve breakfasts and usually close about 7 p.m. when the restaurants and bars take over. In summer, and where space is available, there are tables in the open air. Most cafés are thoroughly respectable, rather middle-class, and unaccompanied girls and women use them frequently. In them the local matrons meet for morning and afternoon chats and older schoolgirls for gossiping or meeting boy-friends, businessmen use them for informal discussions and on Sundays whole families patronize them. All cafés (and most bars and restaurants) provide copies of national and local newspapers and the illustrated weekly magazines and the papers are often fixed to sticks and hung by hooks from racks. Customers can sit for as long as they wish over a cup of coffee or a beer without being importuned to order again. Many towns have large modern office blocks and *Dachcafés* 'roof cafés' have been opened on the flat roofs; such cafés are usually open until the early hours.

Clinomobil (n -e). 'Mobile clinic'.

Clou (m -s). 'The high spot', 'the main event' *Der Clou des Abends war das Feuerwerk*, 'The high spot of the evening was the fireworks'.

D

dämlich. The innocent foreigner should beware as it means 'stupid' or 'imbecile' not 'ladylike' (which is *damenhaft*). *Herrlich* is also not 'gentlemanly' (*ehrenhaft, ritterlich*) but 'wonderful'.

Dämmerschoppen (m -). The colloquial name for the evening drink that men take shortly before supper, as opposed to the *Frühschoppen*, the one taken in the morning particularly on Saturdays and Sundays when it is frequently accompanied by a game of cards. (v. SCHOPPEN)

daneben. 'On the side (of it)', 'beside'; it is often used to express the idea of 'wrong': *er hat sich danebenbenommen* is a nice way of saying 'he misbehaved'. When something goes wrong, you will hear people say *es ist danebengegangen*, 'it was a flop', 'it failed'.

dankbar. 'Grateful, 'thankful' but also means 'of good quality', 'advantageous to the user'. A garment can be *dankbar*, i.e. it is long-wearing, needs little looking after or can be worn on many occasions. *Ein dankbares Publikum* is not necessarily a grateful audience but one that is interested and responsive; *eine dankbare Aufgabe* is a task of much scope or quick returns.

danken. This is a rather formal verb for 'to thank' and the more familiar *sich bedanken* is the one most often used but should not be used in letters and when thanking a person directly except in connection with *möchten*, e.g. *ich möchte mich bei Ihnen für . . . bedanken,* 'I should like to thank you for . . .'. Colloquially *danken* and *sich bedanken* can express rejection, e.g. *Zehn Stunden täglich arbeiten? Ich danke* or *Na, ich danke* or *Da danke ich,* 'Work ten hours a day? No thank you'.

Datterich (m). A nervous trembling caused by age or a hangover; *Er hat einen Datterich,* 'He's got the shakes'.

Dauer (f). 'Duration', but in compound words it indicates 'long-term' e.g. *Dauermieter* is a tenant of a flat or rooms who takes them for at least a year; *Dauerkarte* (f -n) is a 'season ticket' for swimming pools, tennis courts etc. A season-ticket for the theatre is *ein Abonnement für das Theater*. A railway season ticket is a *Wochenkarte* for a week, *Monatskarte* for a month.

Dauerbrenner (m -). Humorous for a very long kiss.

Dauerlutscher (m -). Also *Lutscher,* a 'lollipop'.

Decke (f -n). 'Ceiling' and also 'blanket'. Three often heard idioms with 'ceiling': *an die Decke gehen,* 'to climb up the wall' (blow one's top); *an die Decke springen* equivalent to 'to jump for joy'; *sich nach der Decke strecken,* 'to try to make ends meet'. The meaning of 'blanket' could be the cause of some discomfort to the English as it is just what they will not find on German beds. In summer, the bed is covered with a *Steppdecke,* a 'duvet',or its modern counterpart the *Rheumadecke* (a quilt filled with wool) and in winter these are replaced by a *Deckbett* (n -en) often also referred to as *Bett* or *Federbett,* a voluminous 'sack' filled with feathers. A *Daunenbett* is filled with down and so is a *Daunendecke,* but the latter is quilted. Do not confuse *Deckbett* with *Bettdecke* (or *Tagesdecke*) which is a 'bedspread'.

delikat. It can never be used in the sense of 'delicate lace' or 'a delicate child'; it is used almost exclusively in the sense of 'difficult': *eine delikate Angelegenheit,* 'a difficult affair' or 'a ticklish business'. The word sometimes means 'delicious': *Das Abendessen war delikat,* 'The supper was delicious'. *Die Delikatesse* (-n) is the 'delicacy', e.g. *Kaviar ist eine russische Delikatesse,* 'Caviare is a Russian delicacy'. The 'delicatessen (shop)' is *das Feinkostgeschäft* (-e) or more rarely *das Delikatessengeschäft*.

denken. 'To think'. Care must be taken with phrases such as *Sie sind hier? Ich denke, Sie sind im Kino* which means 'Here you are, I thought you were at the pictures' and the use of the present tense *ich denke* implies that you are accusing the person spoken to of having misled you; if you wish to indicate that you have been wrong in your own assumption, you must use the past tense *ich dachte, Sie sind im Kino* and this absolves the person spoken to of blame.

Dentist (m -en). A false friend as a 'dentist' is *ein Zahnarzt* (m ¨-e).
Der Dentist is one without a university degree, rather like the
unqualified dentists who were allowed to practise in England until
the mid-1930s and like them, the German *Dentist* will eventually
disappear as no new ones are permitted to practise.

deplaciert. (Often spelt *deplaziert* but this version is considered
incorrect.) A false friend as it does not mean 'displaced' but 'out of
place' or 'awkward': *in diesem Kleid komme ich mir deplaciert
vor,* 'I feel out of place in this dress'.

deutsch. 'German' and can be figurative: *Mit dem muß man deutsch
reden,* 'You must be blunt with him'. *Der deutsche Michel* is the
traditional German figure comparable with 'John Bull' and is a
rather simple but frank fellow always depicted wearing a night-
cap.

deutsche Schrift. 'Gothic handwriting' that is now rarely used save by
the elderly; most youngish people have difficulty in reading it and
it is no longer taught in schools except in art lessons. Some newspapers still use Gothic print in headings and their own names but,
with the exception of the devotional literature issued by some
churches, books are no longer printed in it; it can, however, be
read by all literate people and unlike Gothic handwriting, it is not
difficult to decipher.

Diakonisse (f -n). Member of a Protestant sisterhood. *Die
Diakonissen* are trained as nurses in centres called *Mutterhäuser*
but rarely remain in them after having qualified. Most of them
work in secular institutions but their salaries are paid to the
Mutterhaus from which they receive pocket money and sufficient
for expenses. Their habits vary slightly from one *Mutterhaus* to
another but always retain the distinctive white bonnet and ankle-
length dark blue dress. You will often see *Diakonissen* going about
on public transport, scooters or *Volkswagen* (if they have a car, it
never seems to be of any other make). The order is not very strict
and it is possible to leave it easily.

dick. 'Thick'; *dicke Freunde,* 'fast friends'. *Dem dicken Wilhelm
spielen* is 'to throw one's weight about' and to say of a person *er
hat es faustdick hinter den Ohren* means either that he is cleverer
(smarter) than he appears to be or that he is a 'smooth operator'.

dienen. 'To serve' and shop assistants usually greet a customer:
womit kann ich Ihnen dienen? 'what can I get you?' or 'can I help
you?'. If you want to buy something you answer with *ich suche
. . .* 'I'm looking for . . .' or *ich möchte . . .* 'I should like . . .' or
können Sie mir . . . zeigen? 'can you show me . . .?' If you merely
want to look around then say *danke, ich möchte mich nur umsehen*
and you had best learn this by heart as you are rarely left in peace to
look around even in large stores. Note the idiomatic *damit ist mir
nicht gedient,* 'That doesn't help me' or 'serve my purpose'.

Dienst (m -e). 'Service'. The *Kundendienst* of a shop (customer service) can either refer to the shop's delivery van or a technician who can come to your home to repair an appliance of a particular brand; thus you ask for a *Siemens-Kundendienst* or a *Philips-Kundendienst* etc. For cars the word *Dienst* suffices and you often see signs on roads indicating the nearest garage with a *Volkswagen-Dienst* etc. *Kundendienst* often appears written above automatic vending machines outside a shop. *Nachtdienst* 'night duty' and *dienstbereit* 'on duty' are useful words to know in case of illness because they refer to chemists and doctors available after normal hours and details appear in local newspapers under the headings *Ärzte mit Nachtdienst* (or *Sonntagsdienst*), *Apotheken mit Nachtdienst* and *Apotheken dienstbereit am* . . . Most chemists have a small illuminated indicator outside the shop stating *dienstbereit* if they are and indicating *die Klingel* (-n) 'bell' or giving the address of the nearest duty chemist if they are not. There is usually an extra fee of DM 1.- added to prescription charges outside normal shopping hours. The adjective *dienstlich* is opposed to 'private': *ich bin dienstlich hier,* 'I'm here on (official) business'; *Möchten Sie ihn dienstlich oder privat sprechen?* 'Do you want to speak to him on a private or business matter?' A phrase to use when thanking someone for a present is *es leistet mir gute Dienste,* literally 'it renders me good service' but equivalent to the English 'I find it very useful'.

Ding (n -e, -er). 'Thing'; the plural depends on the meaning: *die Dinge* when referring to 'things' but *die Dinger* when used colloquially to mean 'silly girls' (it can be used to mean just a girl but it usually is uncomplimentary and indicates without an adjective that the girl spoken of is silly): *Es war ein dummes junges Ding, das mich bediente,* 'It was a silly little thing who served me'; *ihr albernen Dinger!* 'you silly creatures!'. The plural *Dinger* can also refer to 'things' when the word is derogatory and then has the sense of 'stuff' (and can be replaced by *Zeug* (n)): *Was soll ich mit den komischen Dingern (mit dem komischen Zeug)?* 'What am I supposed to do with this strange stuff?'. An *s* added to the singular gives the meaning of 'gadget' *das Dings* and also forms the compound word *Dingsbums* 'thingumibob' or 'what's-its-name'. Colloquially *Ding* can also mean 'crime' and is then used in the singular only and with *drehen*: *Er hat ein dolles Ding gedreht,* 'He pulled off a good job'.

dir. Dative of *du*. It figures in *mir nichts dir nichts* which means 'without preamble' or 'just like that': *Er ist mir nichts dir nichts aufgestanden und gegangen,* 'He upped and went just like that'.

direkt. With *können* it means 'almost': *Ich konnte ihn direkt vor mir sehen, als sie von ihm sprach,* 'I could almost see him in front of me when she was speaking about him'.

Direktion (f -en). A false friend as it is only used to mean the 'management' of a firm or organization; it does not even mean 'direction' in the English sense of 'the orchestra is under the direction of . . .' which in German is *das Orchester steht unter der Leitung von* . . . 'Direction towards' is *Richtung* (f -en).

Dirn (f). A rather old-fashioned and poetic word for 'girl' used mostly in the singular and not often heard save in its North German form of *Deern* (f -s). From *Dirn* is derived *Dirndl* (n -) the peasant dress in bright colours and with puffy short sleeves and an apron which is worn by many women and girls in the Southern parts of Germany. *Dirn* is mentioned here in case the reader might confuse it with *die Dirne*, 'the prostitute'.

diskret. 'Discreet'. *Diskreter Versand* in advertisements means 'under plain cover'. The phrase 'at one's own discretion' must be rendered by *nach eigenem Gutdünken (Ermessen)*.

doch. As an expletive *doch* conveys disbelief, doubt, emphasis or is the equivalent of the question tag: *Das ist doch nicht Ihr Ernst!* 'You can't be serious'; *Wenn er doch käme!* 'If only he came'; *Sie kommen doch?* 'You're coming, aren't you?'. Note also *Ja doch!* 'Yes, for Pete's sake'; *Denk doch,* 'Just imagine'; *Nicht doch!* 'Don't do that'. The answer *doch, doch* to a negative question is not, as you might think, doubly strong but much weaker than one *doch* and equivalent to a drawn-out 'well, yes . . .'.

doll. A mispronunciation of *toll* (q.v.) which has come to mean 'bad' or when used adverbially 'very much'; it is highly colloquial but by no means bad or vulgar: *Das war eine dolle Arbeit*, 'That was a heck of a job'; *Wir haben doll gelacht*, 'We laughed until it hurt'.

Double (n). When spelt without an accent on the *e* it means an actor's 'stand-in', with an accent it means 'gold-plated'; in both cases the pronunciation is French.

Drachenfutter (n). 'Dragon fodder', a colloquial name for the sweets, chocolate, flowers or other gifts that husbands bring their wives as peace offerings when they have stayed out late. At lunch-time on Saturdays you can often see men drinking in bars or cafés with their *Drachenfutter* bought and ready beside them. A similar construction is *Studentenfutter* which can be bought in cinemas and kiosks and is a mixture of raisins and nuts alleged to be a food upon which poor students exist.

dran. The colloquial abbreviation of *daran* 'at it' and idiomatic expressions with this word are numerous. Some of the most important are: *Er ist arm dran,* 'He is in a bad way' or 'Things are going badly for him'; *Du bist dran,* 'It's your turn'; *Drauf und dran sein,* 'To be within an ace of'; *Mit allem Drum und Dran,* 'With all the trimmings'.

drankriegen. 'To make a fool of somebody' by misleading him. *Da habt ihr mich schön drangekriegt,* 'You led me nicely up the garden path'.

drauf. Colloquial abbreviation of *darauf*, 'on it' and also used to mean 'later', *ein Jahr drauf*, 'a year later'. *Ein Draufgänger* is a 'go-getter'.

Dreck (m). 'Dirt' but has various figurative uses especially in a number of rather impolite phrases all much stronger than their English equivalents: *Müssen Sie mit jedem Dreck zu mir kommen?* 'Must you badger me with every triviality?'; *Das geht Sie einen Dreck an!* 'That's none of your damn business'; *Kümmern Sie sich um Ihren eigenen Dreck*, 'Mind your own business'. *Da haben wir den Dreck*, 'We've got ourselves into a fine mess' can be more politely expressed by replacing *Dreck* with *den Salat* or *die Bescherung*.

dreckig. 'Dirty' also means 'badly off': *Es geht ihm dreckig*, 'He's badly off'.

dreschen. 'To thresh' and colloquially 'to thrash' and *Dresche kriegen* is 'to get a good hiding'. As card players are apt to slam their cards on the table when excited so *Karten dreschen* is often used instead of *Karten spielen*, 'to play cards'. Another frequently heard phrase is *wir dreschen leeres Stroh*, 'We're getting nowhere fast'. *Phrasen dreschen* is 'to mouth empty phrases' and *abgedroschene Redensarten* are 'hackneyed phrases'.

drin. Often used only as a superfluous expletive, e.g. *Das Wort ist nicht in dem Buch drin*, 'The word isn't in the book', but in the very colloquial phrase *das ist (nicht) drin* it means 'that is (not) possible': *Beim Autofahren ist es drin, daß man einen Unfall baut*, 'There is always the possibility of an accident when driving'.

Drogerie (f -n). Is not an *Apotheke* (f -n) 'chemist's'. It sells cosmetics, photographic equipment, toilet articles and the things required for festivals and carnivals such as candles, tinsel, fireworks, lead for New Year (v. BLEI), confetti etc. but cannot sell medicines or fill prescriptions, these are obtainable at the *Apotheke* only. *Die Apotheke* also sells cosmetics and toilet requisites but only as a side line. Both shops sell wines and spirits, the one for carnival purposes, the other for health reasons.

drüben. 'Over there' and is a euphemism for the *Deutsche Demokratische Republik* (*DDR*) or East Germany. In post offices you might see posters at Christmas and Easter asking you to send letters and parcels *nach drüben*. It was once used to refer to the USA but this usage is dying out. It is considered bad form to refer to the DDR without expressing some doubt about it and children in school are taught always to speak of *die sogenannte DDR*, 'the so-called DDR'.

Druck (m). 'Pressure', 'print'. On forms and coupons *bitte drucken* or *in Druckschrift, Druckbuchstaben* or *Blockschrift* mean 'please complete in block letters'. 'Printed matter' by post is *Drucksache* (f -n). *Ich bin in Druck* means 'I'm pressed' (for money or time etc.).

drücken. 'To push' or 'press' and on doors it is the opposite of *ziehen* 'to pull'. It is a very useful word when buying shoes as it is the only way to describe that a shoe is uncomfortable and it is also used figuratively: *Wo drückt der Schuh* or *Wo drückt's?* 'Where does the shoe pinch?' or 'What's the trouble?' *Sich drücken vor* means to succeed in getting out of doing something and *der Drücke-berger*, 'shirker' or 'slacker' is derived from this verb. *Sich verdrücken* means 'to make yourself scarce' and 'to take French leave' and is rather colloquial as is the non-reflexive form *verdrücken* 'to eat', 'to polish off'.

duftig. An adjective used to describe a girl's hair or clothes; it is highly complimentary and conveys the notion of clean, fresh, frilly, feminine, sweet and youthful. 'She wore a light summery frock' is an inadequate rendering of *sie trug ein duftiges Sommerkleid. Ein duftiges Nachthemd* could be translated as 'a diaphanous nightie' but you would not describe *ein Schlafanzug* (pyjamas) as *duftig.* Do not confuse *duftig* with the slang term *dufte* which is vulgarly used to mean 'luscious': *eine dufte Biene* is 'a peach of a girl'.

duhn. A word much favoured in North Germany as a euphemism for *betrunken,* 'drunk', 'sozzled'.

dumm. 'Stupid' and the origin of the American 'dumb'. *Zu dumm,* 'what a pity'; *der Dumme sein* means literally 'to be the dummy' but could be translated as 'the joke is on him (her)'. 'To treat someone as if he were a fool' is *jemand für dumm verkaufen.*

Dunkelziffer (f -n). The number of crimes remaining unsolved annually by the police; *v.* also AUFKLÄRUNGSQUOTE.

Dunst (m ¨-e). 'Haze', 'vapour', 'steam' and gives two useful idioms: *ich habe keinen Dunst,* 'I haven't the foggiest idea' and *jemandem blauen Dunst vormachen,* 'to deceive someone' or 'befog the issue'.

durch. 'Through', 'past'; *Es ist schon fünf durch,* 'It is gone (past) five (o'clock)' instead of *es ist schon nach fünf.* When used of meat it means 'done': *Ist das Fleisch durch?* 'Is the meat done?' In a restaurant it is better to say *gut durchgebraten* rather than *gut durch* for 'well done' and if you want your steak underdone then you can say *nicht zu sehr durchgebraten* or *auf englische Art* as all English people are assumed to like their steaks almost raw.

durchgehend. A sign often seen outside restaurants *durchgehend warme Küche* indicates that you may obtain hot meals from opening to closing time. Another shop sign is *durchgehend geöffnet* which means that the shop etc. does not close at lunch-time or is open day and night.

dürfen. Generally translated as 'may' but its use in conversation is declining steadily and, except for servants and children, is being replaced by *können.* When you really want to help someone or offer a service you still say *darf ich Ihnen behilflich sein?* 'May I help you?' Shopkeepers in smallish shops often say *was darf's sein?* which is like the English 'what can I get you?'. If he hopes for more than one purchase he will probably say *darf's noch was sein?* or *was darf's noch sein?* 'will there be anything else?'. A waiter will say *was darf ich Ihnen bringen?* 'What can I bring you?' but if you wish to open the window in a railway carriage you would ask your fellow passengers *kann ich das Fenster aufmachen?*. *Gestatten* is an ultra-polite and elegant substitute for *dürfen* and *können*: *gestatten Sie, daß . . .* 'please permit me to . . .'. In business letters *dürfen* is frequently thrown in for politeness but without any particular meaning: *Wir freuen uns, Ihnen mitteilen zu dürfen, . . .* 'We are pleased to inform you . . .'.

dürftig.   Has no connection with *dürfen*; it is an adjective meaning 'poor', 'scanty' or 'wanting': *Der Erfolg war recht dürftig*, 'It was rather a poor show'.

Durststrecke (f -).   Slack period in business.

duster.   Colloquial and derived from *düster* 'gloomy', 'dismal' but means simply 'dark' (i.e. little light present) and does not connote 'dismal'.

E

echt.   'Genuine' but *echte Farben*, 'fast colours'. The phrase 'that's typical of so-and-so' or 'that's just like so-and-so' can be expressed by *das ist echt* (and then the person's name).

Edelfreßwelle (f -n).   Another term for *Freß- und Saufwelle*, refers to the over-eating and drinking that has accompanied the *Wirtschaftswunder*. Similar word formation is *Pornowelle*, almost past now, for all the photos and articles in the 'good-class' magazines like *Quick* etc. which were really pornographic.

egal.   Does not mean 'equal' except colloquially in *unegal* 'not matching', e.g. *Er hat zwei unegale Socken an*, 'He's got two odd socks on'. *Egal* generally means 'it doesn't matter' or 'no matter': *Egal, was es kostet*, 'No matter what it costs'; *Es ist mir egal*, 'I am indifferent' or 'it doesn't matter to me' and *es ist mir völlig egal* has something of the significance of 'I couldn't care less'.

Ehe (f -n).   'Marriage' but *in wilder Ehe leben* is 'to live in sin'.

ehe.   'Before' as in *ehe ich wußte, was geschah*, 'Before I knew what was happening'. It has a comparative and superlative: *eher* 'earlier', 'sooner' and *am ehesten*, 'earliest'. To express 'at the earliest' the adverb *ehestens* is recommended: *Ich komme ehestens morgen* (though *frühestens* is commoner), 'I'll come tomorrow at the earliest'. Very strangely, *am ehesten* can also convey the idea of 'easiest': *So geht es am ehesten,* 'That's the easiest (best) way to do it'.

Eile (f). 'Hurry'. 'I'm in a hurry' can be translated literally into *ich bin in Eile* but everyday usage prefers *ich hab's eilig.* 'There's no hurry' about something can be *das ist nicht eilig, es eilt nicht* or *damit hat es keine Eile.* The verb 'to hurry' (of people) is reflexive *sich (be)eilen.*

Eimer (m -). 'Bucket'; *im Eimer sein,* 'to be ruined', 'beyond repair'.

ein. 'A' or 'an' or 'one'. In colloquial usage *ein* provides the genitive, dative and accusative cases for *man* and as Germans avoid the passive and replace it by an impersonal construction whenever possible, *ein* becomes very useful: *das muß man einem doch sagen* is not the best of German but quite acceptable and very common and means 'well, one ought to be told' and implies 'how was I to know?'. *Laß einen in Ruhe* exemplifies a popular use of an impersonal form to refer to oneself and really means 'why can't you leave me alone?'.

einbilden, sich. 'To imagine' but in *darauf kannst du dir etwas einbilden* it means 'proud of' and the phrase is best rendered by 'you can be proud of that'; from this *eingebildet* has come to signify 'conceited'.

Einfall (m ¨-e), **einfallen.** Words for which there exists no exact translation; 'idea' or 'notion' is the nearest and the verb is best rendered by 'to think of': *Was brachte Sie auf diesen Einfall?* 'What gave you this idea?'; *Der Name fällt mir nicht ein,* 'I can't think of the name'; *Da fällt mir ein,* 'By the way, it just occurred to me'; *Was fällt Ihnen ein?* 'What's the idea?'

einigermaßen. 'Quite', 'so-so'.

einleuchten. A frequently used phrase is *das leuchtet mir ein,* 'I can see the point' or 'it's clear to me now'.

einmal. 'Once' often shortened to *mal* (q.v.) but never in *auf einmal,* 'suddenly', 'at once', 'in one go'. *Einmalig,* 'single' can describe an event occurring once only and also means 'unique' and 'wonderful'.

einpacken. A bit of a false friend and means 'to wrap up' and is used of wrapping up goods. In everyday speech it often means the English slang 'pack up' in sense of 'give up': *Wenn er loslegt, dann können wir alle einpacken,* 'When he gets going, we can all pack up'.

einrichten. 'To furnish' and also 'to arrange': *Können Sie es (sich) einrichten, mich um sechs Uhr zu treffen?* 'Can you arrange to meet me at six?'

Einstand (m ˸-e).   There is no exact translation of this word which describes the office party given to his colleagues by a new member of the staff; the phrase used is *seinen Einstand geben* and the party takes place in the office, during office hours and the boss pretends not to notice. *Einstand* was originally a membership fee paid by a new member of a group. *Seinen Ausstand geben* for the farewell party when a member of the staff leaves (basically *Ausstand* is 'strike').

eintragen, sich.   'To register' in a hotel or similar place and *wollen Sie sich bitte eintragen?* 'Will you please register?'

Einwegflasche (f -n).   Throwaway or non-returnable bottle.

einwerfen.   'To throw in' and also 'to insert' and is written on letter-boxes and on automatic vending machines above the coin slot: *1* × 50 Pfg. einwerfen, 'insert a 50 Pfennig piece'.

Eisdiele (f -n).   'Ice-cream parlour' to use an out-of-date equivalent but the *Eisdiele* and *Milchbar* are really coffee-bars for respectable teenagers and on Sundays their parents also. Apart from ice-cream and milk drinks such places sell beer, wines, spirits, coffee and snacks.

Eisen (n -).   'Iron'; *Er gehört zum alten Eisen,* 'He is too old for this' or 'He's ready for the scrap heap'. *Eisern!* is a teenagers' confirmatory exclamation meaning 'yes', 'of course'.

Eisenbahn (f -en).   'Railway' (colloquially shortened to *Bahn*) and included here because of the phrase *es ist höchste Eisenbahn,* 'it is high time'.

Emanze (f -n).   Women's libber. Rather derogatory and condescending for what is neutrally called a *Feministin* (f -nen), a woman active in the women's liberation movement.

Ende (n -n).   'End'; colloquially it can mean 'perhaps' in the phrase *am Ende*: *am Ende hat er Sie falsch verstanden* is 'perhaps he misunderstood you' and not 'in the end he misunderstood you' which would be *zum Schluß hat er Sie falsch verstanden*. When *am Ende* is to mean 'at the end' it should be connected with a noun: *am Ende der Vorstellung,* 'at the end of the performance'.

Endpreis (m -e).   In restaurants, cafés and hotels it means that the price charged includes service and VAT.

Engelmacher/-in (m -, f -nen).   'Angel-maker', a euphemism for an 'abortionist'.

englische Art.   Used in phrase *nicht die feine englische Art,* an idiom meaning 'not done' or 'not fair'.

entschlacken.   To purify the body of noxious matter by *Nulldiät* (q.v.) and *Heilfasten* (q.v.), 'to purge'.

entsprechend.   'According' but 'accordingly' is *dementsprechend*.

entwerten. To cancel a bus or train ticket by inserting one end of it into a machine situated in the bus or on the platform. The machine stamps a date on the ticket so that it cannot be used again.

erbaut. 'Built' and *erbaut sein von* can mean 'built by'; it can also mean 'pleased' as in *mein Vater war nicht sehr erbaut von meinem Benehmen*, 'My behaviour did not please my father much'.

erkundigen, sich. 'To enquire' and an indispensable phrase in offices, railway stations and when asking directions is *ich möchte mich erkundigen . . .* 'I should like to know (enquire) . . .'

erlauben. 'To allow', 'to permit' and one of four similar words needed in everyday life: *gestatten, dürfen* and *können*. You might find the phrase *erlauben Sie mal!* useful when someone does something that offends you as it is a warning phrase indicative of displeasure 'well, I must say . . .!'.

erleben. 'To experience'. *Sie werden Ihr blaues Wunder erleben,* 'You'll get the shock of your life'.

erledigen. 'To settle', 'finish'; *Er ist erledigt,* 'He's done for' or 'He's exhausted'; *Ich habe noch einiges zu erledigen,* 'I still have a few things to see to'.

ernst. 'Serious' and is both adjective and noun (m) 'seriousness'. 'Are you serious?' is *ist das Ihr Ernst?* and the reply 'yes, I am' is *es ist mein völliger Ernst.*

erst. 'First' and 'not before'; *erste Hilfe* is 'first aid'. A commonly heard phrase is *erst recht* in sentences such as *sie hat es mir verboten, aber nun tue ich es erst recht,* 'She told me not to do it but I'll do it to spite her'. Older people are fond of the phrase *wenn Sie erst einmal so alt sind wie ich . . .* 'once you are my age . . . .'; *für's erste genug* means 'enough to begin with'.

Essig (m). 'Vinegar' but not in the phrase *damit ist es Essig* which means 'it's off' or 'nothing doing': *Mit unserem Ausflug ist es Essig,* 'Our trip is off'.

etepetete. 'Precious', 'priggish' and 'affected'; *Er ist sehr etepetete,* 'He is a pedantic prig'; it can also mean 'stickler'.

EWG (f). *Europäische Wirtschaftsgemeinschaft,* 'European Economic Community', the 'Common Market'.

extra. This is not really a false friend as it means in German all that it does in English but it also has a colloquial significance that the English does not have: 'on purpose' or 'deliberately', e.g. *Das haben Sie extra getan,* 'You've done that on purpose'.

F

Fachidiot (m -en). Contemptuous name for a scientific or technological expert or specialist, so narrow that he cannot see the social or cultural consequences of the work that he undertakes.

Fahne (f -n). 'Flag'; *Fähnchen* (n -) 'a gaudy dress' usually cheap and in bad taste; *er hat eine Fahne* means that 'his breath reeks of alcohol'.

fahren. 'To go by some means other than one's own powers of locomotion'; very often it can be translated by 'to go' but in everyday speech it often departs markedly from this basic meaning, e.g. it means 'leave' or 'depart' as in *der Zug fährt um acht nach Köln*, 'The train leaves for Cologne at eight'. The real idiomatic usage which is not readily understandable by a foreigner comes in phrases like *was ist in Sie gefahren?* 'What's got into you?' or 'What's the matter with you?'; *jemandem über den Mund fahren*, 'to interrupt and drown the voice of the speaker'. Some connection with English can be seen in *er ist bei dem Geschäft nicht schlecht gefahren*, 'He did not fare badly in the matter (business)'.

Fahrgestell (n -e). 'Under-carriage'; (coll.) 'legs' particularly of women (not coarse).

Fahrt (f -en). Walking down any German street, you cannot fail to be impressed by the number of *Fahrten* you will see on signs; they all refer to driving, e.g. *Durchfahrt verboten*, 'No entry'; *freie Fahrt* is a sign which cancels the instructions of all previous signs or traffic restrictions; *Ausfahrt*, 'Exit'; *Einfahrt*, 'Entry'; *Ausfahrt freihalten*, 'Don't block the exit for vehicles'. When someone goes on a journey the usual farewell is *gute Reise* but you can just as well wish him *gute Fahrt*. A difficult idiom to understand is *in Fahrt kommen* (or *sein* or *bringen*) and the following example might help to explain it: *Sie war den ganzen Abend sehr still, aber als wir dieses Thema anschnitten, kam sie in Fahrt*, 'She was quiet the whole evening but when we broached this subject she opened up and went ahead (like a house on fire)' or 'she got into her stride'.

Fall (m -e). 'Case', 'matter'. There are a few idioms that might really fox the unwary foreigner such as *gesetzt den Fall*, 'supposing that'; *Das ist ganz mein Fall*, 'That's right up my street' or 'that suits me' and *er ist ganz mein Fall*, 'He's just my type'; note *Knall und Fall entlassen werden*, 'to be sacked on the spot'.

fallen. 'To fall' but there are many idioms in which it is only remotely connected with 'fall'. *Das fällt mir leicht (schwer)*, 'I find that easy (difficult)'; *Er ist nicht auf den Mund gefallen*, 'He is never at a loss for words'; *Er ist nicht auf den Kopf gefallen*, 'He is smart' (not stupid). In English you 'get on someone's nerves' but in German you *jemandem auf die Nerven fallen* and when you speak prematurely about something, you 'fall into the house with the door', *mit der Tür ins Haus fallen. Flach fallen,* 'to fall flat', 'to come to nothing'.

Fasching (m) also called *Karneval* (m), *Fastnacht* and colloquially *Fasnacht, Fassenacht* (f). It begins at 11 minutes past 11 a.m. on 11 November and ends at midnight on Shrove Tuesday. The whole affair is very serious for the many *Karnevalsvereine* (m.pl.) (carnival clubs or associations) that prepare the festivities. Mainz, Cologne and Munich are the chief *Fasching* centres. The *Vereine* often begin holding their festive meetings as early as January and those of the best known *Vereine* are televised; the main item in these *Karnevalssitzungen* (f.pl.) is the *Büttenreden* (f.pl.) which are outwardly humorous speeches satirizing the public and political events of the past year, but often they are savagely critical and have been prepared by masters in the arts of invective as well as ambiguity, the subtleties usually being lost on all save the most perceptive of the audience. The parties, processions and balls usually take place in the week terminating on Shrove Tuesday. The two most important days are *Rosenmontag* and *Faschingsdienstag* (Shrove Tuesday).

fassen. 'To seize' or 'grasp' both figuratively and literally. There are many idiomatic uses, however, e.g. *sich ein Herz fassen,* 'to pluck up courage'; *in Worte fassen,* 'to put into words'. In telephone boxes you may see the injunction *fassen Sie sich kurz!* 'be brief' while *fassen Sie sich* alone means 'pull yourself together'. *Die Fassung (-en)* is 'the setting' of a jewel but *die Fassung verlieren* means 'to lose hold of oneself'. *Fassung* can also mean 'rendering' or 'translation' as in *die deutsche Fassung von diesem Buch. Tragen Sie es mit Fassung,* 'Bear it with stoic fortitude' and *mach dich auf das Schlimmste gefaßt* is colloquial too: 'Prepare yourself for the worst'.

faul. 'Lazy' and as some country people in England refer to bad apples as 'lazy apples' so the German for 'bad fruit' is always *faules Obst. Ein Faulkranker* is 'a malingerer'.

fehlen. 'To lack'; but if you go to a doctor, he might ask you *wo fehlt's?* or *was fehlt Ihnen?* 'what is wrong with you?'. *Weit gefehlt* means 'not by a long shot'. When you want to say that someone is absent, you use *fehlen,* e.g. *Der Schüler fehlt,* 'The pupil is absent'. If you are a smoker you will notice *Fehlfarbe* on some cigar boxes or labels which indicates that the outer wrapper of the cigar is mottled or discoloured, i.e. not 'true' in colour and so the cigars are reduced in price. *Das hat mir gerade noch gefehlt* is 'that was all I needed' (ironic).

Fernstudium (n -ien). 'Correspondence course'.

fertig. 'Ready' and *bereit* also means 'ready'; *fertig* means 'ready' and also 'finished' but *bereit* can never mean 'finished'. *Bereit* describes an attitude of being prepared or willing to do something whereas *fertig* indicates that all the preparations have been completed. The colloquial verbs *fertigkriegen* and *fertigbringen* mean 'to manage' and *fertigwerden mit,* 'to cope with'.

fett. 'Fat', 'greasy' and *Fett* (n -e) 'fat' or 'grease'; (*bei jemandem*) *ins Fettnäpfchen treten,* 'to put one's foot in it' which comes from the pot of grease *das Fettnäpfchen* which used to stand by the doors of farmhouses so that people could grease their boots when going out into the wet.

Feuer (n -). 'Fire'; *Haben Sie Feuer?* or *Können Sie mir Feuer geben?* 'Can I have a light?'

Feuerstuhl (m ¨-e). Slang among the young for a noisy motor-cycle.

FF. Pronounced and sometimes spelt *effeff*; *etwas aus dem FF können,* 'to be extremely good at something'.

filzen. (Colloquial) 'to frisk' (by police when searching for weapons, drugs, etc. on a person). It can mean 'to steal', i.e. from searching a person's pockets and taking something; it also refers to stealing unimportant objects, 'to pinch': *Wer hat meinen Kugelschreiber gefilzt?* 'Who's pinched my ballpoint pen?' Very different is the adjective *verfilzt* ('tangled' as is dirty hair) which newspapers use to describe corruption in the business world, where so many interests intervene in the aims or purposes of a project that the true objective is lost. It is also used as a noun, *Filzokratie* (f -n), e.g. *die Filzokratie in der heutigen Eisenindustrie . . .* 'the conflict of interests in the iron and steel industry today . . .'

fisselig. An untranslatable colloquial adjective meaning either a permanent state of inexactitude and sloppiness or a temporary one of nervousness and absence of composure brought about by another person's nagging. 'Jittery', 'flustered' give some idea of its meaning.

fix. 'Quick', and is also used to strengthen *fertig* which cannot take *sehr* so that the combination *fix und fertig* means 'completely finished' or 'quite ready'.

Flitterwochen (f.pl.). 'Honeymoon'. In recent years the English word honeymoon has crept into German in the translation *Honigmond* (m -e) which is sometimes used in place of the traditional name.

Flosse (f -n). 'Fin', 'flipper'; (coll.) 'hand': *Nimm die Flossen weg!* 'Take your paws off'.

flott. 'Quick'. When applied to women, girls and clothes it means 'chic', 'smart'.

Fluchtgeschwindigkeit (f -en). Escape velocity.

flüchtig. 'Fleeting', 'fleeing' and *Flüchtigkeitsfehler* (m -) the kind of slip of the tongue or hand that you make because you speak or do something too quickly. *Flüchtig kennen* 'to know somebody slightly' and *flüchtig lesen* means 'to skim through (a book)'.

Fluchtkapital (n -e and -ien). 'Hot money'; capital invested in pursuit of profit from changes in exchange rates and the withdrawal of which creates economic problems.

Flur (m -e). 'Hall' and poetically 'meadow' (in which case it is feminine and take -en in the plural). The poetic meaning has given rise to a modern colloquialism meaning 'isolated', e.g. *Der Kanzler steht allein auf weiter Flur*, 'The chancellor is isolated'.

flüssig. 'Liquid' and *flüssiges Brot* is one way of describing 'beer'.

Flüsterwitz (m -e). Satire directed at the government or other authorities.

Föhn (m -e). A warm and unpleasant wind from the Alps felt especially in Southern Germany and the cause of much irritability and depression. *Der Föhn* is also a 'hairdrier', not the large kind found at the hairdresser's but the smaller variety used at home.

Forelle (f -n). 'Trout'. *Lebende Forellen* 'live trout' is a sign often seen in restaurants and the fish themselves are usually visible swimming in a large tank in the main room or vestibule. Many restaurants include 'trout' in their names: *Forellenhof, Haus Forelle, Restaurant zur Forelle* etc.

Format (n -e). This is related to *Form* but refers to the 'size' rather than shape of an article. Colloquially it is used to express 'good quality' or 'greatness' in the phrase *von Format*: *ein Staatsmann von Format*, 'a statesman of high calibre'.

fort. 'Away', 'off' and can replace the more colloquial *weg* in such phrases as *ich muß fort*, 'I must be off'; *es ist fort*, 'it's gone' or 'lost'. As a verbal prefix it indicates 'away' or 'continue' as in *fortfahren* which can mean 'to go (drive) away', 'continue going' or just 'continue' according to the context. *Fort* appears in *in einem fort*, 'without interruption'.

fortkommen. 'To advance' and colloquially 'to be (become) lost' and in the latter sense the *fort-* can be replaced by *weg-*. *Meine Uhr ist (mir) fortgekommen*, 'I've lost (mislaid) my watch'. Note the resemblance between English and German in the colloquial *machen Sie, daß Sie fortkommen!* 'get lost!' 'make yourself scarce!'

Frauchen (n -). 'Little woman' (humorous); also the female owner of a dog. Many foodshops have a sign at about dog's eye level outside the entrance *Frauchen darf mich nicht mit reinbringen.* (The male owner is *Herrchen*.)

Frauengasse (f -n). A street name found in many old German towns and derived from the existence in such streets, many years ago, of brothels. In some cases the prefix of *Frau* in the names of streets and buildings means 'of Our Lady' e.g. *die Frauenkirche*, 'the church of Our Lady'.

frech. 'Cheeky', 'impudent' and one of those words like *dumm* that have been absorbed into American and appear in an anglicized form: *Werden Sie nicht frech* or *Kommen Sie mir nicht frech,* 'Don't get fresh with me'; *Was für eine Frechheit!* 'What cheek!'

frei. 'Free', 'not engaged' and forms many compounds and idioms. *Ich bin so frei* is an answering phrase that is going out of fashion and means 'I don't mind if I do'. On cinema posters you often see *freigegeben ab* . . . 'children or adolescents permitted to see this film from such and such an age'. When *frei* is combined with verbs you must be careful of misunderstandings: *frei sprechen* means 'to speak freely' (even extempore when referring to a speech) but *freisprechen* means 'to acquit': *sich freimachen* is 'to free oneself' from an obligation or thing, but it is also what a doctor might say to you if he wants you to undress: *machen Sie sich bitte frei.* *Freimachen* is officialese for 'to put a stamp on a letter'. *Frei stehen* is 'to stand without support' and *freistehen* 'to be free to' as in *es steht Ihnen frei zu gehen,* 'You are free to go'. *Frei nach . . .* (plus an author's name) is a phrase introducing a quotation that has been modified by the speaker to suit some particular occasion or purpose.

freilich. Not 'freely' but a confirmatory expression common in the South and meaning 'of course' or 'indeed'; when used within a sentence as in *das ist freilich nicht sehr einfach* it means 'to tell the truth'.

Fremdeingriff (m -e). An amateur's bungling attempt at repairing a radio or television set or similar piece of complicated apparatus.

fressen. 'To eat' and refers to animals eating while *essen* describes humans eating but although the textbooks usually say that *fressen* when referring to humans is always derogatory, this need not be so when the speaker is referring to somebody closely related or an intimate friend; a mother might say of her son *er ißt nicht, er frißt* meaning that he consumes large quantities, 'he doesn't eat, he stuffs himself'. German women are often loyal supporters of *FDH* which does not stand for a reactionary political party but for *friß die Hälfte* 'eat half' (of what you intended) and is believed to be the best way to slim. Colloquial and also not vulgar is the exclamation *ach du meine Fresse!* equivalent to 'good heavens!'. *Etwas gefressen haben,* 'to have understood something at last', which can, very strangely, also mean 'to dislike intensely' but as the latter it usually refers to people only. *Einen Narren an jemandem gefressen haben* describes an exaggerated fondness for a person or a thing and *ein gefundenes Fressen* means 'a heaven-sent opportunity'. To use *Fresse* (f -n) for mouth is very vulgar and *halt die Fresse!* is like the English 'shut your gob' or 'cake-hole'; a forceful but acceptable alternative is *halt die Klappe!*

freuen, sich. 'To be pleased' or 'happy'. It is used personally or impersonally: *Es freut mich (ich freue mich), Sie zu sehen,* 'I'm pleased to see you'. *Sich freuen auf* means 'to look forward to' except in letters where 'to look forward to a reply' is *einer Antwort (gern) entgegensehen. Sich wie ein Schneekönig freuen,* 'to be as happy as a sandboy'.

freundlich. 'Friendly' but much wider in meaning than the English word and means also 'kind', 'good-natured', 'pleasant', 'genial', e.g. *Es ist sehr freundlich von Ihnen,* 'It's very kind of you'.

Frikadellenakademie (f **-n**). Humorous for a domestic science college.

frotzeln. 'To chaff' or 'josh' someone.

früh. 'Early' but can also mean any time in the morning as in *morgen früh* 'tomorrow morning' and *heute früh* 'this morning'. If you want to say 'tomorrow morning early' you have to resort to the rather clumsy *morgen früh sehr früh* or *morgen früh in aller Frühe.*

Frührentner (m **-**). A person who receives old age pension at an early age, i.e. is unable to work because of physical or mental incapacity. To receive any kind of pension is, in officialese, *berentet werden; v.* also RENTNER.

fuffzig. Colloquial pronunciation of *fünfzig* and correct spelling in the phrase *er ist ein falscher Fuffziger,* 'He is two-faced' (literally 'he is a counterfeit fifty Pfennig piece').

fühlen. 'To feel' and when used intransitively it becomes reflexive *ich fühle mich wohl,* 'I feel well'. *Ich fühle mich nicht wohl in meiner Haut* means 'I'm ill at ease'. In everyday speech, the reflexive verb can mean 'to think a lot of yourself', e.g. *Jetzt wo er ein Auto hat, fühlt er sich!* 'Now that he's got a car, he really thinks he's somebody!' *Jemandem auf den Zahn fühlen* is 'to pump someone for information'.

führen. 'To lead' or 'guide' but it can disconcertingly mean 'to have' as in *führen Sie einen Paß bei sich?* 'Have you a passport on you?' or *wir führen nur Damenkleidung,* 'We only have (sell) ladies' clothes'. *Was führt Sie zu mir?* means, as you would guess, 'what brings you here?' Two commonly heard idioms are: *jemand hinters Licht führen,* 'to bamboozle someone' and *etwas im Schilde führen,* 'to be up to no good'. *Die Führung (-en)* is 'the guided tour' and *der Führer* usually means 'guide book' but the compound *der Fremdenführer* is the person who acts as a tourist guide.

fummeln. Vulgar for 'to pet', 'to grope', 'touch up'.

Fundbüro (n **-s**). 'Lost property office'.

funkelnagelneu. 'Brand-new'; in colloquial speech there are quite a few compound adjectives consisting of three (equally stressed) parts; they should be avoided in the written language but are very frequently heard in everyday conversation (*v.* ANIMAL COMPARISONS AND ANALOGIES for further examples).

Funkstreife (f **-n**). Police radio patrol, and (*Funk*)*Streifenwagen* (m -), police radio patrol car.

für. 'For'; *für sich leben* can mean 'to live for oneself only' or 'to live alone' or even 'to keep to oneself'. *Er ist gern für sich,* 'He likes to be left to himself'.

Fuß (m ˮ-e). 'Foot' but there are some idioms: *Fuß fassen,* 'to establish oneself'; *die Füße in die Hand nehmen,* 'to make a quick get-away'; *auf freiem Fuß sein,* 'to be free (not under arrest)'; *auf Freiersfüßen sein,* 'to be an eligible bachelor' or 'on the lookout for a wife'.

futsch. The nearest English equivalent is 'to have had it' or 'to be irretrievably lost' as in 'the watch has had it' ('done for'), *die Uhr ist futsch.*

Futter (n). 'Fodder' and the 'lining' in clothes; *er ist gut im Futter* describes a person looking 'well-fed'. *Futtern* means 'to gobble' and *füttern* 'to feed' human beings or animals.

G

Gammler (m -). 'Long-haired hippy'. The word is derived from *gammeln* 'not to work' in the sense of being on a permanent binge or just loafing about; the adjectives *vergammelt* and *gammelig* mean 'worn-out' and 'dirty', not because of normal wear and tear but through negligence. The noun *der Gammel* describes a 'row' or 'noise'.

Ganove (m **-n**). A colloquial word for 'thief' or 'crook'. It comes from the Yiddish 'ganeff'. *Ganovensprache* (f) (also *Rotwelsch* (n)), 'thieves' jargon'.

ganz. 'Quite' and like the English 'quite' it can also mean 'not so very much' as in 'quite good but I've seen better'. *Ganz* is often combined with *gar,* e.g. *Das haben Sie ganz und gar mißverstanden,* 'You misunderstood every bit of it'; *ganz und gar nicht,* 'not at all' or 'by no means' but *im großen und ganzen* means 'on the whole'.

gar. As an adjective means 'cooked' but (*v.* GANZ) it is also an expletive and as such figures in the common remark *gar nicht,* 'not at all'. *Nicht gar* combined with *doch* gives the sense of 'I hope not', e.g. *Er wird doch nicht gar verunglückt sein,* 'I do hope that he hasn't had an accident'.

Gardine (f **-n**). 'Curtain' of lace, net or muslin; the heavier kind is

Vorhang (m ¨-e) and the 'iron curtain' is *der Eiserne Vorhang* but oddly enough, 'to be behind bars' is *hinter schwedischen Gardinen sitzen. Gardinenpredigt* (f -en) is the 'ticking-off' a wife gives her husband when he steps out of line.

garni. Used in connection with hotels: *Hotel Garni* offers bed and breakfast only. *Garniert* on menus means that a 'garnishing' of vegetables is served with the meat.

Garnitur (f -en). A 'set' of anything but in clothes shops it usually means a set of ladies' matching underwear.

Gastarbeiter (m -). Foreign (not E.E.C.) national working in Germany under contract.

gebauchpinselt. Colloquial and used in the phrase *sich gebauchpinselt fühlen,* 'to feel flattered', 'to have been buttered up' (from 'stomach' and 'brush', i.e. have one's stomach stroked).

gebrauchen. 'To use' in the sense of 'to make use of': *das kann ich gut gebrauchen* can mean 'that'll come in handy'. Germans very often misuse *brauchen* ('to need') when they mean *gebrauchen* but not vice versa.

gebügelt. Colloquial for 'astonished'.

gebustet werden. Colloquial translation of the American 'to be busted', i.e. arrested.

Gedanke (m -n). 'Thought', 'idea' as in *das bringt mich auf einen guten Gedanken,* 'That gives me a good idea' but some idiomatic usages are not easy to fathom, e.g. *sich Gedanken machen* means 'to worry' and *auf andere Gedanken kommen* is 'to be distracted' or 'diverted' while the exclamation *kein Gedanke!* in answer to a question means 'not in the least'.

gefährliche Begegnung (f -en). Officialese for 'near-miss' referring to aeroplanes.

gefallen. When it means 'to like' it must be used impersonally: *Es gefällt mir,* 'I like it' (it pleases me). Combined with *lassen* the significance changes completely: *sich etwas gefallen lassen* means 'to stand' as in *eine solche Frechheit lasse ich mir nicht gefallen,* 'I'm not going to stand for such cheek' but the colloquial phrase *das lasse ich mir* (*schon eher*) *gefallen* means 'that's more like it'.

gefällig. It can mean 'pleasing to the eye' but in a social context it usually means 'obliging' and 'helpful': *Kann ich Ihnen gefällig sein?* 'Can I help you?' and *ein gefälliger Mensch* is 'an obliging or helpful person'; *Gefälligkeit* (f -en) is both the 'doing of a favour' and the 'willingness to do a favour'. The colloquial use in *noch ein Bier gefällig?* 'Another beer?' dispenses with the common courtesies but is not necessarily rude. *Da war was gefällig!* indicates that there was much excitement or quarrelling, 'there was a carry-on!' *Gefälligst* (originally 'most kindly') in phrases like *mach gefälligst die Tür zu!* 'Shut the damned door!' is rude and threatening.

Gefühl (n -e).   'Feeling' and found in the colloquial *das ist das höchste der Gefühle*, 'That's the best I can do for you' as in *Sie wollen vier Tage Urlaub? Zwei Tage ist wirklich das höchste der Gefühle*, 'You want four days off? Two days is really the best I can do for you'.

Gegendarstellung (f -en).   Denial, contradiction.

gehen.   'To go (on foot)'. Clocks 'go' in England as in Germany but in Germany they go in front when they are fast (*sie gehen vor*) and after when they are slow (*sie gehen nach*). Common everyday phrases with *gehen* are: *Was geht hier vor?* 'What's going on here?'; *es geht*, 'so-so'; *Das geht doch nicht*, 'You can't do that' or 'It's impossible' or 'It won't go (doesn't work)'; *Ach, gehen Sie* (*gehn's* in Southern Germany), 'Go on with you' (disbelief); *es geht hoch her*, 'things are buzzing'; *Darum geht es nicht*, 'That's not the point'; *Wenn es nach mir ginge*, 'If it were up to me'; *wo man geht und steht* (also *auf Schritt und Tritt*) 'everywhere'.

Geisterbild (n -er).   Technical term for the double image or 'ghost' phenomenon on television reception.

Geisterfahrer (m -).   Driver who inadvertently gets into the wrong lane of the *Autobahn* and usually causes serious accidents involving 'pile-ups'.

geladen sein.   Colloquial, 'to be angry' or 'furious'.

Gelenkbus (m -se).   'Articulated bus', common in Europe.

gelinde.   'Slight' or 'light' but mainly heard in *gelinde gesagt*, 'to put it mildly'.

gell.   In this form or as *gelle* or *gelt* it is found in several dialects and is a kind of question tag like *nicht wahr*; it may precede or follow the sentence.

Geltung (f -en).   Does not mean 'validity' which is *Gültigkeit* but expresses how something looks in *das Gemälde kommt in diesem Zimmer nicht zur Geltung*, 'The picture doesn't look good in this room'. *Geltungsbedürfnis* (n -se) is the 'drive for personal prestige'.

gelungen.   From *gelingen* 'to succeed in': *Das war ein gelungener Abend*, 'The evening was a success' (went off well) but when used of a person it means he is 'funny' or 'odd'.

gemein.   *Etwas miteinander gemein haben*, 'to have something in common with another person' though in everyday usage *gemein* means 'wicked' or the American 'mean'.

Generalanzeigerpresse (f -n).   Newspaper(s) without specific political affiliations.

geplättet. Colloquial for 'astonished'. Comes from the colloquial *ich bin platt,* 'I am flabbergasted', which means 'flat' but is humorously derived from *plätten = bügeln,* to press, iron.

gerade. *Gerade heute* is the equivalent of 'today of all days' and *nun gerade* usually means 'just for spite' while *ich komme gerade so aus* means 'I can just about manage'; *Er ist nicht gerade freundlich,* 'He's not exactly friendly'. Note that the meaning of *gerade* can be changed by stress in a phrase such as *er war gerade hier,* unstressed 'he happened to be here', stressed 'he was here a moment ago'.

Geratewohl, auf's. 'At random' or 'on the off-chance'; most Germans tend to mispronounce it so that it sounds like *auf's Geradewohl* but it is derived from the verb *geraten* 'to turn out' not from *gerade.*

Gericht (n -e). 'Law court' and 'meal'; *Tagesgericht* is 'plat du jour' and *Tellergericht* is a meat dish garnished with vegetables and salad and served on a large plate divided into compartments; it is usually available only in inexpensive restaurants.

gern. 'Gladly' and *gern haben* is 'to like' mostly applied to people and implies a degree of affection; colloquially it can be used to imply the opposite: *Sie können mich gern haben!* is like 'You know what you can do!'. *Gern geschehen* is a useful phrase that most foreigners can't remember when they want it and it means 'don't mention it' or the American 'you're welcome'.

Gesamthochschule (f -n). University for *Zweiter Bildungsweg* (q.v.); now many have been retitled *Universität.*

Gesamtschule (f -n). Comprehensive school.

geschehen. 'To happen'. *Das geschieht Ihnen (dir) recht,* 'That serves you right'.

Geschichte (f -n). 'Story', 'history' but in everyday speech it often means 'business', 'affair'. *Machen Sie keine Geschichten* can mean 'no funny business please' or merely express disbelief or a warning. It is also used to describe an illness: *Er hat eine Nierengeschichte,* 'He has kidney trouble'.

Gesellschafterin (f -nen). Hired female escort or sometimes a polite euphemism for a 'call-girl'. The latter frequently advertise as *Fotomodell.*

gesund. 'Healthy', 'sound' and *gesunder Menschenverstand* is 'common sense'. The exclamation *Gesundheit* is still used when someone sneezes and is not 'low class'; the reply is *danke. Sich gesundstoßen* is a colloquialism of recent creation and expresses the energetic and unscrupulous attainment of success as in *bei diesem Geschäft hat er sich gesundgestoßen,* 'He made his pile in this business'.

Gewerkschaft (f -en). 'Trade union'; *Gewerkschaftler* is a 'trade unionist'. Trade unionists address one another as *Genosse* (m -*n*) which can best be rendered as 'mate'; it does, however, also mean 'comrade' and is in use among Communist party members; in recent years an attempt has been made to replace *Genosse* with the neutral word *Kollege* (m -*n*) but this has not been widely accepted. The German equivalent of the TUC is *der Gewerkschaftsbund*. *Das Gewerkschaftswesen* is 'trade unionism'. The German trade unions have a very special legal position because they are represented on the *Aufsichtsrat* (v. AKTIE) of every public joint-stock company. Another word for trade union is *Gewerkschaftsverein* (m -*e*).

Gewissen (n -). 'Conscience' but whereas the English conscience pricks, the German one bites; *Er hat* (*macht sich*) *Gewissensbisse*, 'His conscience is pricking him'.

gewöhnlich. 'Ordinary', 'usual' but take care as it can also mean 'common' in the sense of 'vulgar'.

Gipfeltreffen (n -). Summit meeting.

glatt. 'Smooth'. Much used colloquially when something unexpected happens and it is then often combined with *weg*: *Er hat es mir glatt(weg) ins Gesicht gesagt*, 'He said it straight to my face' (and I did not expect him to); *Das habe ich doch glatt(weg) vergessen*, 'I clean forgot about it'. It can also mean 'cheek', e.g. *Er kam glatt zu spät*, 'He had the cheek to come late'.

glauben. 'To believe' but often used in the sense of 'to think'. *Ich glaube gar!* expresses incredulity. Another very colloquial expression is *daran glauben müssen*, 'to be finished off' applied to things as well as people.

gleich. 'Equal', 'like', 'similar'. *Es ist mir ganz gleich*, 'It's all the same to me'. It also means 'presently' or 'soon' and when you call a waiter in a restaurant, he often replies *komme gleich*, 'I'm coming' and if you are lucky, he will attend to you within the next half-hour. But if he replies *Kollege kommt gleich*, 'my colleague is coming', it would perhaps be better to give up hope and try another restaurant. *Gleichfalls* is used in answer to a greeting or good wish: *danke, gleichfalls*, 'thanks, and the same to you'.

Glocke (f -n). This is generally the 'church bell' and *läuten* 'to ring' describes what it does; the door-bell is *die Klingel* (-*n*) and it, and the phone, *klingeln* 'ring'; in parts of Southern Germany, *Glocke* and *läuten* sometimes replace *Klingel* and *klingeln* in colloquial usage. *Sie brauchen es nicht an die große Glocke zu hängen* is the equivalent of 'you don't need to shout it from the housetops'. *Läuten* provides the phrase *ich habe etwas davon läuten gehört* which means 'I've heard a rumour about it'.

Glück (n). 'Good luck' or 'good fortune' and also 'happiness'; *glücklich* can mean 'lucky' or 'happy' when an adjective but only 'happy' when an adverb; 'I am lucky' must be rendered by *ich habe Glück*. *Glück* forms part of numerous idioms and here are a few that are frequently heard in everyday speech: *ein Glückspilz* ('a lucky mushroom') is someone who is always fortunate; *dein (Ihr) Glück!* a warning exclamation rather like 'lucky for you'; *ein Glück, daß . . .* 'it's a good thing that . . .'; *auf gut Glück,* 'on the off-chance' and not to be confused with the miners' greeting to each other *Glück auf!*. *Von Glück reden* (or *sagen*) *können* is 'to be able to consider oneself lucky' but 'I consider myself happy' is *ich schätze mich glücklich*. Two useful greetings are: *viel Glück!* 'good luck' and *herzliche Glückwünsche zu . . .* 'congratulations on . . .' or 'many happy returns of . . .'

Glühwein (m -e). Mulled red wine.

Goethe-Institut (n -e). German equivalent of the British Council.

goldig. It must not be confused with *golden* 'gold' or 'golden'; *goldig* is equivalent to the American 'cute'.

gönnen. 'Not to begrudge' and *nicht gönnen* thus means 'to begrudge'; 'to begrudge someone the shirt on his back' can be translated into German in two phrases: *jemandem nicht das Schwarze unterm Nagel gönnen* and *jemandem nicht das Weiße im Auge gönnen* 'to begrudge someone the dirt under his finger nails' or 'the whites of his eyes'.

Gott (m ¨-er). 'God' provides Germans with a wealth of exclamations and interjections: *ach Gott* is an untranslatable preamble to many replies and equals the English 'well'; *leider Gottes,* 'unfortunately'; *weiß Gott,* 'really' and this one can also appear in the body of a sentence: *Ich habe weiß Gott keine Zeit für sowas,* 'I really have no time for that sort of thing'. In Southern Germany the greetings *Grüß Gott* and *Gott zum Gruß* often replace *Guten Tag* (in the second form it is mostly used by clergymen). 'To talk about everything under the sun' is *über Gott und die Welt reden*. *Der liebe Gott* is how children are usually taught to refer to Him and it is equivalent to 'the Lord God'.

Groschen (m -). The colloquial name for a ten Pfennig piece and 'the penny dropped' is *der Groschen ist gefallen. Bei dir fällt der Groschen pfennigweise* is a way of telling someone he is stupid as in his case the ten Pfennigs have to drop one by one before he grasps the idea.

Groschenroman (m -e). Colloquial and contemptuous name for a trashy (penny) novelette in garish paper covers. Typical are *Liebesromane* 'love stories' and *Wildwestromane* 'Westerns'.

groß. Besides the usual meanings it can convey the idea of being good at something: *Im Trinken ist er groß,* 'He's great at drinking'. Children refer to grown-ups as *die Großen*.

grün. 'Green'; *eine Fahrt ins Grüne* is 'a trip to nature', and it is from its connection with nature that *grün* has derived the implication of 'good' as well as 'young': *die grüne Seite* of a person is his left, where his heart is; *das ist dasselbe in grün* means 'that is no improvement (on the original suggestion)'. *Er ist mir nicht grün*, 'He doesn't like me'. *Grüner Bericht* is the annual government statement on the agricultural situation in the *Bundesrepublik Deutschland. Eine grüne Witwe* is 'a grass widow'.

Gruselfilm (m -e).   Horror film.

Gruß (m ¨-e).   'Greeting' and 'regards' as in *schönen Gruß zu Hause*. 'My regards to your family'.

gucken.   A colloquial word for 'to peep' or 'look' and usually pronounced as if spelt *kucken*; it can be replaced by *sehen* or *schauen* except in idiomatic phrases such as *der Unterrock guckt vor*, 'Your slip is showing' (*es blitzt* means the same) and *er wird sich umgucken!* 'He'll get a shock!'

gut.   'Good'; *gut und gern* is 'at least' or 'if not more' in estimating an amount; *Sie sind gut!* 'Some hopes'; *Sie haben gut lachen*, 'It's easy for you to laugh'; *Sie haben's gut* (which sounds like *Sie hamms gut*), 'You're lucky'; *Gut so!* 'That's it'. In Southern Germany *jemandem gut sein* means 'to love' or 'be fond of a person' but in Northern Germany it means 'to be no longer angry with a person'.

Gymnasium (n -ien).   'Grammar school' or equivalent to American high school. Pupils enter at 11 and either take the school-leaving certificate *die Mittlere Reife* at 16 or stay on 3 more years to obtain the *Abitur* (n) (also *Reifezeugnis* and *Matura*) which is a prerequisite for university entrance and entry to most professions.

H

haben.   'To have' but forms part of many colloquialisms that are not readily understandable such as the exclamation *das haben Sie davon!* 'That'll teach you!'. *Es hat nichts auf sich*, 'That's not important'; *Es hat's in sich*, 'It has hidden depths' or 'There's more to it than you'd think'; *Dafür bin ich nicht zu haben*, 'I won't lend myself to that'. In Southern Germany *es hat* may replace *es gibt* 'there is (are)' but this usage should be avoided. *Haben* can also be similar to 'having something wrong with' as in *sie hat's an der Galle*, 'She has something wrong with her gall-bladder'. Two often heard remarks are: *Hab dich nicht so!* 'Don't make such a fuss' or 'Don't take on so' and *Hat sich was!* 'That's off!'.

Hackordnung (f -en).   'Pecking-order', term borrowed from zoology.

hakeln. 'To arm-wrestle'; figuratively, 'to fight over trivialities'.

halb. 'Half' and *halbe-halbe machen* is 'to go fifty-fifty'. If someone says *das ist nichts Halbes und nichts Ganzes* he means that something is not done properly. *Ein Halbstarker* is a teenage hoodlum or 'yobbo'.

Hallelujabruder (m ⁻-) and **Hallelujamädchen** (n -). 'Salvation Army lad and lass'.

hallo. Can be used as in English on the phone but it is generally used to attract the attention of waiters and sometimes shop assistants; it is the least polite way of doing so. *Jemand mit großem Hallo empfangen* is 'to greet someone vociferously'.

Hals (m ⁻-e). Both 'throat' and 'neck' as *Nacken* (m -) can only indicate the 'nape of the neck'. 'To have a sore throat' is expressed by *einen rauhen Hals haben*. If you are 'fed up' with something you say *es hängt mir zum Hals (he)raus*. 'To be insatiable' is *den Hals nicht voll kriegen können. Hals über Kopf* is not the same as 'head over heels' but means 'too quickly', e.g. *Er reiste Hals über Kopf ab*, 'He left on the spur of the moment'. There is a superstition in Germany that if you want someone to have good luck you wish him something bad because the opposite of what you wish happens, so instead of saying 'good luck' you say 'may you break your neck and leg', *Hals- und Beinbruch*; this is often said to actors on a first night or students sitting an exam.

halt. 'Stop' but has an odd and widespread use particularly in Southern Germany as an expletive and it cannot be translated except by a longish phrase: *Es ist halt so*, 'Well, that's the way things are and nothing can be done about them' and *Er ist halt ein Dummkopf*, 'He's just a fool and that's that'.

halten. 'To hold' but in combinations and with prepositions it usually means 'think': *Was halten Sie davon?* 'What do you think of it?' Sometimes it means 'keep' as in *Milch hält sich nicht*, 'Milk won't keep' and *Halten Sie sich links*, 'Keep left'. It also translates the English 'to arrange' in sentences like 'What arrangements do you make for dinner?' *Wie halten Sie es mit der Hauptmahlzeit?* and *Das können Sie halten, wie Sie wollen*, 'You can do as you please'. The phrase *sich jemand halten* means 'to cultivate someone's acquaintance'.

Hand (f ⁻-e). 'Hand'. *Die öffentliche Hand* is 'the state' in its benevolent aspect as the giver of 'hand-outs'. *Etwas Handfestes* is 'something substantial' and the German rendering of something having neither rhyme nor reason would be *es hat weder Hand noch Fuß*. In the newspapers you often see the phrase *es kam zu Handgreiflichkeiten*, 'it came to a punch-up' or 'to blows' in the write-up about some incident in a bar. *Der Handkuß*, 'hand kissing' of married women among the upper classes is going out of fashion but provides the origin for a phrase in Northern Germany *mit Handkuß* meaning 'with enthusiasm' and appears in sentences such as *Jede andere Firma nimmt mich mit Handkuß*, 'All the other firms will fall over themselves to get me'. In Southern Germany and Austria *küß die Hand, gnä' Frau* sometimes replaces other greetings to married and single women in non-élite circles but is never accompanied by an actual kiss.

Hans. A common first name which appears in various everyday expressions: *Hans im Glück* is someone who is stupid but lucky; *ein Hansdampf in allen Gassen* is 'a busybody'; *Hanswurst* (m) can be a 'circus clown' or a 'silly fool' in general contexts; *bei uns ist Schmalhans Küchenmeister* means that 'we don't get much to eat at home'.

Hansestadt (f ¨-e). Bremen, Hamburg and Lübeck still proudly proclaim themselves *freie Hansestadt*, 'free Hanseatic town' as former members of the Hanseatic League and put an *H* before the town's initials on car number plates.

Haube (f -n). 'Bonnet' of a car and nurse's little white cap. Once upon a time married women wore bonnets so *ein Mädchen unter die Haube bringen* means 'to marry a girl off'.

Hauptverkehrszeit (m -en). Rush hour.

Haus (n ¨-er). 'House' but do not be misled by advertisements into thinking that the description *das erste Haus am Platz* is an address; it means 'the best establishment in the area (place)' and refers to shops, cafés etc.

Häuschen (n -). *Ganz aus dem Häuschen sein*, 'to be beside oneself' with excitement, joy etc.

hausen. Does not mean 'to house' but either 'to behave badly in another person's property' or 'to live in wretched conditions'.

Hausfrauenkredit (m -e). Loans of up to DM 2,000. -, made to married women by certain loan companies; the company does not require the husband's consent to the transaction.

Haxe (f -n). 'Trotter' (in cooking), e.g. *Schweinshaxen*, 'pigs' trotters'; colloquially it refers to a person's feet or lower legs but mostly in Southern Germany (where it is also often used in the masculine form *der Haxen*).

he. Often also *heda*, a loutish way of saying *hallo*.

Heide (m -n). 'Heathen' but in compounds means 'an excessive amount of', e.g. *Heidenangst*, 'excessive anxiety'; *Heidenarbeit*, 'too much work'.

Heilfasten. Fasting for one's health. *Heilfasten hilft bei vielen Krankheiten*, 'Fasting helps with many diseases'.

Heimatschnulze (f -n). A particularly sickening type of film about life and love affairs in the mountains and forests where clean-living young forester rescues fair maiden from clutches of vile Sir Jasper; such films were made in abundance in the 1950s.

Heini (m -s). Short for *Heinrich* but also means 'silly fool'.

heißen. 'To be called' as in *wie heißen Sie?* 'What is your name?' or *wie heißt das auf deutsch?* 'What's that in German?'. If spoken curtly, *was soll das heißen?* is a reproof meaning 'what's that supposed to mean?'. *Heißen* can also signify 'mean' in *das hieße, ihn im Stich lassen,* 'That would mean leaving him in the lurch' and *hier heißt es, schnell handeln* is 'what's called for here is quick action'. It can also translate 'it is said that', e.g. *Es heißt, er hat Geld,* 'It is said that he has money'. Many English textbooks still teach the archaic use of *heißen* 'to tell (order)' as in *wer hat Sie geheißen, das zu tun?* 'Who ordered you to do that?' which is rare today and replaced by *sagen* and *befehlen*.

heißer Ofen (m -). Humorous for a powerful sports car.

heiter. 'Serene' or 'cheerful' and colloquially used to indicate the opposite: *Das kann ja heiter werden,* 'That's going to be a lovely mess' (in this sense it is usually combined with *ja*).

helau. A *Fasching* version of 'hallo' and used only as a greeting during *Fasching*.

Heller (m -). An old German coin which figures in some often heard phrases: *auf Heller und Pfennig bezahlen,* 'to pay up to the last penny'; *Ich würde dafür keinen roten Heller bezahlen,* 'I wouldn't give a penny for it'.

her, hin. Two prefixes or suffixes; their logic will become apparent if you remember that they are used almost exclusively with verbs of motion; *her* means towards the speaker and *hin* away from him; *Bring es hierher,* 'Bring it here'; *Bring es dorthin,* 'Take it there'. Germans have a fine game adding *hin* and *her* to prepositions but with a little ingenuity you can work out the meaning, e.g. *hinaus,* 'out' and away from the speaker; *heraus,* 'out' but towards the speaker (who ought therefore to be outside also). The word made familiar by so many Anglo-American war films *raus,* 'get out' is short for *heraus* and really incorrect unless the speaker is standing outside; when he is inside, he ought to say *hinaus* but nobody ever does. It is not uncommon for Germans to confuse the two prefixes in other contexts. Phrases worth remembering are: *es ist schon eine Woche her,* 'it's a week (since)'; *vor sich hin,* '(to speak, read etc.) to oneself'; *es ist hin,* 'it's gone, done for'; *hin ist hin,* 'gone is gone'; *hin und wieder,* 'every now and then'; *nichts wie hin!* 'let's go!'; *kein Hin und Her,* 'no hesitation'. *Hin und her* may be used in another sense meaning 'even if', e.g. *Freund hin, Freund her, ich kann ihm nicht helfen,* 'Even if he is my friend, I can't help him'.

Herzinfarkt (m -e). Stroke, heart attack, coronary.

herzlich. 'Cordial', 'sincere' but can be used ironically as in *das ist herzlich wenig,* 'That's precious little'.

Herzschlag (m ¨-e). 'Heart-beat' and also 'heart-failure'.

heute. 'Today' and has an adjective *heutig* 'of today' and likewise *morgen* and *gestern* have adjectives *morgig* and *gestrig*. *Von heute auf morgen* indicates 'quickness': *das kann ich nicht so von heute auf morgen,* 'I can't do it that quickly (i.e. just in a day)'.

hieb- und stichfest. Refers to consistency in an argument: 'holds water'.

hin *v.* HER.

hinkommen. 'To get (yourself) there', 'to approach'; *das kommt hin,* 'that'll be about right (just about do)'.

hinkriegen. 'To get (something) there' and also colloquial for 'to manage to do'. *Das hast du sauber hingekriegt!* 'well done!'.

hintereinander. 'One after the other'; *drei Tage hintereinander,* 'three days running'.

Hinz und Kunz. (In Southern Germany *Krethi und Plethi*) 'Every Tom, Dick and Harry'.

Hitze (f). *Fliegende Hitze* or *Hitzewellen* (f.pl.), 'hot flush', the waves of heat that often afflict women at the menopause.

hoch. 'High'. Colloquially much abused to replace *herauf* or *hinauf* in the sense of 'upstairs': *ich gehe jetzt hoch,* 'I'm going upstairs now' but should be avoided where misunderstandings might arise (*hochgehen* is really 'to explode' or 'blow one's top'). *Hoch* combined with a figure is 'to the power of' in mathematics but in the phrase . . . (a number plus) *Mann hoch* it means '. . . people altogether'.

hochkommen. 'To come upstairs' (*v.* HOCH) and also commonly used for 'to feel sick': *mir kommt's hoch,* 'it makes me sick' (often in a figurative sense); it must not be confused with the standard phrase *wenn's hoch kommt,* 'at the most'.

Hochschule (f -n). Not a 'high school' but a university (*v.* also SCHULE).

Höhe (f -n). 'Height'; *Das ist doch die Höhe (der Gipfel)!* 'That's the limit (last straw)!'

Holz (n ˮ-er). 'Wood' provides the basis for two expressions; *auf dem Holzweg sein,* 'to be on the wrong track' and *Süßholz raspeln,* 'to say sweet nothings' to a girl. *Gut Holz!* an encouragement or greeting among bowlers; indoor bowling *Kegeln* is very popular in Germany and the names of bowling clubs often include the word *Holz* (*v.* also UNBERUFEN).

Honig (m). 'Honey' and used to express the English 'to butter up': *jemandem Honig um den Mund* (or *Bart* or the vulgar form *um's Maul* depending on the region) *schmieren.*

Hopfen (m). 'Hops'. *Bei ihm ist Hopfen und Malz verloren,* 'He is a hopeless case' (because hops and malt are wasted on him).

hören. 'To hear' and 'to listen' though 'to listen to' is *zuhören. So hören Sie doch!* is rather forceful and means 'will you please listen (to me)!'. *Das läßt sich hören* is 'that sounds reasonable'. *Hört, hört!* is an exclamation that does not mean the English 'hear, hear!' but expresses mocking disbelief. *Hören Sie mal* can be a not very polite equivalent to 'I say . . .' but when stressed it is a strong warning something like 'now, look here . . .'.

Hunger (m). 'Hunger'. In German you 'have hunger', *Hunger haben* and 'have thirst', *Durst haben*, but *hungrig sein* and *durstig sein* are not incorrect, merely uncommon.

husten. 'To cough' and in declining to do something, you might hear the rather strong refusal: *Ich werde Ihnen was husten!* which equals 'I won't do anything of the sort'.

I

i. Usually a sound of disgust or loathing, but *i wo!* is a colloquial answer 'of course not'.

immer. 'Always' and 'ever'. In combination with *noch* it is used for emphasis and cannot be satisfactorily translated: *Er ist immer noch hier* (*noch immer hier*) 'He's still here'. Many phrases used to calm contain *immer*, e.g. *Immer langsam*, 'There's no hurry'; *Immer ruhig Blut*, 'Don't get excited'.

imstande. 'Capable' and most commonly used in sentences such as *er ist imstande und vergißt es*, 'I wouldn't put it past him to forget it'.

Inkassobüro (n -s). 'Debt-collecting agency'.

Intensivstation (f -en). Intensive care unit in a hospital.

interessieren. 'To interest'. 'I am interested in . . .' can be expressed in two ways: *ich interessiere mich für . . .* and also *ich bin an . . . interessiert*; 'I have an interest in' can be rendered by *ich habe an . . . Interesse.* 'Disinterested' is *unparteiisch; desinteressiert* and *uninteressiert* mean 'uninterested'.

Intimsphäre (f -n). The most private sector of one's life but refers always to one's sexual life.

intus. *Etwas intus haben*, 'to have something inside oneself', i.e. have eaten something, be drunk or have understood something according to the context.

irgend. 'Any' and sometimes 'in any way' as in *wenn irgend möglich*, 'If in any way possible'. *Irgend so ein* means 'one of those' or 'one of that kind of' as in *irgend so ein Vertreter,* 'Some kind of travelling salesman' or 'one of those travelling salesmen'.

irr(e).   'Insane' but colloquially often means no more than 'confused' as in *du machst mich ganz irr, sei still* which is about equivalent to 'I can't concentrate, be quiet'.

irren.   'To err' and 'to be wrong'. It is reflexive in everyday usage: *Ich habe mich in der Nummer geirrt,* 'I made a mistake about the number'. *Sich um . . . irren* means 'to miscalculate by . . .': *Sie haben sich um zwei Mark geirrt,* 'You've made a mistake of two Marks'. *Sich verirren,* 'to lose one's way'.

Irrtum (m ¨-er).   'Error', 'mistake' and often heard as a single word answer *Irrtum!* meaning 'that's where you're wrong!'

J

ja.   'Yes', probably the most versatile word in the language. As an answer or introductory word it exists in numerous combinations with *aber, ach, also, doch, nun, na, schon* etc. which convey hesitation or emphasis and all of which can be understood from the context or the speaker's intonation. Not so easy to understand are the various uses of *ja* as an expletive and we have tried to classify the most important:

(a) causative or explanatory: 'because' and may be combined with *weil, da* or *denn* or may replace them: *Du mußt ihn mir zeigen, (denn) du kennst ihn ja am besten,* 'You must point him out to me because you know him best' and *Mach dir keine Gedanken, die Vase war ja nicht wertvoll,* 'Don't worry, (because) the vase wasn't valuable'.

(b) surprise: *Es schneit ja!* 'Goodness, it's snowing!'.

(c) calmative intention: *Es muß sich ja eines Tages bessern,* 'Don't worry, it'll have to improve one day'.

(d) impatience: *Ich komme ja schon!* 'All right, all right, I'm coming!'

(e) reservations (in combination with *aber*): *Ich weiß es ja, aber was kann ich denn tun?* 'I know, I know, but what can I do (then)?'

(f) question tag: *Habe ich recht, ja?* 'I'm right, am I not?'; *Du weißt ja, wie es ist,* 'You know how these things are, don't you?'

(g) warning but only if the spoken emphasis is on the *ja,* e.g. *er darf ja nicht ans Telephon* with stress on the *ja* means that the *er* referred to is on no account to be permitted access to the telephone, but without this stress it would only provide an explanation 'because he is not allowed to touch the telephone'; *tu es ja nicht!* 'I warn you, don't do it!'

Jacke (f -n). 'Jacket' and *Strickjacke* 'cardigan'. One way of saying the choice of alternatives does not matter uses *Jacke*: *das ist Jacke wie Hose*; another is *das ist gehüpft wie gesprungen* (pronounced *das's gehüppt wie gesprungen*); both being more or less equal to 'I don't mind (which)'.

Jahrgang (m ¨-e). The year of origin: 'vintage' for wines, 'year of birth' for people but the production year of a car is *Baujahr*.

Jahrmarkt (m ¨-e). Originally an 'annual fair' or 'market' but now an entertainment fair or fun-fair held on a public holiday.

Jammer (m). *Es ist ein Jammer* and *es ist jammerschade* mean 'what a shame'.

Jenaer Glass (n). A trade name but now stands for 'heat-resistant glass' in general.

jucken. 'Itch' and *kratzen* 'to scratch' and Germans often confuse the two. A colloquial meaning of *jucken* is 'to bother': *Wen juckt's?* 'Who is going to bother?'; *Wo juckt's?* 'What's bothering you?'

Junge (m -n). The usual word for 'boy'; *Knabe* and *Jüngling* are literary and rarely used in speaking. The plural varies, although *Jungen* is correct, the plural in Northern Germany is *Jungs* while in other regions *Jungens* is favoured. The phrase 'boy, oh boy' is *Junge, Junge!* and common among young people. *Ein schwerer Junge* indicates a criminal, 'a bad egg'.

Jux (m -e). 'Joke', not an anecdote or story but practical: *Wir wollen uns einen Jux mit ihm machen,* 'We want to play a joke on him'.

JWD. A colloquial abbreviation (pronounced 'yott-vay-day') which stands for *janz* (dialect pronunciation of *ganz*) *weit draußen*: *Er kommt von JWD,* 'He comes from the back of beyond'.

K

Kaffee (m -s). 'Coffee' is usually served plain and with a tiny jug of condensed milk or *Schlagsahne,* 'whipped cream'; in some cafés white coffee *Kaffee verkehrt* (*Melange* in Austria) is obtainable. Caffeine-free coffee is called *Malzkaffee* or *Kaffee Hag* and colloquially referred to as *Blümchen* or *Muckefuck,* the last name dating back to the Franco-Prussian War of 1870–1 and is a Germanization of 'mocca faux' by the Prussian soldiers. Coffee is generally ordered by the cup: *eine Tasse Kaffee, bitte* or by the pot: *ein Kännchen.*

Kaffeekränzchen (n -). 'Hen party' often called more aptly a *Kaffeeklatsch* (m) ('coffee gossiping'); the members refer to themselves as *Kränzchendamen* or *Kränzchenschwestern*.

Kamelle (f -n). A colloquial corruption of *Kamille* 'camomile' and used derogatorily for a 'hackneyed plot or story'; a similar expression is *kalter Kaffee*: *Das ist eine ganz olle Kamelle* or *Das ist ja alles kalter Kaffee*, 'That's all old stuff'; *Kamelle* refers more to books and plays while *Kaffee* is used for 'news'.

Kanone (f -n). 'Cannon'. Two colloquialisms refer to achievement in any field but especially in sports: *unter aller Kanone* is a very poor achievement but *eine Kanone sein* is 'to be very good at' as in *Er ist eine Kanone im Schwimmen*, 'He is very good at swimming'.

Kanzleideutsch (n). Also *Behördendeutsch* and *Verwaltungssprache* (f) 'officialese'.

kapieren. Colloquial 'to understand'; *schnell* (*schwer*) *von Kapee*, 'quick (slow) on the uptake'.

Kapitel (n -). *Das dunkle Kapitel* is the 'dark chapter' in German history, i.e. the Holocaust.

kaputt. A colloquial word known to most foreigners but one which often sounds a little childish to Germans particularly in the combinations *kaputtgehen* 'to break' or 'break down' (intransitive) and *kaputtmachen* 'to break' (transitive). There is no other alternative to *kaputtgehen* save the very literary *entzweigehen* and in order to avoid both, Germans try to use verbs like *zerbrechen* or *zerreißen* whenever possible.

Karambolage (f -n). 'Pile-up' resulting from cars colliding.

Karte (f -n). 'Card' but in compounds really means 'the paper on which something is printed' as in *Landkarte* 'map', *Speisekarte* 'menu', *Fahrkarte* 'ticket' and *Stadtkarte* 'town plan' (street map).

kaschieren. 'To conceal or lessen a defect' by distracting the attention of the onlooker: *Das gestreifte Kleid kaschiert ihre breiten Hüften*, 'The striped dress makes her hips look slimmer'.

Kasse (f -n). 'Cash box', 'cash register'; *der Kassierer* 'the cashier'. Recently a verb *kassieren* has been devised which means 'to ask for and take payment' and waiters and sales staff often use the formula *darf ich kassieren, bitte?* which is roughly equivalent to 'would you mind paying now?' and usually indicates that the waiter wants to go off duty. *Gut bei Kasse sein*, 'to have a lot of money' and *knapp bei Kasse sein*, 'to be short of money'. *Bei mir stimmt die Kasse*, 'I'm all right for money' (i.e. have enough). The wide coverage given in the German press and television to the London Airport robbery some years ago produced a popular colloquialism: *zur Kasse bitten*, 'to make someone pay up' and it is much used in journalism as well as in irony: *Die öffentliche Hand* (*v.* HAND) *bittet zur Kasse,* 'The state requests you to pay up' (e.g. your income tax). *Kasse* is also short for *Krankenkasse* (health insurance) and *Sparkasse* (savings bank).

Kauf (m ¨-e). 'Purchase'; *ein Gelegenheitskauf,* 'a bargain'. *Etwas in Kauf nehmen,* 'to have to take the bad with the good' or 'you can't have it both ways'.

Kaufhaus (n ¨-er), **Kaufhof** (m ¨-e). Large usually inexpensive department stores.

kennen. 'To know' and *wissen* and *können* also mean 'to know' and cause non-Germans some confusion. *Kennen* is 'to know because you are familiar with'; *wissen* 'to know' in the sense of 'being aware of' or 'understanding'; *können* is 'to know how to' but remember that the verb following is often omitted: *Ich kann es,* 'I know how to do it'; *Ich kann Deutsch,* 'I speak German'.

kennenlernen. 'To get to know', 'make the acquaintance of' and *er soll mich kennenlernen!* conveys the same kind of warning as 'I'll show him!'

Kenntnis (f -se). 'Knowledge'. When it implies knowledge through learning it is always in the plural: 'knowledge of German' is *Deutschkenntnisse.* In business letters the phrase *zur Kenntnis nehmen* means 'to note' (the contents of your letter etc.).

Kind (n -er). 'Child'. The two adjectives derived from it have different meanings: *kindlich* is 'childlike' whereas *kindisch* is 'childish' in the bad sense of 'puerile'. There is an idiom *sich lieb Kind machen bei* which means 'to ingratiate oneself with' (one's superiors), and *wir werden das Kind schon schaukeln* is a calming-down phrase meaning 'don't worry, we'll wangle it somehow'.

Kinderstube (f -n). Not the 'nursery' (which is *das Kinderzimmer*) but 'manners': *Er hat eine gute Kinderstube,* 'He has good manners'.

Kintopp (m or n -s). 'Soap opera', also a colloquialism for 'the cinema'.

Kippe (f -n). Colloquialism for 'cigarette end' and slang: 'fag-end'.

Kirche (f -n). 'Church'; *Man muß die Kirche im Dorf lassen,* 'That is going too far' or 'One mustn't exaggerate'.

Kirmes (f -sen). Village or small town annual open-air dance, fun-fair and fiesta, with side-shows, the owners of which are called *Schausteller.*

Kitsch (m). Sentimental and trashy forms of ornament or art; the adjective is *kitschig.*

Klacks (m -e). Colloquially a small quantity of solid food, never liquid; *ein Klacks Butter,* 'a bit (dollop) of butter'; also with *jeder*: *Warum habe ich einen Assistenten, wenn ich jeden Klacks allein machen muß?* 'Why do I have an assistant, if I have to do every little chore myself?' Also means a 'triviality'.

Klamotten (f.pl.).   'Odds and ends' but is rather contemptuous and usually refers to clothes; for articles in general and non-contemptuously 'odds and ends' is best expressed by *Siebensachen* (f.pl.).

Klappe (f -n).   A slang word for 'bed' and 'mouth'; *in die Klappe gehen* means 'to turn in' or 'hit the sack' while *halt die Klappe* is 'shut up'.

klappen.   A very popular colloquial verb meaning 'to succeed': *Hat es geklappt?* 'Did it work?' or 'Were you successful?'. *Alles klappe wie am Schnürchen,* 'Everything went like clock-work'.

Klaps (m -e).   'Slight slap' or 'smack'. Colloquially, *er hat einen Klaps* means 'he's round the bend' and *eine Klapsmühle* is colloquial for a mental hospital: 'loony-bin'.

klar.   'Evident', 'clear' and often a single word answer 'of course'. *Das geht klar* is equivalent to 'O.K.'; *sich im klaren sein über* means 'to realize' or 'be aware of'. *Schnaps* (m ¨-e) is like gin in appearance, and a rather vulgar way of ordering a *Schnaps* is to ask for *einen Klaren, bitte* and even more vulgar is to ask for *einen Kurzen, bitte*; the colourless liquid is drunk at one gulp and usually washed down with a beer chaser, generally of the light type called *ein Helles* (*v.* BIER).

kleiden, sich.   'To wear clothes' and 'to dress in . . .' but not 'to put on clothes' or 'get dressed' which is *sich anziehen* or more literary *sich ankleiden. Kleiden* can also mean that clothing is 'becoming' thus *Es kleidet mich,* 'It suits me'.

Kleinkredit (m -e).   A loan made by a commercial bank to a customer for his personal (non-business) use; such loans were introduced in 1959 by the Association of Private Banks (*Bundesverband des privaten Bankgewerbes*) and are usually for DM 5,000. – repayable in two years and with a low rate of interest; no security other than a guarantee by the employer or the borrower's husband or wife is required.

kleinlich.   Not 'smallish' but 'narrow-minded' and also 'mean'.

Klimaanlage (f -n).   Air conditioning.

Klubgarnitur (f -en).   Three-piece suite.

Klubjacke (f -n).   Blazer.

klug.   'Clever'; *nicht klug werden aus,* 'not to understand what makes a person tick' or of things 'not to be able to make head or tail of' something.

Knall (m -e).   'Bang'; *Er hat einen Knall,* 'He's off his rocker'. *Knäller* (m -) is a colloquial name for all the noise-producing articles sold for New Year's Eve and festivals, 'bangers'. *Knallen* is 'to bang' or 'slam' and can also mean to smack someone's face. *Knallig* (adj) refers almost entirely to colours and means 'gaudy'.

Knast (m).   A colloquialism for 'imprisonment'; *im Knast sein*, 'to be in prison' and *Knast schieben*, 'to do time'.

kneifen.   'To pinch'; colloquially 'to shirk' or 'dodge'; the thing shirked is not mentioned, if you wish to mention it you must use *sich drücken vor* . . . . *Kneifen* is used in phrases such as *jetzt können Sie nicht kneifen*, 'You can't dodge it now' and *kneifen gilt nicht*, 'There's no shirking it'.

kneippen.   This has nothing to do with *Kneipe* 'pub', 'tavern' or *kneipen* 'to go boozing' but is derived from Sebastian Kneipp (1821–97), a Catholic priest who popularized the use of plain cold water (externally and internally) to relieve or cure a variety of ailments. Most German health resorts offer the *Kneippkur* (f *-en*) as a means of combating 'executive illnesses' and old age.

Knigge (m).   A word meaning a standard work on correct social behaviour or etiquette and derived from Adolf von Knigge (1752–96), the author of one of the first books on this subject.

Knirps (m *-e*).   An endearment; 'little chap' when used of a child but contemptuous when directed at an adult (dictionaries tell us it means 'dwarf' but it is rarely used in this sense). It is the trade name of the best known *Taschenschirm* (m *-e*) 'telescopic umbrella' but has also become the general descriptive term for all umbrellas of this type.

Knobel (m *-*).   'Dice'; *Knobelbecher* (m *-*) the 'leather dice cup'; *knobeln* 'to play dice' or similar games to decide whose turn it is to do something; it also means 'to try and find a solution' as in *wir knobeln schon seit Wochen an diesem Problem herum*, 'For weeks we've been puzzling over a solution to this problem'.

Knüller (m *-*).   Sensational success of something such as a 'hit record'.

Koffer (m *-*).   'Suitcase' but in compound words it means 'portable' e.g. *Kofferradio* (n *-s*), 'portable radio'.

Kohldampf (m).   Colloquial for 'hunger': *Kohldampf schieben* (*haben*), 'to be hungry'.

Kohlen (f.pl.).   'Coal' and a slang term for 'money'. It also provides a much used idiom: *wie auf glühenden Kohlen sitzen*, 'to be on tenterhooks'. The colloquial verbs *kohlen* and *ankohlen* 'to tell lies (to)' derive from the colloquial use of *Kohl* (m), 'cabbage' to mean 'nonsense' or 'gibberish'.

Kohlenpott (m).   A nickname for the *Ruhrgebiet* (n).

Kohlepfennig (m *-e*).   An invention of June 1976; an extra amount is charged on every unit of gas and electricity. The money is used to subsidize the coal industry.

Kolleg (n *-s* or *-ien*).   Only a 'college' when referring to a Catholic seminary; generally it means a 'university lecture'; *Kollegbedarf* (m) is all the writing materials a student needs at lectures.

kommen. 'To come'; note in particular the variations in meaning when it is combined with *zu*: *Ich kam dazu, als es passierte,* 'I happened to be there when it occurred'; *Wie kommen Sie dazu, das zu tun?* 'What on earth made you do this?' and also 'What gives you the right to do this?'; *Ich komme nicht dazu, es zu tun,* 'I don't get the time to do it'. Some of the commonest idioms are: *Es ist mir abhanden gekommen,* 'I've lost (mislaid) it'; *nichts auf jemand kommen lassen,* 'to think highly of someone'; *auf etwas kommen,* 'to remember (think of) something'; *Wie kommen Sie darauf?* 'What gives you that idea?'; *Das kommt davon!* 'That'll teach you!'; *So können Sie mir nicht kommen!* 'You can't do that with (to) me!'

kontaktarm. Introvert(ed); *kontaktfreudig,* extrovert(ed).

Kopf (m ¨-e). 'Head'; *Geld auf den Kopf hauen,* 'to spend money on drinking or women'.

kosten. 'To cost' and also 'to taste' or 'try' food.

Kosten (pl.). 'Cost', 'expenses'; note the difference between *es geht auf meine Kosten,* 'It's on me' and *auf seine Kosten kommen,* 'to get one's due' (not to be disappointed).

kotzen. Vulgar for 'to be sick' but heard often in the phrase *es ist zum Kotzen,* 'It's enough to make one sick'.

Krach (m ¨-e). 'Row', 'din', 'quarrel' and from the latter meaning *sie haben Krach* (*miteinander*) or *sie sind verkracht,* 'They are not on speaking terms'; *Krach schlagen,* 'to kick up a row'.

Krachledernen (f.pl.). Colloquial for 'leather shorts' for adults.

Kragen (m -). 'Collar' and in idioms 'neck': *Er riskiert seinen Kragen,* 'He's risking his neck'; *Es geht um Kopf und Kragen,* 'All is at stake'. *Das ist genau meine Kragenweite* could mean 'that's just my collar size' but usually it means 'that's right up my street'. 'That's about as much as I'm going to stand for' is *jetzt platzt mir aber der Kragen!*

Krankenhaus (n¨-er). 'Hospital'; *Klinik* (f -en) is either a 'private hospital' or a 'specialized clinic' except that in university towns all the 'hospitals' that are departments of the university are referred to as *Universitätsklinik. Spital* (n ¨-er) is rarely used and means a very small hospital and *Hospital* (n ¨-er) is only used in proper names. *Poliklinik* is 'out-patients' department'.

Kreuz (n -e). 'Cross' and the cross you bear and thus 'suffering'; in some parts of Germany it is used to mean a person's 'back'. *Drei Kreuze machen* is an expression indicating relief: *Ich mache drei Kreuze, wenn es vorbei ist,* 'I'll be glad when it is over'. *Aufkreuzen* is colloquial for 'to arrive unexpectedly' or 'to show up'; 'to cross the road' is *die Straße überqueren.*

kriegen. 'To get' and a colloquial substitute (as popular as 'get') for *bekommen* and *erhalten* but hardly ever used in writing.

Krimi (m -s). 'Thriller', short for *Kriminalroman* (m -e).

Kripo (f). A short form of *Kriminalpolizei*, the detective branch of the civil police.

Kritik (f -en). Not a 'critic' which is *Kritiker* but a 'criticism'. *Unter aller Kritik* is a more elegant way of saying *unter aller Kanone* or *unter aller Sau*, 'beneath contempt'. The verb *kritisieren* 'to criticize' has been corrupted in everyday speech to *bekritteln* or *an etwas herumkritteln*, 'to find fault with'.

krumm. 'Bent', 'crooked' and colloquially it can mean 'illegal' but only in the phrase *eine krumme Tour*, 'a crooked way' of doing something. *Etwas krummnehmen* is 'to take something amiss' or 'be offended by'.

Küche (f -n). 'Kitchen'; on notices outside restaurants and on menus 'meals' e.g. *Kalte (warme) Küche*, 'Cold (hot) meals'.

Kuli (m -s). Short for *Kugelschreiber* (m -), ballpoint pen.

Kulturbeutel (m -). A 'toilet bag' containing cosmetics, washing articles etc.

Kummerkasten (m ¨-). A kind of letter-box outside some churches and welfare institutions into which people in trouble or difficulties put letters explaining their plight; sometimes the letters are anonymous complaints.

kümmern, sich . . . um. Although derived from *Kummer* 'sorrow' this verb (which is indispensable in everyday life) has three main meanings: *Ich werde mich darum kümmern*, 'I'll see to it'; *Ich kümmere mich um ihn*, 'I'm looking after him'; *Kümmern Sie sich nicht um . . .*, 'Don't worry about . . .'.

Kumpel (m - or -s). A dialect word for a 'coalminer' now also equivalent to 'mate', 'buddy', or 'bloke'.

Kunst (f ¨-e). 'Art'. *Nach allen Regeln der Kunst* is a colloquial phrase defying translation but meaning that something is done properly according to all the 'tricks of the trade'. *Kunststück* is a 'clever trick' but can be a single word reply rather like 'so what!'. Note the adjectives *künstlerisch* 'artistic' and *künstlich* 'artificial'.

Kurort (m -e). 'Health resort' usually full of *Kliniken* and nursing-homes and hotels specializing in the popular 'second holidays' of businessmen (usually unaccompanied by their wives) as a precaution against the strains of business life. *Zur Kur fahren (gehen)*, 'to go on a cure' and *zur (auf) Kur sein in . . .*, 'to be on a cure in . . .'. Usually the *Kurort* specializes in a single group of ailments, e.g. Bad Nauheim for heart trouble and Bad Mergentheim for liver and gall, Bad Wildungen for kidneys. *Der Kurschatten* is the person with whom one formed an amorous attachment while on a *Kur* and the continued relationship with whom falls as a 'shadow' across husband and wife.

Kurs (m -e). 'Course' as in direction and also a 'course' in the sense of 'evening class', the latter being a corruption of *Kursus* (m); both words have the same plural *Kurse*. *Kurs* is also the 'rate of exchange' in currency dealings and from it we have the phrase *das steht bei mir hoch im Kurs,* 'I like it a lot'.

Kurzschluß (m ¨-(ss)e). 'Short circuit' but also applied to acts resulting from a mental blackout: *Kurzschlußhandlung* (f -en).

L

lachen. 'To laugh'; *erst können vor Lachen* is a reply to a request that you cannot fulfil: 'but I honestly can't' or 'if only I knew how'.

Ladenhüter (m -). An unsaleable article in a shop, a 'non-selling line', but it is also the old name for a 'shopwalker' or 'store detective'.

Land (n ¨-er). 'Country' and 'countryside' and the official name for the German States (*Länder*) of the Federal Republic.

Landplage (f -n). 'Plague', 'calamity' but also used for something bothersome or annoying: *Im Sommer sind die Gammler eine Landplage in den Großstädten,* 'In summer, the hippies are a damned nuisance in the big cities'.

Landstraßenschreck (m -e). A combination of 'road hog' and generally bad driver.

lang (e). 'Long' and often used to mean 'a long time': *Das ist schon lange her,* 'That's a long time ago'. *Noch lange* can mean 'far from' as in *das ist noch lange kein Beweis,* 'That is far from being evidence'. Care must be taken with the superlative: *längst* means 'for a long time' and is an emphatic version of *seit langem* whereas *längstens* means 'at the longest' or 'at the most' referring to time, e.g. *Das weiß ich schon längst,* 'I've known that for ages' but *Ich bleibe längstens drei Tage,* 'I'll stay for three days at the most'. A frequently heard colloquial use of *lang* to mean 'more than' or 'by a long way' should not be imitated: *Das ist lang gut für ihn,* 'That's more than good enough for him'. *Lang* also stands for 'for' as in 'for three days', *drei Tage lang*.

langen. 'To be enough' and the question *langt's?* 'is that enough?' is often used but the reply *mir langt's!* is 'I've had enough!' or 'I'm fed up with it!' rather than an answer to *langt's?*. *Jemandem eine langen* is a colloquialism having no connection with the above meanings, it is 'to smack somebody's face'.

Lappen (m -). 'Piece of cloth', 'rag' but not in a derogatory sense.

Durch die Lappen gehen means 'to slip through' and comes from the hunting practice of encircling an area to be hunted over with coloured rags tied to sticks as few frightened animals dare to pass between them. *Bei der Feier gestern abend sind mir hundert Mark durch die Lappen gegangen,* 'At the party yesterday evening I spent a hundred Marks' or 'a hundred Marks went west'.

lassen. 'To allow', 'to let' but also translates the English causative form of 'to have' as in 'I have the boy help me', *ich lasse mir von dem Jungen helfen* and 'I have my suit cleaned', *ich lasse meinen Anzug reinigen.* It also translates the English 'he made me wait for an hour', *er ließ mich eine Stunde (lang) warten.* 'Stop' or 'leave off' can also be rendered by *lassen: lassen Sie das!* 'stop it' or 'leave it'. *Das eine tun und das andere nicht lassen,* 'to have your cake and eat it'. *Etwas stehenlassen (liegenlassen),* 'to forget' or 'leave something behind'.

Last (f -en). 'Load', 'charge' but *jemandem zur Last fallen* means 'to bother' or 'trouble someone'; *lästig fallen* or *lästig sein* (in social life) is stronger and means to 'pester' or even 'molest'.

Latein (n). 'Latin' but *ich bin mit meinem Latein am Ende* means 'I'm at my wits' end'. In compounds it means exaggerated or 'tall' stories: *Jägerlatein* 'hunters' tall stories' and 'fishermen's yarns' are *Anglerlatein* but 'sailors' yarns', *Seemannsgarn.*

laufen. 'To run' but colloquially it usually means 'to go on foot' as distinct from riding or driving. *Was läuft im Kino?* 'What's on at the cinema?' *Jemand auf dem laufenden halten* is 'to keep someone up-to-date'. *Laufend* is 'always', 'continually', 'currently'.

Laufmasche (f -n). 'Ladder' in a stocking. *Leiter* (f -n) is also used.

Laufpaß (m ¨-(ss)e). 'Brush off' in girl-boy relationships: *Ich gab ihm den Laufpaß,* 'I told him we were through'.

Laufpraxis (f -xen). Doctors' jargon for 'casual patients' i.e. a doctor's 'passing trade', derived from *Laufkundschaft* (f -en), 'casual custom' of shops and restaurants.

lavabel. Washable.

Lebensgefährte (m -n), **Lebensgefährtin** (f -nen). Euphemism for lover with whom one lives.

Leberwurst (f ¨-e). To say of someone that *er ist eine* (or *spielt die*) *gekränkte Leberwurst* means that he is offended and refuses to join in the fun and is equivalent to a 'wet blanket'.

Lehre (f -n). 'Doctrine' and 'apprenticeship' but gives rise to two frequently used remarks: *Das wird ihm eine Lehre sein,* 'That'll be a lesson to him' and if someone says to you *lassen Sie sich Ihr Lehrgeld zurückgeben* he is indicating that your training premium should be returned to you as it was wasted and you are incompetent. *Lehrjunge* (m -n) 'apprentice' is often replaced by *Stift* (m -e).

lehren. 'To teach' and do not imitate the uneducated use of *lernen* 'to learn' for *lehren*. *Ein gelehrtes Haus* is a term for an educated person and similar to 'egg-head'.

leicht. 'Light' and 'easy'; *man hat's nicht leicht* is a common complaint 'life isn't easy' but *aber leicht hat's einen,* 'but it catches up with you easily enough'. 'That's not so easy' is rendered by *das geht nicht so leicht.*

leid. All foreigners learn *es tut mir leid* but not when to use it; it should only be used when you are really grieved and not as an apology when *Entschuldigung* is more appropriate; it also means 'to feel sorry for' or 'pity' as *er tut mir leid,* 'I pity him'. When *leid* is conjugated with *sein* in colloquial German it means 'to be fed up with', e.g. *Ich bin ihr ewiges Gerede leid,* 'I'm fed up with her eternal chatter'.

leiden. 'To suffer' but when used with *können* (or *mögen*) it means 'to like': *Ich kann ihn gut leiden* (in Northern Germany *Ich mag ihn wohl leiden*), 'I like him well'.

Leim (m -e). 'Glue' and 'bird-lime' and the latter meaning provides the idiom *jemandem auf den Leim gehen* which is best translated by the American 'to fall for somebody's line'; *aus dem Leim gehen* means 'to fall apart'.

leise. 'Soft' for noises, so *seien Sie doch leise!* is 'don't make such a noise'. *Leisetreterei* (f -en) is 'pussy-footing'.

leisten. 'To achieve' though with a noun it means no more than 'to do' or 'make': *gute Arbeit leisten,* 'to do a good job'. It has many idiomatic uses such as *Gesellschaft leisten,* 'to keep company'; *Hilfe leisten,* 'to assist' or 'help'; the reflexive form *sich etwas leisten,* 'to treat oneself to something' is often ironic: *Da haben Sie sich etwas geleistet,* 'That was brilliant of you'; with *können,* however, it means 'to afford'; *das kann ich mir nicht leisten,* 'I can't afford that'.

Leitung (f -en). 'Management' but also the 'mains' for water and gas and the 'cable' for electricity and the telephone ('line'); *er hat eine lange Leitung* is equivalent to 'he's rather dim (dense)'.

Leitzordner (m -). Originally a trade name but now indicates any file cover.

Lektion (f -en). 'Lesson' as the section of a textbook but an actual lesson at school is *Stunde* (f -n). It is also used in *das wird ihm eine Lektion sein,* 'That'll teach him a lesson' (*v.* LEHRE).

lernen. 'To learn' and 'to study' but 'to study at a university' is *studieren* thus 'I'm studying my lesson' is *ich lerne meine Lektion.* *Gelernt* means 'skilled' (not 'learned') and *ein gelernter Arbeiter* (also *ein Facharbeiter*) is 'a skilled worker'.

Lesezirkel (m -). Firm supplying doctors, dentists, hairdressers and cafés with copies of journals and magazines which are covered by a folder *Lesemappe* (f -n) bearing local advertisements.

letzt. 'Last' and 'latest' so beware of misunderstandings. There is no equivalent for 'few' in phrases like 'in the last few years' and it has to be translated by *in den letzten Jahren*.

Leute (pl.). 'People' but never in the sense of a nation which is *Volk* (n ¨-er) or *Nation* (f -en). In business *Leute* is often used for 'employees'. There is a play on words in the colloquialism *wir sind geschiedene Leute* (lit. 'we are divorced people') meaning 'I don't want to have anything more to do with you'.

Licht (n -er). 'Light'. *Lichtscheues Gesindel*, 'light-shunning rabble', the kind of human flotsam that hangs about the railway stations of large towns all through the night.

Lichtbild (n -er).   An alternative for *Photo* (q.v.).

Lichtspiele (n.pl.), **Lichtspielhaus** (n ¨-er) and **Lichtspieltheater** (n -).   Alternatives for *Kino* (n -s) 'cinema' but appear usually in proper names only.

lieb. 'Dear'. In phrases like *lieber Gott*, the *lieber* has lost its significance as it has also in *er hat seine liebe Not damit*, 'It is very difficult for him'. *Es wäre sehr lieb, wenn Sie . . .*, 'it would be sweet of you if you . . .' but *es wäre mir lieb, . . .*, 'I should like . . .'; *es wäre mir lieber* (the comparative) 'I should rather . . .'. When *lieber* is combined with *hätte* it means 'it would have been better if . . .': *Sie hätten lieber nicht kommen sollen*, 'It would have been better if you hadn't come'. *Am liebsten*, 'best' and *am allerliebsten* is 'best of all'; *allerliebst* is a rather affected expression equivalent to 'adorable', 'gorgeous'.

liebenswürdig. 'Kind', 'pleasant' and indispensable in social life: *Ich danke Ihnen für die liebenswürdige Einladung*, 'Thank you for your kind invitation'; *würden Sie so liebenswürdig sein . . .* 'would you be so kind as to . . .' and is followed by a *zu* or *und* clause.

liegen. 'To lie' but often the best translation is 'be'. It has many idiomatic uses. *Das liegt mir nicht* is 'that's not my line' rather than 'I don't like it' though it includes the latter idea, and *er liegt mir nicht* means 'he's not my type'. When *liegen* is combined with *an* things become complicated and many interpretations are possible: *Mir liegt viel daran*, 'It means a lot to me'; *Das liegt nicht an mir*, 'That's not my fault'; *Woran liegt es?* 'What's the cause of it?' and *An mir soll es nicht liegen*, 'As far as I'm concerned, it is all right' or the slang 'it's all right by me'.

links. 'Left' but it can also mean 'inside out' when referring to clothes: *Sie haben den Pullover auf links an*, 'You have your pullover on inside out'. *Jemand links liegen lassen* is 'to ignore' or 'disregard someone'. *Linkshänder* (m -) is a 'left-handed person'.

Litfaßsäule (f -n).   The advertisement pillars which are such a distinctive feature of German streets; named after their originator, E. Th. Litfaß, who erected the first in Berlin in 1855.

Loden (m).   A greenish-grey woollen material used for the Austro-Bavarian type of hunting and peasant cloaks, coats, jackets and even suits: *Lodenjacke, Lodenmantel, Lodenkostüm* are perennially popular and called *der Trachten-Look*, 'the peasant costume look'.

Löffel (m -).   'Spoon' but also correct for 'ears' of rabbits and hares and gives rise to the vulgar *sperr doch deine Löffel auf!* 'Why don't you damn well listen?' (open your lug-holes).

lohnen.   An archaic verb now only used in *es lohnt sich* (*nicht*), 'It's (not) worth it'. *Lohnend* (adj), 'rewarding', 'profitable'.

Lokal (n -e).   Generic name for places in which you can eat and drink; *Speiselokal* is often used as an alternative to *Restaurant*. *Kneipe* (coll.) is a place selling beer and alcoholic drinks and *Bierstube, Bierkeller, Biergarten* all indicate places selling alcohol; the *Biergarten* often has a real garden and is usually situated on river banks or by a lake. *Bräustübl* is a higher class *Bierstube*. *Stehbierhalle* has little seating and is much used for standing 'quick ones'. *Gasthof,* *Gasthaus, Gaststätte* are usually found in villages and suburbs and serve meals at midday, light meals in the evening and cater for the local drinkers; the *Bahnhofsgaststätte* must be familiar to every railway traveller and is often a local meeting place. *Wirtschaft* and *Wirtshaus* are lower class versions of the *Gaststätte* and although they offer food they rarely have any. The *Weinstube* abounds in the wine-producing districts but sells beer and spirits as well as wine. *Ausschank, Schankstube* concentrate more on wines than beer. All the foregoing could be compared with the English pub but the comparison would be misleading as the *Lokale* resemble the French bistro and Italian osteria rather than anything in England, and you can always get something to eat in them.

los.   'Off' and not to be confused with *lose* 'loose'. It forms many idioms: *Was ist los?* 'What's up?', 'What's the matter?'; *Es ist nichts los*, 'There's nothing going on' and therefore also meaning 'boring'; *er hat etwas los* is a compliment meaning 'he's got what it takes'. In colloquial German *losfahren, losgehen*, 'to drive off', 'to go off' tend to replace *abfahren* and *gehen*. *Los!* is 'off (we etc.) go' and this idea is also expressed by *also los, nun aber los, nichts wie los, los geht's! Jemand loswerden*, 'to get rid of somebody' and *loslassen*, 'to let go'.

Lot (n -e).   'Plumb-line' but there is an often used expression: *Wir werden die Sache schon wieder ins Lot bringen*, 'Don't worry, we'll sort it out' or 'put matters straight'.

Lotse (m -n).   'Pilot' but *Lotsendienst* (m -e) is a service provided by some large towns to visiting motorists who, on paying a fee, can obtain a driver to guide them through the town. *Lotsen* is 'to wangle' a person through something.

Lotto (n). State-run numbers game; *Lottoannahme(stelle)* (f -n) 'Lotto offices' can be found everywhere; the draw is weekly and the first prize considerable.

Luftlinie (f -n). 'As the crow flies': *Es ist 20 Kilometer Luftlinie.*

Lüge (f -n). 'Lie', 'untruth'; *die Auschwitzlüge* is used by neo-Nazis to express their denial of the Holocaust.

lumpen. To drink too much: *Gestern abend habe ich gelumpt,* 'Yesterday evening I drank too much'. *Sich nicht lumpen lassen,* 'to be generous' as regards an invitation or present. *Das Essen war ausgezeichnet, er hat sich nicht lumpen lassen,* 'The dinner was excellent, he certainly spent a lot'.

Lumpensammler (m -). 'Rag-and-bone man' but also the last train or bus for home at night.

Lust (f ¨-e). This can mean 'lust' but the latter is usually rendered by *Wollust.* In everyday speech, *Lust* is generally found in phrases meaning 'to feel like', e.g. *Haben Sie Lust, ins Kino zu gehen?* 'Do you feel like going to the cinema?'; *Ich hätte fast Lust,* 'I have half a mind to . . .'; *Mir ist die Lust vergangen,* 'I no longer feel like it'. *Lustig* is 'jolly', 'funny' but *sich über jemand lustig machen,* 'to make fun of someone'.

M

machen. 'To make', and as *tun* is rarely used, *machen* frequently replaces it as 'do'. In colloquial speech a noun plus *machen* often substitutes for a verb, e.g. instead of *arbeiten* we find *die Arbeit machen* for 'to work', *den Anfang machen* for *anfangen* 'to begin', but this usage is condemned by purists. *Mach's gut* is 'so long', 'cheerio' between intimate friends. Commonly heard phrases are *ich mache mir nichts aus . . .,* 'I don't much care for . . .'; *Er macht sich,* 'He's getting good'; *Nun machen Sie aber (ei)nen Punkt!* or *Machen Sie's halblang!* 'Come off it!'; *Nun machen Sie schon!* 'Hurry up and get done with it!' *Das macht Spaß* is 'that's fun' but *ich mache Spaß* means 'I'm joking'. *Gemacht* (adj) is often a single-word reply similar to 'right' or 'O.K.'

Machtwort (n -e). Only used in *Sie müssen ein Machtwort sprechen,* 'You must put your foot down'.

Macker (m -). Vulgar term for male friend used by a woman. There is a slight indication of *Zuhälter* ('pimp') but not necessarily.

Magen (m ¨-). 'Stomach'; *auf nüchternen Magen,* 'on an empty stomach'. *Magenbitter* (m -) is a potent alcoholic drink good for hangovers and upset stomachs.

Magenfahrplan (m ˝-e). 'Stomach timetable', colloquial for *Speisekarte,* 'menu'.

Mahlzeit (f -en). 'Meal' and replaces the poetic *Mahl* (n ˝-er) now only found in *Abendmahl*, the 'Lord's Supper'. *Gesegnete Mahlzeit* is something like 'good appetite' but only used among intimates and said before or after meals by the host; the greeting *Mahlzeit!* is often heard in factory and office canteens at lunch time. *Na dann prost Mahlzeit!* is a colloquial and ironic expression like 'now you've let yourself in for something, haven't you'.

mal. Colloquial abbreviation for *einmal* 'once' and it conveys friendliness; it converts an order into a request, e.g. *Kommen Sie her*, 'Come here' but *Kommen Sie mal her*, 'Can you come here for a moment'. It can be an encouraging expletive as in *gehen Sie mal hin, er wird Ihnen sicher helfen*, 'Go ahead and see him, I'm sure he'll help you'. *Mal* (n -e) 'time' as in *das letzte Mal*, 'the last time'; with figures it is combined to form *fünfmal*, 'five times', *ein paarmal*, 'a few times' etc.

Mann (m ˝-er). 'Man' but in the general sense of a 'human being' *Mensch* (m -en) is used. If you want to inquire about the sex of animals you can ask *ist es ein Männchen oder ein Weibchen?* 'Is it male or female?' 'To hold one's own' in a job is *seinen Mann stehen* and this provides a play on words in *im Berufsleben muß die Frau ihren Mann stehen*, 'In business (professional) life women must be efficient'. *Etwas an den Mann bringen* is a colloquialism meaning 'to succeed in getting rid of something'.

Martinshorn (n ˝-er). The 'hee-hawing' police car siren also used by ambulances and fire-engines and combined with a flashing *Blaulicht* (blue light) on the roof. On hearing this sound, other vehicles should draw in to the right and stop.

Maß (n -e). 'Measurement'; *nach Maß*, 'made to order'; *Maß-Anfertigung* or *Maßarbeit* is 'bespoke' or 'custom-made (clothing)'. In Bavaria and Austria *ein Maß, bitte* is a request for a beer. *Das Maß ist voll!* 'That's going too far!', 'That puts the lid on it!' Words derived from *Maß* tend to be confusing, e.g. *maßlos* is 'extremely' and *mäßigen Sie sich* is 'control yourself'. *Mäßig* is 'moderate(ly)' but *massig* is derived from *Masse* and is colloquial for 'very': *massig viel* 'very much'; the High German meaning is adjectival, 'bulky', 'big'.

Mattscheibe (f -n). The screen of a television receiver. When you say of a person that *er hat Mattscheibe* you mean that he is having one of his dimmer or less inspired moments.

Maul (n ˝-er). The mouth or maw of an animal and vulgar and offensive when applied to persons; not so the verb *maulen* which although colloquial is not rude and means 'to gripe' or sulk vociferously about something.

Maulkorberlaß (m -e). Literally 'muzzle decree'; a government decree that forbids people mentioning certain things to which the government is sensitive, e.g. there is an official decree that does not allow pilots to inform the public about near-misses they have experienced. Somewhat like the British Official Secrets Act.

Mehrwertsteuer (n -). 'Value added tax, VAT'.

meinen. This verb creates difficulty for both Germans and Englishmen as the former think the English 'mean' is *meinen* and the latter that *meinen* is 'mean'. *Meinen* is only 'mean' in the sense of 'to intend' as in *das habe ich nicht gemeint,* 'I did not intend (mean) that'; *meinen* is 'to think' or 'be of the opinion' (*der Meinung sein*) and *was meinen Sie (dazu)?* is 'what do you think (of that)?' *Meinen Sie nicht auch?* 'Don't you agree?'; *Meinen Sie?* 'Do you think so?' *Das will ich meinen,* 'I should think so'; *Ich will meinen . . .* 'I dare say . . .'; *Meinen Sie das im Ernst?* 'Do you really think so?' or 'Are you serious?' and *Meinen Sie das ernst?* 'Do you really mean it?' *Ich meine nur so . . .* 'I was only thinking . . .'.

meinetwegen. 'For my sake' but in reply it means 'it's all right with me', e.g. *Er kann meinetwegen noch heute gehen,* 'For my part he can go today'; *Kann ich gehen? Meinetwegen.* 'May I go? All right.' The same idea can be expressed by *von mir aus.*

Melissengeist (m). A patent medicine with a high alcoholic content, and drivers failing an *Alcotest* often use the taking of this tonic or similar medicines as a defence to the charge.

Mensch (m -en). 'Man as 'human being'. It is often used as an exclamation indicating surprise and so is *Menschenskinder! Sei ein Mensch* is an appeal to someone's better nature: 'don't be so hard'; *ein Unmensch* is an inhuman or brutish person.

merken. 'To notice' but reflexively it means 'to remember' and always has an air of warning or menace about it: *Merken Sie sich das für die Zukunft!* 'Remember that in future (or else)!'

merkwürdig. This no longer means 'noteworthy' or 'remarkable' but 'strange', 'odd', 'curious' while 'remarkable' is *bemerkenswert.*

meschugge. A dialect word derived from Yiddish meaning 'mad' or 'daft', frequently used with *machen: Dieser Krach macht mich ganz meschugge,* 'This row is driving me silly'.

Mieder (n -). 'Bodice' and an important element in all regional costumes (*Trachten*) for women. *Miederwaren* (f.pl.) are 'foundation garments'.

Milchmädchenrechnung (f -en). 'Milkmaid's calculation', a colloquial name for any speculation based on false reasoning.

Minna. *Die grüne Minna* or *der grüne Heinrich,* 'Black Maria'. The colloquial phrase *jemand zur Minna machen* is 'to come down on someone like a ton of bricks'.

Mist (m). 'Manure' but does not have the same coarseness as its use would have in English: *das ist der reine Mist* is about equivalent to 'that's tommyrot'. *Das ist nicht auf seinem Mist gewachsen* means 'he didn't do that off his own bat' and *da haben Sie Mist gemacht* is not much stronger than 'you've made a mistake there' or 'you've boobed there'.

Mittag (m -e). 'Midday' and sometimes means 'lunch', e.g. *Was gibt's zum Mittag?* 'What's for lunch?'

Mittagstisch (m -e). A kind of restaurant for more or less permanent customers which is usually inexpensive but the dishes are restricted to one or two; (*gut*) *bürgerlicher Mittagstisch*, 'good homely cooking'.

Moderator (m -). The chairman of any discussion, especially on TV; the verb is *moderieren*.

möglich. 'Possible' and has a superlative *möglichst* . . . 'as . . . as possible'. In commercialese and officialese there is *baldmöglichst* (for *möglichst bald*), 'as soon as possible' which should be avoided.

mollig. A colloquial adjective meaning either 'chubby' for women or 'warm and cosy'.

montan. Appertaining to mining and smelting; hence *Montanindustrie*: mining and smelting industry, and the *Montanunion*: the European Coal and Steel Community.

Mord mit Messer und Gabel. Death from overeating.

Morgen (m -). 'Morning' but *das Morgen* is 'the tomorrow' or 'future'.

Most (m -e). Slightly fermented fruit-juice but in most cafés it means unfermented apple juice unless you specify something else when ordering. Not completely matured wines are popular in Germany and in restaurants that specialize in wines the following terms are used: *der Most*, freshly pressed grape juice with fermentation only just beginning; *der Brauser, Bitzler, Rauscher, Sauser, Witzler* (depending on region), the vigorously fermenting cloudy wine which quickly goes to your head; *der Federweißer*, still cloudy but fermentation coming to an end; *der Jungwein*, fermentation finished but still 'gassy'; *der heurige Wein*, the finished young (this year's) wine.

Muffel (m -). Lifeless person, a 'drip'; the adjective *lahm* 'lame' describes such a boring individual; a 'wet blanket'.

Mumienschänder (m -). An apt but coarse name for a young man who toadies to rich elderly women.

Mund (m ¨-er). 'Mouth' and forms part of many idioms, some of which are very pointed as *sich den Mund fusselig reden*, 'to talk so much that one's mouth begins to fray'. *Mundraub* (m) is a theft caused by the need for the bare necessities of life. *Mundart* (f) is 'dialect'.

Musiker (m -). A serious instrumentalist who has studied music and his instrument properly; *Musikant* (m *-en*) is an amateurish musician, a street musician or a fair-ground fiddler, and the word can be derogatory; *Musikus* (m *-ici*) indicates that the user of the word has a poor opinion of musicians, of music as a way of earning a living or of a particular musician whom he describes with this term.

Mußehe (f -n). 'Shot-gun wedding'.

müssen. 'Must' but note that it can be used alone and another verb is implied: *ich muß in die Stadt,* 'I have to go into town'; *es muß gehen* is a useful phrase meaning 'it must be possible' or 'it has to work'.

mutterseelenallein. 'Completely alone', 'all by oneself' (*v.* FUNKELNAGELNEU).

N

na. A preamble equivalent to 'well', 'and' or 'so' but most examples are so idiomatic that they must be explained before they can be grasped, e.g. *na, wenn schon,* 'even so'; *na und?* 'so what?'; *na, und ob!* 'of course!'; *na, dann nicht!* 'all right, have it your way' but *na!* alone means 'stop it' *Na ja, es ist ja egal* is a wonderful example of expletives and means 'oh well, it doesn't really matter anyway'; *na, wird's bald?* 'well, how much longer are you going to take?' The self-satisfied *na bitte* has the same significance as *na also* (*v.* ALSO).

nachsehen. *Das Nachsehen haben* means 'to be disappointed' or literally 'to follow your wishes with your eyes as they disappear': *Der allzu Bescheidene hat immer das Nachsehen,* 'Too much modesty will never get you what you deserve'.

nachsenden. *Bitte nachsenden* on letters is 'please forward'.

Nacht (f ¨-e). 'Night' and can never mean 'evening' e.g. 'I met him last night' meaning about 10.30 p.m. would be *gestern abend*. It is never quite certain what a German means by *heute nacht* or *diese Nacht*; he could mean the night just passed or the one approaching unless the context makes it clear as in *heute nacht habe ich schlecht geschlafen* and *heute nacht werde ich gut schlafen* 'last night I did not sleep well' and 'tonight I shall sleep well'; *gestern nacht* and *letzte Nacht* are also ambiguous whereas *morgen nacht* is clearly 'tomorrow night', i.e. the night following tomorrow. *Gute Nacht* is a farewell and sometimes replaced by *angenehme Nachtruhe* or *angenehme Ruhe*.

nachträglich. 'Additional', 'supplementary'; often used when you have forgotten an anniversary: *Nachträglich herzlichen Glückwunsch,* 'Belated best wishes'.

nah(e). 'Near', 'close' and *die Nähe,* 'vicinity' or 'nearness'. 'It is quite near' is best rendered by *es ist ganz in der Nähe* or *es liegt ganz in der Nähe* whereas *es liegt nahe* (literally 'it is situated near by') can also be used figuratively 'it stands to reason' (followed by a *daß* clause). *Jemandem zu nahe treten* is 'to offend somebody' but *bitte, treten Sie näher* is only a very formal 'please come in'. *Nächst* can mean 'nearest' or 'next': *Wo ist die nächste Tankstelle?* 'Where is the nearest (next) service station (garage)?' *Demnächst* and *nächstens* mean 'some time in the near future' and on cinema posters mean 'coming' or 'forthcoming'.

nämlich. 'Namely' but colloquially it can replace 'because' and have the same significance as 'you see', e.g. *die Sache ist nämlich die . . .* 'it's like this you see . . .' and *ich kann nicht kommen, ich habe nämlich noch zu tun,* 'I can't come because I've still got some work to do'.

nanu. A verbal equivalent of a surprised look; said alone or as a preamble.

naschen. 'To eat sweets (on the sly)' and the origin of the Yiddish-American 'nosh', 'nosher' and 'noshery'.

Nase (f -n). 'Nose' and there are many expressions with 'nose' but one of the oddest and frequently heard is *auf der Nase liegen,* 'to be laid up (ill in bed)'. Another is *pro Nase,* 'per head'.

Naseweis (m -e). A young *Besserwisser,* 'know-all'.

Nassauer (m -). 'Sponger' but does not refer to the inhabitants of Nassau; at the beginning of the nineteenth century, the students at Göttingen University (in Nassau) were given free meals by the state and if one of those entitled could not attend, then a non-Nassau born student would take his place. *Nassauern* is 'to sponge'.

Neger (m -). 'Ghostwriter'.

nehmen. 'To take'; a colloquialism is *die nehmen's von den Lebendigen,* 'they make you pay through the nose'.

Nepplokal (n -e). 'Clip-joint'.

Nerv (m -en). 'Nerve' but *die Nerven verlieren* is 'to lose one's head' and 'to lose one's nerve' is *den Mut verlieren. Sie haben Nerven!* is a colloquialism meaning the same as 'you've got a nerve!'.

neu. 'New' but *das neueste* is 'the latest' as well as 'the newest'. *Neuheit* (f -en) is 'novelty' and *Neuigkeit* (f -en) is 'personal news' though the singular *Nachricht* (f) can also mean this; political or general news is *Nachrichten* (pl.). Beware of *neulich*, it is not 'newly' but 'the other day'.

neumodisch, neumodern. 'New-fangled'.

Neuzugang (m ¨-e). A 'new admission' to hospital, prison, etc.

nicht. 'Not'. The construction *es ist nicht zu . . .* is best rendered by 'un-' (plus adj) as in *es ist nicht zu glauben*, 'It is unbelievable'. In *nicht einmal* the meaning depends on the stress; if stress falls on *einmal* the phrase means 'not once' but when *nicht* is emphasized it means 'not even'.

Nickerchen (n -). 'Nap', 'snooze' and *ein Nickerchen machen* (*halten*) is 'to take a nap'; *einnicken*, 'to drop off'.

niedergeschlagen. This is the usual word for 'depressed' but *deprimiert* is also used.

Niere (f -n). 'Kidney'. *Es geht mir an die Nieren*, 'It puts me out' and refers to the feeling that comes with being angry because of a disappointment.

Nippfigur (f -en). A porcelain figurine of the type popular in the nineteenth century and until recently considered *kitschig* (*v.* KITSCH). Recently the new rich élite has begun collecting them as status symbols.

Niveau (n -s). 'Standard' but in a cultural context it implies 'high standard': *Er hat Niveau*, 'He is a man of culture'; *Das Theaterstück hat Niveau*, 'The play is of a high standard'.

noch. 'Still' but when added to a measure of quantity means 'more' or 'another' as in *noch einen Kaffee, bitte*, 'Another cup of coffee please'. In shops one hears *noch was?* 'anything else?' *Schon noch* with the future tense expresses 'don't worry, it's only a matter of time'. *Noch* can mean 'again' as in 'what was his name again?' *wie war* (*doch*) *noch sein Name?* Some idioms with *noch* are: *Noch vor zwei Tagen*, 'As little as two days ago'; *noch am selben Tag*, 'on the very same day'; *noch heute*, 'even today' and also 'before today is over'.

Normaluhr (f -en). 'Electric master-clock' and *Normalzeit* the 'standard time' set by it.

Not (f ¨-e). 'Trouble', 'distress' and 'emergency' and forms compounds in which it means 'emergency', e.g. *Notbremse*, 'emergency brake', *Notruf*, 'emergency call' but *Notgroschen* is 'savings for a rainy day' and *Notwehr*, 'self-defence'.

Note (f -n). Not a written 'note' but an official or diplomatic note or memorandum. In schools etc. *Noten* are marks and they range from one, the highest mark, to five or six (depending on regions), the lowest mark. *Note* can also mean a 'characteristic' or 'feature' as in *etwas eine mehr zeitgemäße Note geben*, 'to give a more up-to-date look to something'.

Notiz (f -en).   Not a 'notice' but a 'note' or memorandum except in the phrase *keine Notiz nehmen von,* 'to take no notice of'; *sich Notizen machen* is 'to take notes'.

Nulldiät (f -en).   A calorie-free diet.

Nulltarif (m -e).   When some service does not cost anything, e.g. *am Wochenende fahren Kinder bis zu 6 Jahren zum Nulltarif,* 'at weekends children up to 6 years travel free'.

Nummernschild (n -er).   'Licence number plate' of a car and has letters indicating the town of registration.

nur.   'Only'. Often the addition to a sentence of *nur* is equivalent to 'I wonder': *was hat er nur?* 'I wonder what's wrong with him?'

O

oben ohne.   'Topless'; *ein Kleid oben ohne,* 'a topless dress'.

Ober (m -).   When addressing or calling a waiter you should always use *Herr Ober* (short for *Herr Oberkellner*) and never just *Kellner*. A waitress is *die Bedienung* (the service) or *die Kellnerin* but when calling her you should always use *Fräulein*. When those who serve you are clearly the proprietors you ought to address them as *Herr Wirt* and *Frau Wirtin*.

Offene Handelsgesellschaft (f -en).   Abbreviated forms *OHG* or *oHG*, a legally recognized and registered form of business enterprise without any restrictions on its liability for debt.

offenherzig.   Humorous for low neckline or deep cleavage.

öffentlich.   'Public' and public telephone booths bear the words *öffentlicher Fernsprecher*; an *öffentliches Haus,* however, is not a 'public house' but a euphemism for a brothel.

ohne.   'Without'; *ohne weiteres* is 'just like that' or 'without more ado'. A colloquial usage is to describe a thing or person as *(gar) nicht so ohne* and means that there is more to it than you think, e.g. *Er ist gar nicht so ohne,* 'Be careful, he's smart'.

Ohr (n -en).   'Ear' and in various idioms it implies deceiving or cheating, e.g. *jemand übers Ohr hauen,* 'to cheat a person'; in English you 'pull the wool over someone's eyes' but in German you 'pull it over his ears': *jemandem das Fell über die Ohren ziehen,* and the rabbit's ears (v. LÖFFEL) reappear in the equivalent *jemand über den Löffel barbieren.* The English 'keep a stiff upper lip' but the Germans keep their ears stiff: *die Ohren steifhalten.*

Ohrwurm (m ¨-er). A tune that continues to run through one's head.

oll. A colloquial corruption of *alt* 'old' with the connotation of 'bad' or 'worn-out' and often translates the English 'silly old . . .' as in *wo habe ich nur das olle Ding hingetan?* 'I wonder where I've put that silly old thing?'; *je oller je doller,* 'the older, the sillier' which is equivalent to 'there is no fool like an old fool'.

Ölpest (f -en). A ship or tanker that discharges polluting oil.

Ölverknappung (f -en). Oil shortage.

Onkel (m -, coll. -s). 'Uncle'; the colloquial *über den großen Onkel gehen* has nothing to do with uncles but means 'to walk pigeon-toed' and is a corruption of the French 'grand ongle' big toe-nail, and so means to tread on one's own big toes.

ordentlich. 'Tidy', 'proper' and often used like the English 'properly' as in *sie haben ihn ordentlich übers Ohr gehauen,* 'They cheated him properly'.

Ort (m -e). 'Place' but in everyday speech it is used instead of *Ortschaft* (f -en) 'village' or 'small town'. *An Ort und Stelle* is 'on the spot' or 'in the proper place'.

Örtchen (n -). In 1966 this word appeared in an official English booklet prepared for Germans visiting Britain for the World Football Cup and readers were advised of many *hübsche Örtchen* 'beauty spots' which they could visit by bus or train. *Örtchen* can no longer be used for a 'nice little spot' as it has become a generally accepted but rather childish euphemism for 'lavatory' so the tourists were being advised to visit 'pretty lavatories'; the authors should have used *Fleckchen* for nice little spots near a town or even better *Ausflugsziel* (n -e).

P

packen. 'To pack' but a real portmanteau word as it can mean 'to grab' in colloquial speech: *Er packte mich am Arm,* 'He grabbed my arm', and it can also mean 'to help' as in *können Sie mal mit anpacken?* 'Can you give me a hand?' In some parts of the country it is used in the sense of 'manage to do' or the American 'make', e.g. *Der Zug geht in zehn Minuten, packen wir das noch?* 'The train leaves in ten minutes, can we still make it?' but this should not be imitated as a much better rendering is . . . *schaffen wir das noch?*

Palme (f -n). 'Palm (tree)' and part of a colloquialism: *Es bringt mich auf die Palme,* 'It infuriates me'.

Panne (f -n). 'Breakdown' of a car but has gradually been extended so as to refer not only to motoring but to anything going wrong for an individual, a 'mishap'.

Pantoffelkino (n -s). Humorous for television set, 'goggle box'.

Papierkrieg (m). The complicated official paperwork connected with a problem or complaint.

Pappenstiel (m). A colloquial word used only in the singular and meaning a small sum of money, e.g. *Ich kriegte es für einen Pappenstiel,* 'I got it for a song'; *tausend Mark sind kein Pappenstiel* is 'a thousand Marks is not chicken-feed'.

parken. 'To park' and parking-places are indicated by blue signs bearing a white P; *Parkhaus, Autohaus* and *Autosilo* are names for multistorey covered car-parks.

Parkstudium (n -ien). Because of the long waiting list for popular university courses such as medicine and dentistry, intending students often have to wait as much as six years before commencing the course of their choice; they therefore fill in their time studying something else, hence they 'park' and the study is a *Parkstudium*. This is a byproduct of *numerus clausus* that limits the number of students in a faculty.

Partie (f -n). Not a 'party' (for which the English word is used) but the playing of a game, e.g. *eine Partie Schach,* 'a game of chess'. *Ich bin mit von der Partie* is equivalent to 'you can count me in' and *sie hat eine gute Partie gemacht* means 'she has married well'. In commerce *Partie* has two different meanings: *eine Partie Hemden,* 'a consignment of shirts' but *Partiewaren* are 'seconds', i.e. sub-standard goods.

passen. Not 'to pass'; the verb has variations in meaning but all contain the basic notion of 'to be good (suitable) for the purpose intended' as in *das Kleid paßt nicht,* 'the dress doesn't fit' and *das Kleid paßt nicht hierher,* 'the dress doesn't suit the occasion'. It is useful in making appointments: *Paßt es Ihnen am Montag?* 'Is Monday all right for you?'; *Wann paßt's denn?* 'What time would suit you?' Only in playing cards does the verb have a different meaning and *ich passe* then means as in English 'I pass'.

Patron (m -e). Colloquially it means 'customer' in the English figurative sense as in 'a shrewd customer', *ein schlauer Patron.*

Patsche (f -n). 'Fix' in the sense of a predicament: *Ich sitze in der Patsche,* 'I'm in a fix'.

Pech (n). 'Bad luck' but also 'pitch' and when two friends stick together this is expressed by *sie halten zusammen wie Pech und Schwefel.*

Pendlerverkehr (m). 'Commuter traffic'.

Penne (f -n). Colloquial for a 'school' and *Pennäler* a 'pupil'. The verb *pennen* means 'to sleep' or rather 'to doss down' and *Pennbruder* is 'tramp' as *eine Penne* also means a 'doss-house'.

Pension (f -en). 'Retirement pension' but also 'board' in the combination 'room and board', *Zimmer mit Pension* (*Vollpension*); it can also mean a 'boarding-house'.

Peterwagen (m -). Nickname for a police patrol car.

petto. Used in the idiomatic phrase *etwas in petto haben* which means 'to have something up one's sleeve (in reserve)'.

Pfeffer (m). 'Pepper' but also forms part of a phrase which is a euphemism for 'you can go to hell', *Sie können bleiben, wo der Pfeffer wächst! Gepfeffert* is used figuratively for 'strong', 'sharp' as in *ich schrieb ihm einen gepfefferten Brief,* 'I wrote him a stiff letter'; with prices it is 'exorbitant'. *Pfeffern* is 'to throw violently'.

pfeifen. 'To whistle' and *auf etwas pfeifen* is the nearest approach to 'couldn't care less'.

Pflaster (n -). A useful word to know as its most important contemporary meaning is a 'small adhesive wound-dressing'.

Pflaume (f -n). 'Plum' but colloquially also 'teasing remark'; 'to make teasing remarks' is *pflaumen* and 'to tease somebody', *jemand anpflaumen.*

pfuschen. When used in the context of games and examinations, it means 'to cheat' by not observing the rules but when referring to work it means 'to botch'.

Photo (n -s). As in English, short for photograph *Photographie* (f -n); the latter can also mean 'photography' but *Photograph* (m -en) is the 'photographer' and not the picture. (There is a tendency to replace all these ph's with f.) Film is developed in either a *Drogerie* or a *Fotogeschäft* and if you want prints, it is useful to know the descriptive terms used, otherwise the question *ohne Rand, mit Büttenrand?* may fox you. The main types of print are *schwarzweiß* 'black and (a very pure) white'; *chamois* a yellowish tinge to the print; *Hochglanz* 'shiny'; *matt* 'matt'; *mit Rand* 'with a white margin'; *ohne Rand* 'without a margin'; *Büttenrand* 'serrated edge'.

Pillenknick (m -). Drop in birth rate since 1965, since the 'Pill' became popular.

Pimpf (m -e). Derogatory for a young man, i.e. too young in the speaker's opinion, but no connection with 'pimp'.

pingelig. A Rhenish word made popular by the late Chancellor Adenauer; it means 'fussy' or 'pernickety' and corresponds to the *penibel* of other parts of Germany.

platzen. 'To burst' (lit. and fig.) and colloquially 'to be cancelled', e.g. *die Party ist geplatzt* 'the party is off'.

Pleite (f -n). 'Bankruptcy' and also 'failure' in general and so *das war eine Pleite* can mean 'that was a washout'. *Ich bin pleite* means 'I'm broke'.

plötzlich. 'Suddenly'; to emphasize a command or request the colloquial *aber etwas plötzlich, wenn ich bitten darf* or *aber etwas plötzlich, bitte* is added 'and get cracking'; it can be quite offensive depending on the tone.

Plürre (f -n). 'Dishwater', i.e. weak coffee or tea.

Polente (f). Colloquial for 'police', used with a singular verb.

Politesse (f -n). 'Uniformed policewoman'.

Polizei (f). 'Police' and is singular so that the translation of 'the police are . . .' must be *die Polizei ist . . . .Polizeistunde* is the time after which alcoholic drinks cannot be served in bars.

Polterabend (m -e). The eve-of-wedding ceremony when friends make a row outside the bride's house by breaking crockery etc., and then the *Polterer* are invited inside.

Pontius. *Von Pontius zu Pilatus* is the German equivalent or 'from pillar to post'.

popelig. 'Stingy' or 'mean'.

Postleitzahl (f -en). Postal district code number.

praktizieren. 'To practise' (a profession) only when speaking of doctors and sometimes of lawyers, but it has a colloquial meaning 'to manage to put something somewhere without being observed': *Ich weiß nicht, wie er den Zettel in meine Tasche praktiziert hat,* 'I don't know how he managed to slip that note into my pocket'.

Preisausschreiben (n -). A sales promotion competition; the customer receives a prize for the correct solution.

Probe (f -n). 'Test' or 'sample'. *Auf (zur) Probe,* 'on test' but *laut Probe* is a commercial phrase meaning 'according to sample'. *Probe* also means 'rehearsal' and *Generalprobe* is 'dress rehearsal'. There are two verbs *proben* 'to rehearse' and *probieren* 'to try' or 'to sample'.

Probemann (m ¨-er). Colloquial for 'ticket inspector' on buses; the correct term is *der Kontrolleur.*

problematisch. A much more widely used adjective than the rarely used English 'problematic' and in German it means 'questionable', 'uncertain', 'dubious', 'difficult'. *Die Lage ist problematisch,* 'The situation is grave'. When used about people it means they are 'difficult to understand or handle'.

prost. (Short for Latin 'prosit'.) A toast like 'cheers' and politeness requires a slight nod in the direction of the person you are addressing before and after drinking. *Prost allerseits* is 'cheers to everybody'. A more polite general toast than *prost* is *auf Ihr Wohl* and specific versions are *auf Ihr Glück* or *auf Ihren Erfolg* etc. (*v.* ANSTOßEN).

Prozeß (m -(ss)e). This can be 'process' but its commonest meaning is a 'trial' or 'legal proceedings'; *prozessieren*, 'to conduct a trial', 'to take proceedings'. *Kurzen Prozeß machen* (*mit*) is 'to make short work (of)'.

prüfen. Not 'to prove' (which is *beweisen*) but 'to examine' or 'check'. *Geprüft* can mean either having passed an official check: 'certified', or 'tried', i.e. having survived many hardships.

Publikumsverkehr   (m -). 'Personal callers', contact with the general public. Offices are described as having or not having *Publikumsverkehr*.

Puddingabitur (n -e). *Das Abitur* (colloquial abbreviation is *Abi*) is the equivalent of GCE 'A' and 'S' levels and gives entrance to the university. *Das Puddingabitur* is humorous for the school-leaving examination in domestic science and is taken by many girls, but it does not provide entrance to university and is a bit of an academic joke.

Puff (m ¨-e). 'Nudge' or 'push' but should be avoided except in the stock phrases such as *es kann einen derben Puff vertragen*, 'It can stand rough treatment' because it is also slang for 'brothel'.

Pulle (f -n). A colloquialism for 'bottle'.

Pulli (m -s). Short for *Pullover*.

pumpen. 'To pump' but colloquially 'to borrow' or 'to lend'; *auf Pump,* 'on tick'.

Pustekuchen. An exclamation used in some parts of Germany and meaning 'nothing doing', 'some hopes', 'that's what you think'.

Putzfrau (f -en). 'Charwoman' but with the social changes of the last few years *Putzfrau* has gradually been replaced by a succession of substitutes: *Reinemachefrau, Aufwartefrau* and finally the *Raumpflegerin* which is something like 'room cosmetician', but *Putzmacherin* is a 'milliner' as *Putz* (m) also means 'finery' and *sich putzen* 'to dress up'.

Q

Quasselstrippe (f -n). 'Prattler', 'chatterbox' and often used ironically for the 'telephone'.

Quatsch (m). 'Bosh', 'twaddle', 'nonsense' and very frequently used rather like the English 'rubbish' or 'tripe'. *Quatsch machen* or *verzapfen* is 'to do something nonsensical'; *quatschen* is colloquial and rather coarse for 'to talk' or 'chat' but not necessarily 'to talk nonsense'.

Quittung (f -en). 'Receipt' and in restaurants you might be asked if you require a *Quittung mit Stempel* when paying your bill as this rubber stamped receipt can be used as evidence for tax-deductible expenses.

R

Rabatt (m -e). 'Rebate'; most German supermarkets give a 3 per cent rebate in the form of stamps, *Rabattmarken* (f.pl.) or *Rabatt-märkchen* (n.pl.), which customers save by sticking in booklets, *Markenheft* (n -e) provided by the shops. They are exchangeable for cash.

Radfahrer (m -). 'Cyclist' but colloquially used as an equivalent for someone who flatters his superiors and browbeats his subordinates, one who bows to above *der nach oben einen Buckel macht* and who kicks downwards *der nach unten tritt*.

radschlagen. 'To turn a cartwheel' and Düsseldorf children are renowned for their skill at this and are reputed to do it for tourists especially in Königsstraße known as *die Kö*, the main shopping street with many cafés with outside terraces. *Die Düsseldorfer Radschläger* appear on most Düsseldorf souvenirs.

Raffinesse (f -n). In the singular it means 'artfulness', 'cunning' but in the plural it is used in the phrase *mit allen Raffinessen,* 'with all refinements'.

Rage (f -). Pronounced as in French this colloquial word does not mean 'rage' but a nervous excitement or anger produced when someone presses or pesters you: *Nun habe ich in der Rage den Schirm vergessen,* 'Now you've made me forget the umbrella with all your pestering and hurry'.

Rahmen (m -). 'Frame' and found in two common idioms: *aus dem Rahmen fallen,* 'to be out of keeping with the rest' and *in großem Rahmen,* 'on a big scale'.

Rand (m ¨-er). 'Edge', 'brink', 'margin', and can be a vulgar term for the 'mouth'. *Etwas am Rande erwähnen,* 'to mention something in passing'; the expression *mit etwas zu Rande kommen* is colloquial and means 'to cope with something'.

Rasthaus (n "-er), **Raststätte** (f -n).   These are rather posh, usually on the *Autobahnen* and are open day and night seven days a week. They often have bathrooms, showers and small rooms like ships' cabins in which the traveller can rest for a few hours or less. Alcohol must not be sold after a certain time (midnight, 1 a.m. or 3 a.m. depending on the area) but the waiters can often be 'persuaded' to ignore the regulations. These places are for motorists (not *Fernfahrer*, 'lorry-drivers') but are frequented also by people who just like to stay up late and, of course, by a good number of drunks. A *Rasthaus* on a main road is used mostly by lorry-drivers.

Rat (m).   *Rat* in sense of 'advice' has no plural and when you want to say 'pieces of advice' you have to use the plural *Ratschläge*. *Rat* can also mean 'council' and 'councillor' and the plural is then *Räte*; *Geheimrat* is an honorary title like 'Privy Councillor'.

Ratskeller (m -).   An upper- or upper-middle-class restaurant always more or less expensive and with a reputation for good cooking. You may linger as long as you like over your wine after a meal or you may go in solely for a bottle or half-bottle of wine. The *Rats* . . . prefix always seems to denote good food whereas the *Gast* . . . prefix denotes food but it might be prepared badly or unwillingly if the place is patronized more by drinkers than eaters.

Räuberzivil (n -).   Humorous for what the British call 'leisure wear' (clothes).

rauh.   'Rough' and often used of climates 'raw'. The colloquial *in rauhen Mengen* is 'lots and lots of', i.e. in great quantities.

rausbekommen.   The colloquial form of *herausbekommen* and sometimes replaced by *rauskriegen* and means 'to get back change when paying' as in *einen Moment, Sie bekommen noch was raus,* 'Just a moment, you have some change coming'. It has a second meaning: 'to find out', e.g. *Haben Sie rausbekommen (rausgekriegt), wer es war?* 'Have you found out who did it?'

rausgeben.   Colloquial for *herausgeben* 'to return the change to the one who pays' as in *Sie haben mir zu wenig rausgegeben,* 'You've given me too little change' and *haben Sie es nicht kleiner? Auf zwanzig Mark kann ich nicht rausgeben,* 'Haven't you anything smaller? I haven't change for twenty Marks', but remember that *rausgeben* is only used for change due after payment; if you only want to change a twenty Mark note then you must use *wechseln*.

recht.   'Right'; it can mean 'quite' in a rather negative sense as in *es war recht nett, aber . . .*, 'It was quite nice but . . .' and note that this use of *recht* is not the English 'right nice'. *Rechtzeitig* is 'in time'.

Rede (f -n).   'Speech', 'talk', 'conversation' and the verb *reden* 'to talk', 'converse', 'discourse' offer few problems but there is a colloquial phrase used when interrupting someone: *Vergessen Sie Ihre Rede nicht,* 'Don't forget what you were going to say'.

Reformhaus (n ¨-er). 'Health foods shop' specializing in vegetarian foods and herbal remedies.

Regenbogenpresse (f -n). Popular newspapers and magazines.

reichen. 'To pass' as in *können Sie mir das Salz reichen?* 'Can you pass me the salt?' It also means 'to be enough' as in *danke, es reicht,* 'Thanks, that's sufficient' when you have had enough of a food or drink but *jetzt reicht's mir aber!* means 'that's going too far!'

reichlich. 'Ample', 'plentiful' but it can also mean 'rather' so that *das ist ja reichlich wenig* is not as illogical as it seems because it means 'that is rather little'.

Reihe (f -n). 'Row', 'rank', 'line', 'queue'. *Aus der Reihe tanzen* is 'to step out of line' and *er ist an der Reihe* or *er kommt an die Reihe* mean 'it is his turn'.

rein. 'Clean', 'pure' and 'sheer' and often used emphatically as is the English 'clean', e.g. *Sie ist rein verrückt danach,* 'She's clean daft about it' (in this sense of 'completely' *reineweg* often replaces *rein*). *Mit jemandem im reinen sein* is 'to be in the clear with somebody' about some problem or business.

reinfallen. Colloquial for *hereinfallen* and used in the phrase *auf jemand reinfallen,* 'to be taken in (cheated) by somebody', 'to fall for somebody's line'. *Der Reinfall,* 'flop', 'failure'.

Reisefieber (n -). The excitement engendered by preparing for a journey.

reißen. 'To tear' but it also denotes eagerness in the construction *sich um etwas reißen*: *Er reißt sich um jede Gelegenheit, sie zu sehen,* 'He jumps at every chance of seeing her' and ironically in *ich reiße mich nicht darum, ihn kennenzulernen,* 'I'm not exactly dying to make his acquaintance'.

reizen. 'To excite', 'stimulate' but can cause confusion because it is often used in the bad sense of 'irritate' or 'annoy' and *gereizt* means 'annoyed', 'irritated' whereas *reizend* means 'charming', 'delightful'.

Reizüberflutung (f -en). Over-abundance of stimuli in the environment of today, noise etc. *Bei der heutigen Reizüberflutung sind auch Kleinkinder merklich aggressiver als vor Jahren,* 'With today's over-stimulation, even infants are noticeably more aggressive than they were years ago'.

Reizwäsche (f). Ladies' frilly underwear.

Reklame (f -n). 'Advertisement' or 'advertising' and *Reklame machen* is 'to advertise' but *reklamieren* is 'to complain' or 'protest' and *die Reklamation* is the 'complaint', 'protest' or 'objection'.

rentieren, sich. 'To be profitable' and *rentabel,* 'profitable'.

Rentner (m -). According to the dictionary a variant of *Rentier,* 'a person with private means' but in modern usage *Rentner* means someone drawing a pension (usually old-age).

Reptilienfonds (m sing. & pl.). Secret funds used by a government for political purposes, 'slush fund'.

revisibel. Contestable.

Röhre (f -n). 'Pipe', 'tube' and also a small recess in the oven used for roasting or keeping food hot and from the latter meaning comes the phrase *in die Röhre gucken,* 'not to get one's due' from the idea of looking into this recess and finding it empty.

Rolle (f -n). 'Roll' and also 'role' and in the last sense it is widely used; *aus der Rolle fallen* means 'to misbehave' as in *wenn er betrunken ist, fällt er immer aus der Rolle,* 'When he's drunk he always forgets his manners'.

Roman (m -e). 'Novel' and *Novelle* (f -n) is a 'short story' for which there is also the word *Kurzgeschichte* (f -n) although this is usually a 'short' short story. A science fiction novel is *ein utopischer Roman.*

rücken. 'To move' and commonly heard in buses or trains: *Können Sie etwas rücken?* 'Could you move over a bit?' *Aufrücken* is 'to move up'.

Rückgang (m ¨-e). Although mostly used in commerce to mean a 'decrease' or 'falling off' (in sales) it forms part of an everyday phrase: *etwas rückgängig machen,* 'to cancel' or 'undo' something.

ruck-zuck. A colloquialism describing a quickly completed action; *Die Arbeit war ruck-zuck erledigt,* 'The work was done before you could say Jack Robinson'.

Rufmord (m -e). This word is much favoured by the newspapers and means 'character assassination', the destruction of a person's reputation by rumour and innuendo.

Ruhe (f). 'Rest', 'repose', 'silence'. German restaurants have 'a day of rest' once a week and put up a little sign *heute Ruhetag.* Phrases with *Ruhe*: *Er ist immer die Ruhe selbst,* 'He's as cool as a cucumber'; *Er hat die Ruhe weg,* 'He takes his time'; *Immer mit der Ruhe,* 'keep calm'.

Ruheständler (m -). 'Retired person'.

Rumtreiber (m -). 'Lay-about'; the verb is *sich rumtreiben.*

rundweg. 'Flatly'; *rundweg abschlagen,* 'to refuse flatly' (note that the *eg* is not pronounced as in *der Weg,* 'the way', but short as in *der Weck,* 'the roll', and there is no connection with 'going round' or a 'roundabout').

Rutsch (m -e).   *Einen guten Rutsch (ins neue Jahr)!* is a popular greeting used only on New Year's Eve (*Silvester*).

S

Sachbuch (n ¨-er).   A book by a specialist for non-specialist readers; a popularization.

Sache (f -n).   'Matter', 'thing', 'affair', though idiomatic and stock phrases containing this word are sometimes hard to grasp as the following show: *Es tut nichts zur Sache,* 'It is of no account'; *Das gehört nicht zur Sache,* 'That's beside the point'; *Kommen wir zur Sache,* 'Let's get down to brass tacks'; *das ist Ihre Sache,* 'That's your problem'; *Das ist nicht jedermanns Sache,* 'That's not to everybody's taste'. In the plural the noun is used to refer to one's belongings or clothes. Also note the two colloquial uses: *mit 120 Sachen,* 'at 120 kilometres per hour' and *machen Sie keine Sachen!* 'Don't be (do anything) silly' in disbelief or as a warning.

Sack (m ¨-e).   'Sack' but in many regions it is used, also in compound words, for 'pocket' (instead of *Tasche*), e.g. *Sacktuch,* 'handkerchief', *Hosensack,* 'trouser pocket'; it is rather coarse and should be avoided.

Saft (m ¨-e).   'Fruit juice' and normally one of the very popular bottled juices such as *Apfelsaft, Traubensaft* or *Johannisbeersaft* (apple-juice, grape-juice, red- or black-currant-juice) although when offered in a shop it may also refer to concentrated juice and replace the word *Sirup* (m -s) (syrup), e.g. *Himbeersaft* is normally raspberry syrup. *Apfelsaft* is so popular that it might almost be considered Germany's second national drink. *Der Apfelwein* is very similar to cider and alcoholic and should not be confused with *Apfelsaft*; it is characteristic of the Frankfurt area and frequently served with *Zwiebelkuchen* (m), a warm onion pastry, and when a Frankfurter orders this it sounds like *Eppelwoi un Zwiwwelkuche*. *Apfelsaft* is often served in a large yellowish or greenish glass goblet with a knobbed or twisted stem called a *Pokal* (m -e).

Saftladen (m ¨-).   Inefficiently run shop, restaurant or similar establishment (and can be very offensive).

sagen.   'To say', 'to tell' and in most cases 'tell' translates into *sagen,* not *erzählen* which, in everyday speech, is only used in the sense of 'narrate'. The combination of *sagen* with *zu* means 'to think about' as well as literally 'to say to', e.g. *was haben Sie zu ihm gesagt?* is 'what did you think about him?' or 'what did you say to (tell) him?' (to avoid confusion, the latter can be *was haben Sie ihm* *gesagt?*). *Zusagen* (sep.) means 'to accept an invitation' or 'to like': *Das Bild sagt mir zu,* 'I like the picture'; *Sie hat mich eingeladen, und ich habe zugesagt,* 'She invited me and I accepted' (*N.B.* the separable verb *absagen* is 'to cancel an invitation' but cannot express dislike). *Sagen* combined with *lassen* is 'to have a message conveyed' and when reflexive 'to hear': *Ich habe ihm sagen lassen . . . .* 'I had word sent to him . . .'; *Ich habe mir sagen lassen . . . .* 'As far as I've been told . . .', 'as far as I've heard . . .' but the reflexive form in the negative means 'not to listen to advice or reason', e.g. *Er läßt sich nichts sagen,* 'He won't listen to reason'. There are also some slightly confusing infinitive constructions with *sagen*: *Er hat nichts zu sagen,* 'He has no say in the matter' (as well as literally 'he has nothing to say'); *Es hat nichts zu sagen,* 'It is not important (of no account)'; *Es ist nicht zu sagen, wie schön es war* (also: *es war unsagbur schön*), 'It was too beautiful for words'. *Sage und schreibe* is an expression used for emphasis (mostly with figures) 'really and truly'.

Sakko (m -s). A man's sports jacket or jacket with pattern different from the trousers.

Sammeltasse (f -n). A popular form of gift consisting of a cup, saucer and small plate, all of extravagant shape and decoration; the set is mostly sold already gift-wrapped.

Samstag (m -e). 'Saturday' in Southern and Central Germany; in the North *Sonnabend* (m -e) is preferred.

Sandlerin (f -nen). Girl who entices men into a 'clip-joint' (*Nepplokal*); derives from *Sand in die Augen zu streuen,* 'to throw sand into one's eyes'.

sanieren. Much used for the clearing of slums or restoration of old parts of a town or old houses. Noun: *Sanierung* (f -en).

Sarg (m ¨-e). 'Coffin' and to tell someone *Sie sind ein Nagel zu meinem Sarg* is therefore hardly complimentary. *Sargnagel* (m ¨-) 'coffin nail' is a colloquialism for 'cigarette'.

saufen. 'To drink' for animals but a vulgarism for excessive drinking when referring to humans as is also *Säufer* instead of *Trinker* for an alcoholic or drunkard; *er säuft wie ein Loch* is a vulgar version of 'he drinks like a fish'.

Sauregurkenzeit (f -en). ('Pickled cucumber time') an ominous lull in political activity or an unhealthy slack period in business.

schade. (*Wie*) *schade!* 'what a pity' or 'that's a shame'. *Es ist schade um . . .* expresses that you feel sorry for something that is going to waste or has been lost, thus you might say about savings that are not invested *es ist schade um das schöne Geld,* 'What a shame that such money should go to waste'; a rather hard-hearted remark is *um den ist es nicht schade,* 'He's no great loss' or 'The world can easily do without him'. *Zu schade für* means 'too good for', e.g. *Ich bin mir für solche Machenschaften zu schade,* 'I won't lower myself and take part in such intrigues'; *das Buch ist für ein so kleines Kind zu schade,* 'the book is too valuable to be given to such a young child'.

schaffen. A common verb in everyday life when meaning 'to manage to do' something: *Schaffen wir es allein?* 'Can we manage to do it (cope with it) alone?'; on having completed a difficult job you might say *wir haben's geschafft,* 'We've done it'. In dialect, the verb is used to mean 'to work': *Wo schafft er?* 'Where does he work?' or sometimes 'do': *Ich will nichts mit ihm zu schaffen haben,* 'I don't want to have anything to do with him' and also 'to get' in the sense of 'move': *Können Sie das Paket zur Post schaffen?* 'Can you get (take) this parcel to the post office?'. Note the difference in meaning of *er macht sich im Garten zu schaffen,* 'He's pottering about in the garden' and *der Garten macht ihm zu schaffen,* 'The garden is giving him a lot of trouble'. When the verb is conjugated strongly (*schuf, geschaffen*) it is 'to create' and in noun combinations 'to make' e.g. *Raum schaffen,* 'to make room' but colloquial speech disregards such subtleties and *er schaffte Raum* is preferred to *er schuf Raum.*

Schale (f -n). 'Peel', 'skin'; *sich in Schale werfen,* 'to put on one's Sunday best', i.e. dress as nicely as possible.

scharf. 'Sharp' but often means 'keen' as in the colloquial phrase *ich bin nicht scharf darauf,* 'I'm not very keen on that', or *scharfer Verstand,* 'keen intellect'.

Scharfmacher (m -). As a noun is always used in a political and negative sense as 'agitator'. The verb *scharfmachen auf . . .* can be used in a positive sense: *Er hat mir soviel über Sizilien erzählt, daß er mich ganz scharf auf einen Urlaub dort gemacht hat,* 'He told me so much about Sicily that he has made me quite keen on spending a holiday there'.

schassen. To throw someone out, to 'sack' someone.

Scheck (m -s). 'Cheque'; a 'bearer cheque' is *Barscheck,* a 'crossed cheque' *Verrechnungsscheck* which is not actually crossed, the words *zur Verrechnung* (meaning the amount may only be credited to a bank account) are written on it. A 'bounced cheque' is a *geplatzter* (colloquial for *ungedeckter*) *Scheck. Postkartenscheck* is a crossed cheque in the form of a postcard and can be sent through the mail at ordinary postal rates.

schicken. 'To send'; colloquial 'to be sufficient (enough)': *Schickt das?* 'Is that enough?'

Schickse (f -n). A colloquial word meaning a 'baggage', 'trollop' or a girl who is a bit of a tart.

Schieber (m -). 'Pusher' but colloquially 'racketeer' and the cry *Schiebung!* 'sharp practices' or 'shady transactions' is often heard from hecklers at meetings. *Schiebermütze* is a 'peaked cap'.

schief. 'Crooked' or 'slanted' and colloquially used to mean 'bad' or 'wrong' but not 'illegal', e.g. *Wenn er glaubt, ich helfe ihm, dann ist er schiefgewickelt,* 'If he thinks I'm going to help him he's got another think coming'; *Heute geht mir alles schief,* 'This is an off-day for me'. An encouraging remark is *es wird schon schiefgehen,* 'Don't worry, everything will go wrong nicely' which is supposed to induce the opposite (*v.* HALS).

Schikane (f -n). *Ein Auto mit allen Schikanen,* 'A car with all the contemporary gadgets'.

Schippe (f -n). Colloquial for *Schaufel* (f -n) 'shovel' and *jemand auf die Schippe nehmen* is 'to pull someone's leg'.

Schlachtfest (n -e). A village custom by which a farmer, on having slaughtered a pig, gives a dinner of fresh meat, fresh home-made sausages with *Sauerkraut* etc. to neighbours and friends. Restaurants have adopted the word and quite frequently you find the sign *heute Schlachtfest* in the window of a restaurant or a *Schlachtplatte* offered on the menu; the sign indicates that the main dish for the day is a *Schlachtplatte,* a selection of fresh pork and pork sausages with *Sauerkraut.* Should you ever be invited to a genuine *Schlachtfest* in a village it is an occasion not to be missed if you are fond of good food; the *Schlachtplatte* in restaurants is no comparison and often of poor quality.

Schlafmütze (f -n). 'Night-cap' but usually means a 'sleepyhead' or 'absent-minded person'; never a 'final drink', or 'bedtime drink'.

Schlag (m ¨-). 'Blow', 'electric shock', and also 'stroke' (med.) as an abbreviation of *Schlaganfall* (m ¨-e). In colloquialisms and idioms it describes shock or surprise, e.g. *Ich dachte, mich rührt der Schlag,* 'I was as if struck by lightning'; *ein Schlag ins Kontor* refers to an unexpected occurrence which entails a loss (mostly monetary).

Schlager (m -). 'Pop song' and also colloquially a 'hit' in a general sense, e.g. *ein Verkaufsschlager,* 'a good selling line'.

schlagskaputt. 'Dead beat' and very colloquial but not bad.

schlau. 'Clever', 'artful' but never used in a derogatory sense; *aus etwas nicht schlau werden* is 'not to be able to make head or tail of something'.

schlecht. 'Bad' and as an adverb it can also mean 'not very well': *Das kann man schlecht machen,* 'One can't very well do that'.

Schleichweg (m -e). Secret (and probably illegal) means to achieve something. Can be used in the singular and plural.

schleierhaft. 'Like a veil' and often used as 'mystery': *Es ist mir völlig schleierhaft, wie . . .,* 'It's a complete mystery to me how . . .'.

Schlemihl. A well-intentioned but rather simple fellow whose own acts get him into trouble; the word is derived from the hero, Peter

Schlemihl, of a short novel of the same name by Adalbert von Chamisso which was first published in 1814; the word is Hebrew in origin.

Schliff (m -e). 'Cut' of precious stones or glass and for a less delicate object it is 'grinding'. Figuratively it refers to a person's social manners: *Er hat keinen Schliff* (*er ist ungeschliffen*), 'He has no manners (is crude)'; *einer Sache den letzten Schliff geben* is 'to put the finishing touches to something'.

schlimm. 'Bad' and often 'sore' or 'infected' e.g., *Ich habe einen schlimmen Finger*, 'I have a sore finger' (*schlecht* cannot have this significance). *Aber, aber, es ist doch halb so schlimm*, 'Come, come, it's not as bad as all that'.

Schmarren (m -). An omelette with sugar and cinnamon common in Bavaria and Austria often called *Kaiserschmarren*; colloquially it means 'not a thing' as in *er versteht einen Schmarren davon*, 'He doesn't know a thing about it' or *das geht Sie einen Schmarren an*, 'That's none of your business'.

schmecken. 'To taste' as well as 'to taste good', e.g. *Schmeckt's?* or more formal *Schmeckt es Ihnen?* 'Do you like it?' (with food) and *Es schmeckt schlecht* (*süß, gut* etc.), 'It tastes bad (sweet, good etc.)'.

Schmiere (f -n). 'Grease', 'lubricant'; it is also an itinerant theatrical company of low standard, thus *Schmierenkomödiant*, 'ham actor'. *Schmiere stehen* is an expression derived from crime 'to keep a look out while your companions are doing the job'.

Schmierfink (m -en). A libellous, scandal-mongering journalist.

Schmock (m -s). Corrupt, unscrupulous journalist, from the novel *Die Journalisten*, by Gustav Freytag.

Schmu (m). A colloquial word for 'cheating' or 'unfairness'; *Das ist Schmu*, 'That's cheating'; *Er macht Schmu*, 'He's cheating'.

schmusen. 'To neck' or 'cuddle'; the noun *Schmus* (m) is colloquial for 'nonsense' or 'empty talk': *Machen Sie nicht so einen Schmus*, 'Don't talk such a lot of nonsense'.

Schnapsidee (f -n). 'Stupid suggestion'.

Schneebesen (m -). Not a snow broom but an 'egg whisk' which is occasionally also called *Schneeschläger* (m -); the correct instrument for removing snow is a *Schneeschippe* (f -n).

Schneider (m -). 'Tailor'; *aus dem Schneider sein*, 'to have overcome the greater part of the difficulties so that failure is unlikely'; but of a woman, it means she has passed her prime.

Schnitt (m -e). 'Cut' but often an abbreviation of *Durchschnitt*, e.g. *im Schnitt*, 'on the average'.

schnodderig. 'Snotty'.

Schnulze (f -n).   A trashy and sentimental song or film (v. HEIMAT-SCHNULZE).

schnurstracks.   A colloquialism referring to time or direction: 'straight away' or 'in a bee-line'.

schofel.   Colloquialism for 'mean', 'stingy'.

schon.   'Already' but also a very common expletive and highly idiomatic e.g. *Er wird schon kommen*, 'He'll come, don't worry'; *Schon der Gedanke*, 'The very idea', 'The idea alone'; *Was ist schon dabei?* 'What of it?'; *Schon gut*, 'That's all right' or 'That'll do'; *Das ist schon möglich*, 'That might well be (possible)'; *Morgen schon gar nicht*, 'Tomorrow least of all'; *wenn schon, denn schon*, 'If I'm going to do it at all then I'll do it properly(!)'.

schön.   'Beautiful' but often just 'nice', e.g. *schönes Wetter*, 'Nice weather'. As an introduction it means 'all right': *Schön, was machen wir jetzt?* 'All right, and what do we do now?'; *Na schön, dann eben nicht*, 'all right, have it your way'.

Schönheitsfarm (f -en).   'Beauty farm'.

Schoppen (m -).   Originally a measure but now means a 'drink' or 'a glass of' beer or wine; *zum Schoppen gehen*, 'to go out for a drink' (v. DÄMMERSCHOPPEN).

Schorle (f -n).   White wine or cider in mineral water; a typical summer drink although the mixture with cider is characteristic of Hessen where it is also called *ein gespritzter*; in other regions *ein gespritzter* means a *Schnaps* with a dash of bitters.

schräg.   'Slanted'; *schräge Musik*, 'pop (jazz) music'.

Schrebergarten (m ¨-).   Originally a children's open-air playground named after the man who established the first in about 1840, Daniel Gottlob Moritz Schreber; now it means an 'allotment'.

Schreckschraube (f -n).   Unpleasant and intimidating woman.

Schuld (f -en).   Both 'debt' and 'fault' and it can also mean 'guilt'. The adjective is indispensable when you want to pay: *Was bin ich Ihnen schuldig?* 'What do I owe you?' 'It is my fault' can be rendered in two ways: *Es ist meine Schuld* or more colloquially *Ich bin schuld (daran)*; *Ich bin schuldig* means 'I'm guilty'.

Schule (f -n).   'School'; *die höhere Schule* or *die Oberschule* is a *Gymnasium* (q.v.); *die Hohe Schule* is used figuratively for 'the art of . . .', e.g. *die Hohe Schule des Kochens*, 'the art of cooking'.

Schülerlotse (m -n).   Schoolboy (or girl) acting as school crossing warden.

Schund (m).   'Rubbish(y quality)' and usually refers to literature. Every so often there is a campaign against *Schmutz und Schund*, obscene and trashy literature, during which youngsters may exchange trashy books for good literature in specially opened book centres.

Schupo (m -s). A colloquial abbreviation for *Schutzpolizist* (m -en), 'policeman'.

Schuppe (f -n). 'Scale' and the plural is used for 'dandruff'.

Schuppen (m -). 'Barn' but particularly in compounds (e.g. *Jazz-schuppen, Beatschuppen*) it is a teenage name for a bar with dancing.

Schuß (m ¨-(ss)e). 'Shot' also in the sense of a 'shot' of whisky; *Tee mit Schuß*, 'tea with a dash of rum' is a popular drink in the North. *Ein Schuß ins Schwarze* is a 'bull's-eye'; the colloquialism *etwas gut in Schuß haben* means 'to have something in good working order or perfect condition' and the expression *weit vom Schuß* is also colloquial, 'far removed from the scene of activity or attraction'.

Schutz (m). 'Protection'; *Ich will ihn nicht in Schutz nehmen,* 'I hold no brief for him'.

Schwamm (m ¨-e). 'Sponge'; a colloquial answer to an apology is *Schwamm drüber,* 'It's O.K., let's forget it'.

Schwarm (m ¨-e). 'Swarm', 'host' but also somebody with whom one is infatuated; the verb is *für jemand schwärmen,* 'to be infatuated with a person'.

schwarz. 'Black'; it also means 'illegal'; *schwarzarbeiten* is 'to work outside normal working-hours' and conceal this income from the tax authorities; *schwarzsehen* and *schwarzhören* are verbs of recent creation and refer to the use of a television or radio receiver without a licence but note that *schwarzsehen* is also 'to be pessimistic about a future event'. *Schwarzmalerei* is a pessimistic presentation of future possibilities and *jemand anschwärzen* is 'to slander somebody'.

schwer. 'Heavy' and also 'difficult' and 'hard'. Colloquially it is used for 'very' : *Ich muß schwer aufpassen,* 'I have to be very careful'; the literary *schwerlich* is 'hardly'.

Schwester (f -n). 'Sister'; in a hospital it is a 'nurse' and the ward sister is *die Stationsschwester;* the matron is *die Oberschwester. Schwesterstadt* means a 'sister' (twin) town abroad and many German towns have such links for school and other exchanges.

schwül. 'Oppressive' for weather but it must be pronounced carefully as *schwul* is a vulgarism for 'homosexual'.

schwummerig. 'Queasy', also figuratively *mir wird (ist) ganz schwummerig, wenn ich daran denke,* 'I feel quite uncomfortable when I think of it'.

sein. 'To be'; pronounced *Was is* (spelt *ist*)? 'What's the matter?', also *Is was?* 'Is something wrong (the matter)?'

Seitensprung (m ¨-e). 'Amorous escapade by a married man'.

selbstbewußt. Not self-conscious but 'self-assured'.

Semmel (f -n). Another word for *Brötchen* and in various regions it is also called *Weck* (gender and plural depending on the region, in most it is masculine and *-e* or *-en*); *Semmel* is used in the expression *es geht weg wie warme Semmeln*, 'It sells like hot cakes'.

Senf (m). 'Mustard', an accompaniment to *Frankfurter Würstchen* and also to boiled pork but considered inappropriate for any other kind of meat; a common idiom is *seinen Senf dazugeben*, 'to give one's unasked-for opinion or advice'.

Sense (f -n). 'Scythe'; *damit ist's Sense* is colloquial for 'that's off' or 'nothing doing'.

Silberblick (m -e). *Einen Silberblick haben*, 'to be slightly cross-eyed'.

Sitte (f -n). 'Custom' or 'habit' with a negative form: *eine Unsitte*, 'a bad habit'; it also means 'morals' in the plural and in compounds; *Sittenpolizei*, 'vice squad'; *Sittlichkeitsverbrechen*, 'sex crime'.

sitzen. 'To sit' and *jemand sitzenlassen* is 'to jilt somebody' or 'to leave somebody in the lurch' whereas *etwas auf sich sitzenlassen* is not to object to an accusation or 'take it lying down'. A very colloquial expression for being drunk is *einen sitzen haben*. *Die Bemerkung saß*, 'The remark was very apt' and *Das Kleid sitzt nicht*, 'The dress doesn't hang properly'.

so. A word with a thousand meanings and almost none similar to the English: *so!* 'there you are'; *so so* an uninterested comment, 'is that so?', 'oh well . . .' but never means 'so so'; *Na so was!* 'Well, did you ever . . .!'; *sowieso* 'anyhow'; *so oder so* 'one way or another'. *So sehen Sie aus!* 'That's what you think!'; *Ich will mal nicht so sein*, 'Well, all right, but just this once' (finally conceding to a request one has declined earlier on).

sollen. Note that the main verb may be left out, e.g. *Was soll das?* 'What's that supposed to mean?' or 'What do you think you're doing?' or 'What's the point of that?' depending on the verb implied by the context; *Was soll ich hier?* 'What am I here for?', 'What am I supposed to do here?'; *Was soll's?* 'What's the use of it?' or 'So what?'

sonst. 'Otherwise' and 'else' as in *sonst noch was?* 'Anything else?'

sozialschwach. An adjective meaning that someone is not really responsible for his social and moral shortcomings because his environment (home, neighbourhood, etc.) was not able to provide the example and support conducive to the development of a sense of civic and social duty. It is an explanation often used by social workers (*Sozialarbeiter*) and psychotherapists to indicate why an individual behaves anti-socially. *Er stammt aus einem sozialschwachen Milieu*, 'he comes from an anti-social environment'.

spanisch. 'Spanish'; *Es kommt mir spanisch vor,* 'It seems fishy to me'.

spannen. 'To stretch' or 'to make tense'; the adjective *gespannt* is common with *sein: Ich bin gespannt,* 'I wonder', 'I am anxious to know'.

Sparkasse (f -n). Germany is liberally provided with savings-banks; they came into existence to promote savings by the poorer sections of the community but have rapidly developed into the 'ordinary man's bank'. *Sparkassen* are members of a national association and are usually run by a municipality or a district (*Stadtsparkasse* or *Kreissparkasse*) and provide full banking facilities in addition to those of a savings-bank. The commercial banks tend to be associated with big businesses; private individuals such as doctors and lawyers and small businesses tend to prefer the *Sparkasse*. In many towns, local patriotism makes people support their *Sparkasse* rather than use the commercial banks. Most wages or salaries are paid directly into *Sparkasse* accounts. There is also a post office savings-bank, *die Postsparkasse,* but this does not provide general banking facilities.

Spätentwickler (m -). 'Late developer'; used as in English to denote a person whose intellectual abilities manifest themselves later than usual.

Spätheimkehrer (m -). From *Heimkehrer,*'repatriated prisoner of war' and refers to those whose repatriation from the USSR occurred many years after 1945.

Spätzünder (m -). *v.* SPÄTENTWICKLER.

Spätzündung (f -en). 'Retarded ignition' but colloquially *er hat Spätzündung,* 'He is slow on the uptake'.

spenden. Not to spend but 'to donate' and in towns you will frequently be stopped by children or youngsters with collection boxes asking for *eine keine Spende für . . ., bitte.* The word must not be confused with *spendieren: seinen Freunden eine Runde Bier spendieren,* 'to treat one's friends to a round of beer' and derived from this is *spendabel,* 'generous' 'open-handed'.

sperrangelweit offen. 'Gaping wide open' (*v.* FUNKELNAGELNEU).

Sperrmüll (m -). 'Bulky rubbish', such as old furniture and household appliances. About twice a year, municipal authorities collect such rubbish, and the giant collection is advertised in the press. When the stuff is piled outside the houses, 'looters' go round and take away what they want before the dustmen arrive; this 'looting' has become an honourable and established custom to which no opprobrium is attached.

Spiegel-Deutsch (n -). German that is full of foreign or esoteric words similar to the prose of the weekly *Der Spiegel*.

spitz. 'Pointed'; *etwas spitzkriegen* or *spitzbekommen,* 'to find out', 'get wind of' or 'get the point of'.

Spitzbubenleiter (f -n). A 'step' made by joining hands.

Spitzenkandidat (m -en). 'Favourite candidate for office'.

splitterfasernackt. 'Stark naked' (*v.* FUNKELNAGELNEU).

Sprechstunde (f -n). A doctor's consulting hours or surgery; a doctor's receptionist is *die Sprechstundenhilfe.*

springen. 'To jump'; *etwas springen lassen* is colloquial and means 'to pay for something' when inviting others. *Springen* is also 'to crack' (intr.), e.g. *Dünnes Glas springt leicht,* 'Thin glass cracks easily'.

Sprung (m ¨-e). 'Jump' or 'crack'; *jemund auf einen Sprung besuchen* is 'to pay somebody a short visit'. When a person has little money it is said *er kann keine großen Sprünge machen,* 'He can't go very far on that', 'He can't make a big splash'.

Spucke (f). A colloquial word for *Speichel* (m) 'saliva', and particularly common in Berlinese in the phrase *mir bleibt die Spucke weg,* 'Well, I never did!'; *große Töne spucken* is 'to boast', 'to talk big'.

Spur (f -en). 'Trace' or 'vestige' and a frequently heard answer is *keine Spur* or *nicht die Spur,* 'Not in the slightest'.

Stadtstreicher (m -). One of the hundred thousand or so young people who roam the cities of the *Bundesrepublik Deutschland* and sleep 'rough'. They are jobless and uninsured. The analogy is with *Landstreicher,* tramp.

Stamm (m ¨-e). 'Tree-trunk' and figuratively the 'regulars' when a shop or restaurant speaks of its customers. Derived from this is *Stammkunde,* 'regular customer' and *Stammplatz,* 'one's accustomed place' in a bar or restaurant. Many bars and restaurants also have a *Stammtisch,* a table reserved for a regular group meeting there; often the group calls itself a club and the club's emblem is kept in the restaurant and placed on the *Stammtisch* whenever the club meets; colloquially *Stammtisch* has come to stand for drinking as such: *Er ist zum Stammtisch gegangen,* 'He's gone off for a drink with his mates'. Some restaurants offer a *Stammessen* on their menu which is for those customers who have an *Abonnement,* i.e. advance payment for a number of meals, but the *Stammessen* may be ordered by other guests as well. The verb *stammen* has a completely different meaning and is related to the English 'to stem from' but it is used very widely and translates best into 'to come from': *Das Rezept stammt von meiner Tante,* 'I got this recipe from my aunt' or 'This recipe comes from my aunt'.

Stange (f -n). 'Pole' and an uncomplimentary description of tall slim people (it often takes the form of *Bohnenstange* 'bean-pole' as well). *Ein Anzug von der Stange* is 'a suit off the peg'; *eine Stange*

Zigaretten, 'a carton of cigarettes'. The colloquial *eine Stange Geld* means 'an awful lot of money (that is being spent)'.

stark. 'Strong' and a euphemism for 'big' or 'corpulent'. *Das ist ja ein starkes Stück!* is a reproof, 'that's really a bit thick!'

stärken, sich. Basically 'to strengthen oneself' and thus 'to have something to eat or drink'; *eine kleine Stärkung* is a 'refreshment' 'a light snack'.

starkmachen. *Sich starkmachen für* . . . is 'to defend' an idea, or person or actively to promote a thing or person.

Station (f -en). A false friend in general as it is rarely used in the sense of *Bahnstation* for which the word *Bahnhof* is preferred. It is the 'ward' in a hospital and in *Gehalt und freie Station* it means 'salary plus board and lodging'; it may also describe a short stay as in *wir haben in Berlin zwei Tage Station gemacht,* 'We stopped over in Berlin for two days'.

Staub (m). 'Dust'; *sich aus dem Staub machen* is a common idiom 'to make off'. Humorously *feuchter Staub* is used as a euphemism for *Dreck,* e.g. *Das geht Sie einen feuchten Staub an,* 'That's none of your business'. A common newspaper cliché is *Staub aufwirbeln:* *Diese Angelegenheit hat viel Staub aufgewirbelt,* 'This affair has raised quite a dust'.

stecken. 'To stick' and in colloquial usage the transitive and intransitive are both conjugated with regular endings *steckte, gesteckt.* The verb is very common in everyday speech and the best translation for the transitive is 'to put' and the intransitive 'to be', e.g. *Wo haben Sie gesteckt?* 'Where have you been?'; *stecken Sie den Brief in Ihre Tasche,* 'Put the letter in your pocket'.

Stegreif (m). Used only in the stock phrase *aus dem Stegreif,* 'without preparation', 'on the spur of the moment' or 'off the cuff'.

stehen. 'To stand'; *sich mit jemandem gut stehen,* 'to be on good terms with somebody' or, when applied to things, e.g. *mit diesem Mantel stehen Sie sich gut* it describes a good choice, 'this coat is a (good) bargain'. *Wie steht's?* is colloquial 'how is it going?'; *Es steht nicht gut um ihn,* 'Things don't look too bright for him'; *Das Kleid steht Ihnen (gut),* 'The dress suits you'. *Auf etwas stehen* (very colloquial) is 'to like something'.

stehenbleiben. 'To remain standing' but also 'to stop' (intr.).

stehlen. 'To steal'; the phrase *er kann mir gestohlen bleiben,* 'I couldn't care less about him' is a common colloquialism.

Stein (m -e). 'Stone' and not as many English people think the name for a container in which beer is served; beer is usually served in a glass or a 'glass mug' *Krug* (m ¨-e); in Southern Germany an earthenware mug with or without a lid is preferred, *ein Maß* (*Steinmaß*) (n -e) or *ein Seidel* (n -) and if it is large *ein Humpen* (m -).

stellen. 'To put' and often used phrases are *eine Frage stellen,* 'to ask a question'; *etwas auf den Kopf stellen,* 'to turn something upside down'; *eine Uhr stellen,* 'to set a watch or clock'. The reflexive verb with a present participle means 'to pretend to be', e.g. *Er stellte sich schlafend,* 'He pretended to be asleep'.

stempelfreudig. 'Stamp-happy' and refers to the mania for rubber-stamping documents.

stempeln. 'To stamp' and *stempeln gehen* is a colloquialism for 'to draw the dole'.

sternhagelvoll. 'Dead drunk' (*v.* FUNKELNAGELNEU).

Stich (m -e). 'Thrust' with a sharp object and it can also refer to a sharp pain. A much used colloquialism is *er hat einen Stich,* 'He's round the bend' derived from *die Milch hat einen Stich,* 'The milk is off'. In compound words the significance of *Stich* is often 'key' thus *Stichtag* 'key-date', *Stichwort* 'key-word' etc.

Stiefel (m -). 'Boot'; also a large glass tankard for beer in the shape of a boot ranging in size from an *ein-Liter-Stiefel* to an enormous thing of some four or five litres; it is often used at parties or at the *Stammtisch* (*v.* STAMM) and is handed round, the aim being to empty it without producing a gurgling sound, something that requires great skill because of the tankard's shape. The idiom *er kann einen (ordentlichen) Stiefel vertragen* derives from this and means that 'he can take quite a lot' (of alcohol).

Stift (m -e). 'Spike' or 'pin' and also an abbreviation of *Bleistift* 'pencil'. *Stiftekopf* is ironic for a 'crew-cut'.

stiftengehen. (Coll.), 'to beat a hasty retreat' although it comes from the verb *stiften* 'to donate' and implies ironically that your hurry comes from a keen desire to make an immediate donation to charity.

Stimme (f -n). 'Voice' and also 'vote'; *Stimmvieh* (n) is an ignorant and stupid electorate.

stimmen. A verb that is very common in everyday speech and means 'to be correct'; *stimmt das?* 'is that true (right, correct)?'; *es stimmt so* is the phrase used to tell the waiter that he may keep the change; *stimmt's* at the end of a statement is equivalent to question tag 'right?'

Stirn (f -en). 'Forehead' and as the English use 'cheek' for effrontery so the Germans use 'forehead' for 'cheek', e.g. *Er hatte die Stirn, mir so etwas zu sagen,* 'He had the cheek to tell me that'.

Stoßburg (f -en). Colloquial for an apartment building occupied by bachelors and single women.

stoßen. 'To push' and idiomatically used in *jemand vor den Kopf stoßen,* 'to offend' or 'snub' somebody; *sich stoßen (an)* is 'to knock (into)' something and the equivalent to 'mind your head' or some similar warning is *stoßen Sie sich nicht*; figuratively *sich an etwas stoßen* means to take offence at something or to dislike it.

Stoßzeit (f -en).   'Rush hour'.

Straßenfeger (m -).   A television programme that is so popular that it keeps people at home and the streets empty, i.e. 'street sweeper'.

Straßenkreuzer (m -).   Humorous for a large saloon car or limousine.

Stressor (m -en).   Usually in plural, 'stress-producing factors'.

Strohhalm (m -e).   'Drinking straw'.

Strohwitwer (m -).   'Grass-widower'; the feminine used to be *Strohwitwe* (-n) but recently the expression *grüne Witwe* has become popular.

Strom (m ¨-e).   'Stream' and also 'electric current' (the word *Elektrizität* is hardly ever used in everyday language).

Stück (n -e).   'Piece' and common expressions are: *aus freien Stücken*, 'voluntarily'; *große Stücke auf jemand halten*, 'to think highly of someone'.

studieren.   'To study at a university' or in its figurative use 'to look closely' at something but not 'to study' a lesson (*v.* LERNEN).

Stunde (f -n).   'Hour' and also a 'lesson' which need not be for an exact hour. Note that the verb *stunden* has no connection with the noun but means 'to give somebody credit or time in which to repay an amount due': *Können Sie mir den Betrag bis zum nächsten Ersten stunden?* 'Can you give me until the first of next month to repay you the amount?' *Stunde der Hetze* is 'rush hour'; also *Hauptverkehrszeit* (m -en) and *Stoßzeit* (f -en).

Suchdienst (m).   'Tracing service' and is the designation of a Red Cross Organization in Hamburg which is devoted to tracing the parents, nationality, name and other personal details of children found parentless and nameless in Germany in 1945 and the immediate post-war period. They also seek to re-unite families of prisoners-of-war.

suchen.   'To look for'; *Er hat hier nichts zu suchen*, 'He has no business here'.

süffig.   The connoisseur's word for a very 'drinkable' or excellent wine although *Suff* (m) is slang for 'drinking'.

T

Tante Emma.   Characterizes, in compounds, something like 'the good old...' e.g. *Tante-Emma-Laden*, a small, cosy shop where the shopkeeper chats with every customer and knows every customer's name. Usually used with shops and *Kneipe*.

Tanzdiele (f -n). For dancing in respectable surroundings and without paying exorbitant prices as in *Tanzbars*. The *Tanzdiele* is not usually a 'clip-joint'. There is very often an admission charge which is deductible from the price of drinks consumed. The *Tanzcafé* is very similar but caters for the older generation rather than for youngsters.

Taschenrechner (m -). Pocket calculator.

Tasse (f-n). 'Cup'; *er hat nicht alle Tassen im Schrank* is similar to 'he's got a screw loose'.

Tauchsieder (m -). It is a portable electric immersion heater that can be plugged into a light socket or power point and the insulated heating element can then be immersed in water in a saucepan, jug or even a cup. *Der Reisetauchsieder* is a little one about five inches long and packed in a case with a tiny water container just big enough for a cup of tea or coffee and very handy in hotel bedrooms. Big *Tauchsieder* can heat a bucketful of water in a few minutes.

täuschen. 'To deceive' and the reflexive form means 'to be wrong' or 'mistaken': *Ich glaube ja, ich kann mich aber auch täuschen,* 'I think so, but I may be wrong'.

Taxi (n -s). 'Taxi' also spelt *Taxe* (f -n); an old name is *Droschke* (f -n) but nowadays it is only used on street signs indicating the *Taxenstand* (m ¨-e) 'cab or taxi rank' (the sign also means that other vehicles may not park there). *Funktaxi* 'radio cab'. *Eine Lasttaxi* is a small van or estate car, often a *VW Kombiwagen*, which will transport personal effects and bulky items for short distances. *Der Mietwagen* (-) as a name for taxi is old-fashioned but it is the correct word for a car hired by the day or week, with or without a driver.

Telefonseelsorge (f -n). Telephone counselling service for the distressed, Samaritan organization.

telegen. 'Telegenic', equivalent to 'photogenic', but on TV.

Tempotaschentuch (n ¨-er). A trade name now generally used for any kind of 'paper handkerchief'.

Tesafilm (m). Equivalent to 'Sellotape' and similar transparent adhesives.

Teufel (m -). 'Devil'; in compound words or combinations it may be abusive or frequently an expression of admiration. Very common and inoffensive colloquial expressions are: *den Teufel an die Wand malen* literally 'to paint the devil on the wall' means 'talk of the devil and he's sure to appear'; *in Teufels Küche kommen* or *gebracht werden,* 'to get into trouble' and *es ist zum Teufel,* 'It's gone' or 'lost' or 'ruined'.

Theater (n-). 'Theatre' but colloquially used for 'fuss'; *Machen Sie nicht so ein Theater, es handelt sich ja nur um ein paar Minuten*, 'Don't make such a fuss, it's only a matter of a few minutes'. The adjective *theatralisch* is only used figuratively as in *eine theatralische Geste*, 'a theatrical gesture'.

Thema (n -ta or -men). 'Theme' but more frequently 'topic', e.g. *Das Wetter ist ein beliebtes Unterhaltungsthema*, 'The weather is a popular topic of conversation'; *Kommen wir zum Thema bitte*, 'Let's get to the point'.

Tip (m -s). A false friend because it never means the tip you give to a waiter or taxi-driver but is related to the English 'to tip somebody off' or 'give someone a pointer or lead' as in *können Sie mir nicht einen Tip geben, an welchen der Herren ich mich wenden muß? Sie kennen sie doch . . .*, 'Couldn't you advise me which of the gentlemen I should approach, seeing that you know them . . .'. Backing horses is not a popular pastime in Germany but some people do it and then they use *Tip* and *Tipster* (m -) exactly as do the English and *ein todsicherer Tip* is 'a dead cert'.

tippeln. 'To tramp'; *Tippelbruder* (m ¨-), 'tramp'; *Tippelschickse* (f -n), 'female tramp' or 'vagabond'.

tippen. The verb has various meanings all colloquial and very common; *auf etwas tippen*, 'to reckon' or 'guess'; *tippen*, 'to type' and a colloquial and slightly derogatory name for a 'typist' is *Tippse*, 'silly little typist'; *tippen* can also mean 'to tap lightly' and in games it is 'to bet'.

Tochter (f ¨-). 'Daughter' and *Tochtergesellschaft* is a 'subsidiary firm'. *Haustochter* is an 'au pair girl'.

toi, toi, toi. An encouraging exclamation when a person undertakes a difficult task.

toll. 'Mad' and *Tollwut* (f) is 'rabies', but the adjective *toll* is also equivalent to the English 'crazy', 'daft', 'giddy', 'dizzy' (not 'mentally deranged'); *es ging toll her* means 'it was a riot' or 'there were wild goings-on'; *Das Tollste dabei ist . . .*, 'The most incredible part about it is . . .'; *Das ist das Tollste, was ich je gehört habe*, 'That beats everything I've ever heard'.

Ton (m ¨-e). A word frequently used to mean 'etiquette': *Das gehört zum guten Ton*, 'That's how the best people do it'. A common saying is *der Ton macht die Musik*, 'It doesn't matter what you say (do) but how you say (do) it'. Note also the phrase *etwas in den höchsten Tönen loben* (*in allen Tonarten loben*), 'to praise something to high heaven'. A colloquial expression of surprise: *hat man Töne* (or in the familiar form *hast du Töne*), 'have you ever . . .'.

Torschlußpanik (f). 'Door-shutting panic', a colloquialism which describes the fear and increased efforts of some women in their late twenties or early thirties to find a husband.

Toto (n). *Länder*-controlled football pools; there are no private football pools in Germany.

Tour (f -en). 'Tour' or 'excursion' and not really a false friend but it has various colloquial usages not easily understandable; *an* or *in einer Tour* is 'continuous(ly)' e.g. *Sie redet an einer Tour,* 'She talks continuously'; *Er macht es auf die gemütliche Tour,* 'His motto is "easy does it" '; *Tour* here means the 'way' in which one handles a matter thus the colloquial *jemandem die Tour vermasseln* is 'to mess up somebody's plans'; *krumme Touren* are 'sharp practices'. In the plural it also stands for 'revolutions' and *auf Touren kommen* may mean literally that an engine is increasing the speed of its revolutions or figuratively that a person is increasing whatever he has been doing thus 'getting more excited', 'working harder' etc.; *auf Hochtouren arbeiten* is a commonly used phrase 'to work as quickly and as well as possible'.

Tracht (f -en). 'Regional peasant costume' but it usually refers to the Bavarian or Austrian style if not otherwise qualified.

traktieren. Actually 'to treat' but nowadays only used to mean 'to maltreat' or force something onto a person, e.g. *Sie traktierten mich mit Wein und Likör, bis ich nicht mehr stehen konnte,* 'They forced wine and liqueur on me until I couldn't stand up any longer'.

Trampel (n -). An uncomplimentary colloquial word for a female lout and could be the origin of the American 'the lady is a tramp'.

Tratsch (m). 'Gossip' and pronounced with a long *a*; *tratschen* with a long *a* is 'to gossip', with a short *a* it is a dialect word for very heavy rain, 'to pelt down'.

Traum (m ¨-e). 'Dream' and often used in the exclamation *aus der Traum!* 'Well, that was that!' (the end of a plan or project).

treffen. 'To meet' and also 'to hit' something aimed at, and a very common phrase in everyday conversation is *es trifft sich gut, daß* . . . 'It's good that . . .' or 'It is a lucky coincidence that'. . .'.

treiben. Colloquially 'to do': *Was treibt er denn so?* 'Well, what's he been up to lately?'; the noun *Treiben* (n) is 'bustle' or 'goings-on'.

Treppenwitz (m -e). The clever remark that you think of when it is too late (on your way downstairs and out) and the word is still used in this sense and seems to be a translation of the French 'esprit de l'escalier', but it also derives from a book by W. Lewis Hertslet published in 1882 and entitled *Treppenwitz der Weltgeschichte* and can refer to an event that seems to be the result of a joke played by fate or history ('history' seems to discover the correct course when it is too late).

trimm dich. 'Keep fit', and *ein Trimm-Dich-Pfad* is 'a keep fit path', a kind of obstacle course found in some public parks and recreation grounds.

Trinkgeld (n -er).   A 'tip' and in Germany it is always handed to the person concerned except in restaurants where it is never left on the table but added on to the amount by telling the waiter or by telling him that he may keep the change: *danke* or *es stimmt so*. Service in restaurants is usually 10 or 15 per cent and it is either included in the prices stated on the menu (*einschließlich Bedienung, Bedienung inbegriffen*) or charged separately (*zuzüglich Bedienung, Bedienung nicht inbegriffen*) but it is always added on before the bill is presented so that any additional tip is completely up to you. A tip is almost obligatory in a hairdresser's where very often it is not actually handed to the person who attended to you but dropped into one of the conveniently large and numerous pockets of his overall; taxi-drivers don't normally expect a tip unless they have had to handle your luggage and are always pleased when a passenger gives them a little extra.

Trockenhaube (f -n).   'Electric hair-drier' as used by hairdressers.

Trost (m).   'Consolation' but note the colloquial *Sie sind wohl nicht ganz bei Trost,* 'You must be out of your mind'.

tun.   'To do' or 'to make'. Rather colloquial is the use of *tun* to mean 'put', e.g. *etwas auf den Tisch tun,* 'to put something on the table' and in the sense of 'to be sufficient', e.g. *Zwanzig Mark tun's auch,* 'Twenty Marks should (will) also do'.

Tür (f -en).   'Door'; *Tür an Tür mit jemandem leben* is 'to live next door to somebody'; *vor der Tür stehen,* 'to be on the door step' is much used figuratively, e.g. *Weihnachten steht vor der Tür,* 'Christmas is almost upon us'.

Tüte (f -n).   'Paper bag' as used by shops to pack up your purchases; in self-service shops they also come in the form of a carrier bag, *eine* (*Papier*)*Tragtasche*. A colloquial expression is *das kommt nicht in die Tüte!* 'That's out (of the question)!'

U

überfragt sein.   (Coll.) 'to be asked a question one cannot answer': *Tut mir leid, aber da bin ich überfragt,* 'Sorry but I don't know'.

Überführung (f -en).   A 'viaduct' or 'fly-over' for motor traffic as opposed to the *Unterführung,* a 'subway' or 'underpass'; both are quite frequently found in large towns particularly near level-crossings and signs *bei geschlossener Schranke bitte Überführung* (*Unterführung*) *benutzen* request you to use them when the barriers are closed. If a subway or viaduct serves as a means of crossing a busy street for pedestrians it is a punishable offence not to use it. *Überführung* can also mean 'transport to' or 'transference' but *die Überführung eines Verbrechers* is the 'conviction of a criminal'.

Übergangslösung (f -en).   'Provisional solution', 'temporary arrangement'.

übergeben (inseparable).   'To hand over' but used reflexively it means 'to be sick', 'to vomit'.

übergehen.   When separable it means 'to pass over (into)', e.g. *Es geht in meinen Besitz über,* 'It passes into my possession' but the phrase *die Augen gingen ihm über* can have two different meanings, either 'his eyes were almost popping out' or 'his eyes filled with tears'. When inseparable the verb means 'to ignore' or 'to neglect'. The separable verb must not be confused with combinations of *gehen* with *über* as a separate preposition, e.g. *Es geht nichts über ein gutes Glas Wein,* 'There's nothing better than a glass of good wine' or *Ein gutes Glas Wein geht mir über alles,* 'I like nothing better than a glass of good wine'.

überholen.   When inseparable it is 'to overtake' a vehicle or 'to overhaul' something needing repair, but the adjective *überholt* is 'out-of-date' or 'antiquated'.

überhören (inseparable). No t 'to overhear' but 'not to hear', i.e. either to miss something that is being said or not to pay attention because you prefer not to know; the latter is often stressed by the adjective *geflissentlich,* a word hardly ever used in any other context: *Er überhörte meine Anspielungen geflissentlich,* 'He studiously ignored my hints'.

überleben (inseparable).   'To survive' or 'to outlive'; *es hat sich überlebt* means 'it is outmoded' or 'out-dated'.

übermorgen.   'The day after tomorrow'; *den Morgen über,* 'during the morning'.

übernachten (inseparable).   Also the noun *Übernachtung (f -en)* are the correct words for 'to spend the night', thus in a hotel one would inquire *Was berechnen Sie für die Übernachtung?* 'What do you charge for the night?' and friends might ask, *Wo haben Sie übernachtet?* 'Where did you sleep?'

übersehen.   The inseparable verb means 'to overlook', i.e. not to see by accident or on purpose as well as the complete opposite, viz. 'to see everything that is important or relevant to a matter'; this may seem illogical but *über* can be used in the sense of passing over and not seeing it as well as looking across the whole matter and thus seeing it in its entirety so *eine Lage übersehen* means 'to be in full command of the situation' and *einen Fehler übersehen,* 'to overlook a mistake'. Colloquially the verb is used separably to mean 'to see so much of something that one gets tired of it', e.g. *Diese Farbe* *kann man sich leicht übersehen,* 'One can easily get tired of (seeing) this colour'.

um. A rather difficult preposition as it has a great variety of meanings. When referring to time it may mean 'at' an exact time, e.g. *um sechs Uhr,* 'at six o'clock' or 'at about', e.g. *um Ostern,* 'about Easter'; often a *so* or *herum* may be added to make the inexact nature explicit: *um Ostern herum, so um Ostern* but as often as not it is left out; if *so* follows the *um* it means 'all the . . . (comparative)', e.g. *um so mehr,* 'all the more'.

umdenken. To change one's mind, to rethink.

umgucken, sich (separable). A colloquial verb which means literally 'to glance round' but is mostly used in a figurative sense: *Er wird sich umgucken!* 'He'll get a shock!' or 'he's got another think coming!'

umlegen (separable). Acceptable slang for 'to kill' whereas the reflexive form is colloquial for 'to lie down'.

umsonst. 'For nothing', i.e. either 'gratuitous' or 'in vain'.

umspringen. As a separable verb it is used as a stronger form of *umgehen* in the sense of 'to handle' and therefore means 'to handle roughly' or, as it is mostly used to refer to people, 'to treat without consideration', e.g. *So können Sie nicht mit Ihren Angestellten umspringen,* 'You can't push your employees around like that'.

Umstand (m ⸗-e). 'Circumstance' but in colloquial speech 'fuss' in the sense of making things far more complicated than necessary so that it might also translate into 'bother' or 'trouble'. The plural *Umstände* in the sense of 'fuss' is mostly the trouble that other people take to make things pleasant for you and you might say to your host, *Machen Sie sich meinetwegen keine Umstände,* 'Don't trouble yourself on my account'. Note also the colloquial euphemism for 'to be pregnant': *in anderen Umständen sein* reflected as well in the word for 'maternity clothes', *Umstandskleidung.*

Umtausch (m -e). The 'exchange' of something bought in a shop and shops often specify *vom Umtausch ausgeschlossen* or *Umtausch nicht gestattet* when an article cannot be exchanged once it has been sold; even when there is no such statement it is better to inquire *kann ich es umtauschen?* or *ist Umtausch möglich?* 'Is it possible to exchange this?' if you are envisaging the possibility.

Umweltschutz (m, pl. **Umweltschutzmaßnahmen**). General term for environmental conservation.

unbedingt. Literally it means 'unquestioning' or 'absolute' but in everyday speech it is extremely common in the sense of 'really': *Sie müssen unbedingt kommen,* 'You really must come'.

unberufen. A colloquial exclamation which is usually followed by *toi, toi, toi* or *toi, toi, toi, Holz anfassen* and accompanied by knocking against wood; the English equivalent is 'touch wood', the American 'knock on wood'.

unerhört. 'Unheard of' and when used in a good sense such as in *unerhört talentiert,* 'exceedingly talented (gifted)' has a teenage sound and is rather enthusiastic. In a pejorative sense it is often used alone or in short phrases: *unerhört!* 'honestly . . .!'; *Das ist ja unerhört!* 'That's the limit!'

ungefähr. 'Approximately', 'about'; the educated but archaic meaning of *ungefähr* 'by chance' or 'by accident' is still retained in the phrase *nicht von ungefähr* which is a cautious rendering of 'on purpose' or 'with an ulterior motive', e.g. *Ich sage das nicht von ungefähr,* 'I have my reasons for saying this'.

ungelegte Eier. As in the phrase *kümmern Sie sich nicht um ungelegte Eier* which does not mean 'don't count your chickens before they are hatched' but is equivalent to 'don't worry about that now, we'll cross that bridge when we come to it'.

ungelogen. A colloquial addition to statements equivalent to 'and that's the honest truth', e.g. *Hierfür habe ich ungelogen zwei Stunden gebraucht,* 'This took me two hours, and that's the honest truth'.

ungemein. This is not the opposite of *gemein* 'mean' (in the American sense) but is an emphatic word meaning 'extremely' or 'exceedingly'.

unheimlich. Though *heimlich* means 'secret(ly)' *unheimlich* has no connection with this meaning; it is an emphatic and slightly colloquial word for 'tremendous(ly)'. Apart from this it can mean 'uncanny' or 'eerie': *Mir ist unheimlich* is 'I'm afraid' because of eerie surroundings or circumstances, e.g. in a dark house.

unsicher. 'Unsafe', 'insecure', 'uncertain'. A colloquialism is *etwas unsicher machen* meaning 'to make a place unsafe for other persons' and it is not easy to find a good English equivalent for the idea that the phrase expresses; it can sometimes be translated by 'at large' as in *heute abend machen Soldaten die Stadt unsicher,* 'Soldiers are at large in the town tonight' and the implication is that they will molest civilians. Often it can mean something like 'up to no good' when referring to someone hanging about or loitering: *er macht die Gegend unsicher.* When teenagers go out in a group they sometimes ask each other *Welches Lokal wollen wir unsicher machen?* but the implication of this question is only 'what coffee bar should we liven up?'

unter. 'Under' but also 'among' which most foreigners forget; but *wir sind unter uns* is 'we are by ourselves (no outsider is present)'.

unterbringen (separable). 'To find room for' something and thus it often translates 'to put a person up' for the night.

Unterhalt (m). 'Livelihood' and the verb is *unterhalten* (inseparable) 'to support' or 'to maintain' a person or a business. The verb can, however, also be derived from *Unterhaltung* (f -en) 'conversation' or 'diversion' and mean 'to entertain' someone; *sich unterhalten* is 'to converse' or 'to amuse oneself' (with a hobby etc.).

Unterhosen (f.pl.). 'Underpants'; often they are called *die Unaussprechlichen,* 'the unspeakables' as a euphemism because *Unterhosen* is not a very elegant word. *Schlüpfer* (m -) is preferred when they are short; '(ladies') panties' are called *Slip* (m -s) and 'slip' is *Unterrock* (m ¨-e) in German. A rather blunt colloquialism is *etwas in Unterhosen zeigen,* 'to debunk'.

untersagen (inseparable). A very common officialese euphemism for *verbieten,* 'to prohibit' particularly on signs and notices.

Untersatz (m ¨-e). 'Support', 'base'; colloquially *einen fahrbaren Untersatz haben* 'to have a car (at one's disposal)'.

Urburschenschaft (f -en). This refers to the original fraternity of German students formed in the years 1812 to 1815 in the struggle against the French. A *Burschenschaft* is a student fraternity.

Ursache (f -n). *Keine Ursache,* 'Don't mention it'.

V

Verabredung (f -en). 'Appointment' and 'to have an appointment' can be rendered by: *ich habe eine Verabredung* (*mit*) or *ich bin verabredet* (*mit*); it is , however, not quite so easy to find a translation for 'to make an appointment with . . .': *sich verabreden mit* . . . is 'to arrange a meeting' away from the participants' homes; *sich anmelden bei* is 'to make an appointment' at somebody's business premises, e.g. *sich beim Friseur für vier Uhr anmelden,* 'to make an appointment at the hairdresser's for four o'clock'. If the arrangement is suggested by the hairdresser he will ask, *Darf ich Sie für vier Uhr bestellen* (*vormerken*), 'May I ask you to come at (put you down for) four o'clock?'. Doctors' name plates may have the note *Sprechstunde nach Verabredung* (*Übereinkunft*), 'consultation by arrangement'.

verändern, sich. 'To change' one's character or appearance and it is also used to mean 'to change one's job'.

veräppeln. A colloquialism 'to pull somebody's leg' or 'to mock'; it has nothing to do with *Äppel* (m.pl.), the colloquial pronunciation of *Äpfel* 'apples', it is a corruption of *veralbern* 'to mock' or 'ridicule'.

verballhornen. A colloquial word derived from the Lübeck book printer Johann Ballhorn (1528–1603) who altered and 'improved' on his own initiative, manuscripts entrusted to him. Another colloquial equivalent is *verschlimmbessern,* a combination of *verschlimmern* 'to make worse' and *verbessern* 'to improve' or 'to correct' thus 'to bowdlerize'. Ballhorn printed *vermehrt und verbessert durch Johann Ballhorn* on the title-pages of his publications.

verbieten. 'To forbid' and the verb is often combined with a noun, e.g. *jemandem den Mund verbieten,* 'to forbid a person to speak'. The participle is used colloquially to refer to a person's appearance: *In dem Kleid sieht sie verboten aus,* 'She looks a sight in that dress', or 'She looks quite impossible in that dress'.

verflixt. A colloquial 'nice' version of the swear-word *verflucht,* 'cursed' and it is about equivalent to 'damned', 'blasted' and 'confounded'. *Verflucht* should be used sparingly as it is stronger than its English translation would lead you to suppose but it is quite acceptable in the combination *verflucht und zugenäht* (from *zunähen* 'to sew up'); no similar phrase exists in English and it means 'thoroughly damned'; it originates from a verse in an old students' song.

verfranzen, sich. Colloquial, 'to lose one's way' from World War I in which the traditional nickname for a pilot was *Emil* and for a navigator *Franz*; when *Franz* did not tell the pilot where to go they went off course and lost their way.

vergammeln. 'To go bad' of food, e.g. one speaks of *vergammelte Milch* or *vergammelter Salat*.

vergelten. A highly literary word meaning 'to repay' but common in the South in the phrase *vergelt's Gott* which is equivalent to 'thanks'.

Vergnügen (n -). 'Pleasure' and *mit wem habe ich das Vergnügen?* is a formal way of saying 'who are you?' on the phone or to a person directly.

vergreifen, sich. With *in* it means 'to take the wrong . . .', e.g. *Sie vergreifen sich im Ton,* 'That's the wrong tone to speak to me in' whereas with *an* it is 'to misappropriate' or 'to violate' something, 'to lay hands on' something or somebody with bad intentions. Note that the participle *vergriffen* is 'sold out', 'not available at the moment'.

Verhältnis (n -se). 'Relation' or 'proportion' and in the plural it means 'situation' or 'circumstances'; the phrase *ein Verhältnis haben mit* is colloquial 'to have a (love) affair with'.

Verkauf (m ¨-e). 'Sale' or 'selling' and in order to mean a 'special sale' it takes the following combinations: *Ausverkauf, Schlußverkauf, Winterschlußverkauf, Sommerschlußverkauf*; a

Räumungsverkauf is usually a 'closing-down sale' but it can also mean an *Ausverkauf* or *Schlußverkauf*.

Verkehrsübungsgelände (n -), Verkehrsübungsplatz (m ¨-e). An area provided by the authorities in which people can practise their driving skills without cost and with the advice of experts, i.e. a 'road-sense school'.

verknallt sein (in). A colloquialism particularly common among teenagers for 'to be in love' or 'to be infatuated (with)'; even stronger is *verschossen sein in,* 'to be hopelessly infatuated with'.

verlassen.   The two common meanings of this verb are incorporated in the saying *wer sich auf ihn verläßt, ist verlassen,* 'If you rely on him you've had it' or 'you're left in the lurch'; *sich verlassen auf,* 'to rely on' can also be expressed by a noun: *Auf ihn ist (kein) Verlaß,* 'One can(not) rely on him'; *verlassen* may be just 'to leave' or 'to forsake', 'jilt' somebody.

vermiesen.   Colloquial and derived from *mies* 'bad', it means 'to spoil' things for someone, e.g. *Ich werde mir die Reise von keinem vermiesen lassen,* 'I won't have anybody spoil the journey for me'.

vermissen.   'To miss' only in the sense of feeling or regretting the absence of something or someone; 'to miss a train' is *einen Zug verpassen* or *versäumen* and the same verbs are used for 'you haven't missed anything, it was boring', *Sie haben nichts verpaßt (versäumt), es war langweilig.*

verpfeifen.   *Jemand verpfeifen* (coll.), 'to inform on someone', 'to betray', 'to put the finger on . . .'.

verraten und verkauft sein. (Coll.) 'to be done for' or 'to have had it' and similar to *aufgeschmissen* (q.v.).

Vers (m -e).   *Sich einen Vers auf etwas machen können* is 'to understand something' in the sense of understand 'what makes it tick'. As *Vers* is similar to *Reim,* the idiom also takes the form of *sich einen Reim auf etwas machen können.*

verscheuern.   (Coll.) the sale of goods by a private person to raise money or dispose of unwanted (usually shoddy) effects.

verschieden.   'Various' or 'different' but the phrase *das ist verschieden* does not mean 'that's different' (which is rendered by *das ist etwas anderes*), it is a non-committal answer equivalent to 'that depends', 'that varies (according to the situation)'. The word may also be the past participle of the poetic *verscheiden,* 'to pass away', i.e. 'to die'.

verschludern.   'To lose because of negligence', 'mislay', and the noun *Verschluderung (f -en)* may also refer to 'deterioration because of negligence' (stylists speak of the *Verschluderung der Sprache*). *Schludrig* is 'careless', 'untidy', 'negligent'.

verschüttgehen.   A colloquialism meaning 'to get (become) lost' and it originates from the Low German *schütten* 'to lock up stray cattle in a pound'; this was done by an official called *Flurschütz*, a kind of public guard of fields and meadows, and when an animal was *verschüttet* or *verschüttgegangen* it was irretrievably lost to its owner and could be auctioned off. Thus *verschüttgehen* means 'to be lost' because of carelessness. It does not derive, as most people think, from *verschüttet* meaning 'covered with earth or rubble'.

verschwiemelt. A colloquialism common in the North and East and describes the appearance of someone who has passed the night 'out on the tiles', i.e. bleary-eyed and suffering from a hangover.

verschwitzen. (Colloquial) 'to forget'.

versetzen. Colloquially 'not to come when one has promised to' as in *ihr Freund hat sie versetzt*, 'Her friend stood her up.' In *ich habe meine Uhr versetzt* it is 'I've pawned my watch'.

verspitzen, sich auf. Colloquial, and it means 'to hope very much to get something', e.g. *Wir hatten uns auf einen freien Tag verspitzt, aber es wurde nichts daraus,* 'We had hoped to have (almost counted on having) a day off, but it came to nothing'.

verwaltungstechnisch. *Aus verwaltungstechnischen Gründen,* 'on administrative grounds', 'for administrative reasons'.

verzehren. 'To eat' or 'consume'; the verb and also the noun *Verzehr* (m), 'consumption' are rather high-brow but frequently used by waiters in high-class restaurants.

verzeihen. Socially *verzeihen* is interchangeable with *entschuldigen*: *verzeihen Sie, entschuldigen Sie* and the nouns *Verzeihung, Entschuldigung* all mean 'excuse me', but note that the reflexive *sich entschuldigen für* is 'to apologize for', and the literal meaning of *verzeihen* is 'to forgive'.

Volkshochschule (f -n). 'Adult evening classes'.

Vollkaskoversicherung (f -en). Comprehensive car insurance.

vor. 'Before' and 'ago' so that *vor einem Jahr* is 'a year ago' and never 'for a year' (*für ein Jahr, ein Jahr lang*).

voraus. *Im voraus,* 'in advance'.

vorbei. 'Past', 'gone' or 'finished' and often used as a prefix with the meaning of 'wrong': *sich vorbeibenehmen,* 'to misbehave', *vorbeigehen,* 'to fail', 'to go wrong' etc. Most of these verbs retain their literal significance so *vorbeigehen* also means 'to go past' or 'to walk past' something, when followed by *an*; *vorbeigehen* and *vorbeikommen bei* indicate 'to drop in' or 'to look in on', e.g. *Ich gehe nachher mal bei ihm vorbei,* 'I'll look in on him later in the day'. In the phrase *ich komme nicht daran vorbei* the verb is used figuratively 'I cannot but', 'I have no alternative but' and it is followed by the infinitive with *zu* (the same idea is expressed by *ich komme nicht darum herum* which is stylistically better).

vorerst. Not 'foremost' but 'for the moment', 'for the time being'.

vorgehen. Not 'forgo' but 'to leave before the others', e.g. *Wir gehen schon vor und treffen euch dann am Bahnhof*, 'We'll leave now and we'll see you at the station'; but *was geht hier vor?* means 'what's going on here?'. The noun *Vorgang* (m ¨-e) is often rendered by a verb in English: *Erzählen Sie uns den Vorgang*, 'Tell us how it happened (what happened)' but in some cases 'event', 'incident' or 'process' is better. Note the figurative meaning of the verb as in *die Arbeit geht vor*, 'Work comes first', i.e. 'work is more important'.

vorkommen. 'To happen' or 'to take place' as in the phrase *das kommt vor*, 'Things like that do happen'; with reference to films or writings it often means 'to exist' or 'to be': *Das Wort kommt sechsmal auf einer Seite vor*, 'The word appears (is used) six times on one page'. Note the following uses: *Ich komme mir dumm vor*, 'I feel silly'; *Das kommt Ihnen nur so vor*, 'It only seems (to you) like that'; *Das kommt in den besten Familien vor*, 'That can happen in the best of families' and, to calm someone down, *Das kann ja mal vorkommen*, 'That can happen to anybody' when he has made a mistake.

Vorliebe (f -n). 'Predilection'. The phrases *mit Vorliebe* and *eine Vorliebe haben für* mean 'to like a lot' as in *er redet mit Vorliebe über Politik*, 'He loves talking politics'. Recently some newspapers have begun to use *Vorliebe* ironically to mean 'premarital intercourse'. *Vorliebnehmen mit* is a compound verb that must not be confused with *Vorliebe* as it means 'to have to be satisfied with something less than one hoped for'.

vormachen. This verb has two quite different meanings; *jemandem etwas vormachen* is either 'to show somebody how to do something', i.e. 'to demonstrate' or it means 'to humbug somebody', to act in a way as to deceive him, e.g. *Wir wollen uns doch nichts vormachen*, 'Let's stop pretending' or 'Let's be honest about this'.

vorschießen. 'To advance' a person money; the verb is colloquial whereas the noun *Vorschuß* (m ¨-(ss)e), an 'advance', is an ordinary word used in business.

vorsichtshalber. 'To be on the safe side'.

W

Waisenknabe (m -n). Rarely used, if at all, in its literal sense of an 'orphan boy' as *Knabe* is old-fashioned and high-brow for *Junge* (m -*n*) 'boy', but the colloquial phrase *ich bin ein Waisenknabe gegen ihn* is quite common: 'I'm a beginner compared with him'.

wann. 'When', but 'when' always presents problems in German. *Wann* is used in direct or indirect questions: *Wann kommen Sie?* 'When are you coming?' *Ich weiß nicht, wann sie kommt*, 'I don't know when she is coming'. *Wenn* is used in the present and future tenses (other than in questions): *Wenn mein Freund kommt, geben Sie ihm diesen Brief,* 'Give my friend this letter when he comes'. In the past tense *als* is used: *Als wir aus dem Haus traten, kam er auf uns zu*, 'When (as) we stepped out of the house, he approached us'.

Warentest (m -s). Objective test of a product by consumer organizations similar to the Consumers' Association which produces the magazine *Which* in Britain.

was. 'What' in questions but also often an introductory word conveying disbelief. In combination with *auch* it is equivalent to 'well, why did you have to . . .', e.g. *Was mengen Sie sich auch ein . . .*, 'Well, why did you have to interfere . . .' and the implication is 'whatever happened to you serves you right'. *Was* is also the colloquial form of *etwas* and extremely common as such.

Wasser (n). 'Water' and found in various idioms or common phrases, e.g. *Sie hat nahe am Wasser gebaut,* 'She cries easily'; *Der Ausflug ist ins Wasser gefallen,* 'The excursion is off'; *ein Schlag ins Wasser* is 'a vain attempt' or 'a useless action'; *ins Wasser gehen* can mean 'to commit suicide by drowning'.

W.C. (*Wasser Klosett*), but the commonest word for lavatory is *Toilette* (f -*n*) though the euphemism *Waschraum* (m ¨-e) is becoming popular. In a private house euphemisms are preferred and *möchten Sie sich frisch machen?* is equivalent to asking 'do you want the toilet?'; if you feel that *wo ist die Toilette?* is too direct a question, then *wo kann ich mir die Hände waschen?* will not only remind you of England but also obtain the expected reply.

weg. 'Away' or 'off' and a more colloquial substitute for *fort,* e.g. *Ich muß weg* (*fort*), 'I must be off'; *er ist schon weg* means 'he has already gone' and *weg* can also be 'gone' in the sense of 'mislaid', 'disappeared' or 'lost', e.g. *Meine Uhr ist weg,* 'My watch is gone'. If colloquially a person is said to be *weg* it normally means 'infatuated' or 'very much taken by' but it can describe any kind of enthusiastic loss of control (e.g. youngsters listening to pop music). Note that the word is pronounced with a short *e* and not the long *e* found in *Weg* (m -*e*) 'way'.

wegen. 'Because of' and it should be followed or preceded by a genitive thus 'because of the weather' can be *des Wetters wegen* or *wegen des Wetters*; even educated Germans, however, usually replace the genitive with the dative in speaking, e.g. *wegen dem Wetter* (*N.B.* the dative can never precede *wegen*). The colloquial exclamation *von wegen!* means something like 'nothing of the sort!' e.g. *Hat er Ihnen geholfen? Von wegen! Rausgeworfen hat er mich!* 'Did he help you? Nothing of the sort! He threw me out.'

weghaben. A colloquial verb 'to get the hang of something' or 'to understand' but it also appears in written German as when Novalis wrote *hat man den Rhythmus der Welt weg, so hat man auch die Welt weg* which loses all its neatness in translation; 'if you understand the rhythm of the world you also understand the world'. *Sein Fett weghaben* and *sein Fett wegbekommen* mean 'to get what one deserves' (always indicating something unpleasant). *Weghaben* also has a literal meaning: *Ich möchte das Bild hier weghaben,* 'I want the picture taken away from here'.

wegkommen. 'To get lost' and note the curious construction used in colloquial speech: *Die Uhr ist mir weggekommen,* 'I have lost the watch'. The verb can translate the English colloquialism 'get lost': *machen Sie, daß Sie wegkommen!* A frequent idiomatic combination is *gut (schlecht) bei einer Sache wegkommen,* 'to come off well (badly) in a deal or transaction'.

wegloben. 'To kick (somebody) upstairs' in a job, 'to bowler-hat' someone.

wehe. This is similar to the English 'woe' but unlike it in that it is still widely used but only with people with whom you are intimate: *Wehe, du gehst dahin!* or *Wehe, wenn du dahin gehst!* 'Watch out if you go there!' *Oh weh* and *ach weh* are popular exclamations similar to 'oh dear'.

Weib (n -er). One of the few disconcerting genders in German and an out-dated word for 'woman' that has nowadays a derogatory sound except when used ironically for 'wife', e.g. *Mein teures Weib,* 'My beloved spouse' or when part of an old-fashioned phrase such as *Weib und Kind verlassen,* 'to leave one's wife and children'. Among youngsters the word is also used in a complimentary way: *Ein tolles Weib,* 'A luscious doll', but this use should be avoided as it is both vulgar and ambiguous.

weich. 'Soft'; used figuratively in the colloquial phrases *er macht mich weich,* 'He's driving me silly' and *er wurde weich,* 'He gave in'.

Weihnachten (f or n -). 'Christmas'. 'Christmas Eve' is *Heiligabend* followed by *erster und zweiter Feiertag,* 'Christmas Day and Boxing Day'. Presents are brought by the *Christkind* or the *Weihnachtsmann,* 'Father Christmas', whereas *Sankt Nikolaus, Sankt Ruprecht* or just *der Nikolaus,* 'Santa Claus' arrives a little earlier, on 6 December, and fills the shoes children leave by their beds or outside bedroom doors with sweets. Greetings for these days are: *fröhliche Weihnachten, gesegnete Weihnachten, ein frohes Weihnachtsfest, ein gesegnetes Fest* or similar combinations.

Wein (m -e). German wines are mostly white, *Weißwein,* and come from the Rhineland, *Rheinwein,* or the Mosel area, *Moselwein* or from Franconia, *Frankenwein* or *Steinwein*; there is a small quantity of red wine, *Rotwein*, and rosé, *Schillerwein*, produced in most years; the English word 'Hock' is quite without significance to Germans. *Sekt* is a champagne-type wine native to Germany and bears a tax of one DM per bottle. *Naturrein* is a description indicating that the wine is not adulterated, *verfälscht* or diluted, *gepanscht* or fortified, *verstärkt*. *Südwein* usually describes heavy, sweet wines from Spain or Portugal. Wine sold in a restaurant or café by the glass or carafe is *offener* (*schoppen*) *Wein*. *Moselwein* is in green bottles, *Rheinwein* in brown or amber bottles and *Steinwein* in flagons called *Bocksbeutel*. *Moselwein* has a very low alcoholic content and is very refreshing in hot weather. Common descriptive terms used on wine labels are: *Kabinett* (fine quality estate-bottled), *Spätlese* (made from late gathered grapes), *Auslese* (made from selected late gathered grapes), *Beerenauslese* (like *Auslese* but hand-picked from the bunches), *Trockenbeerenauslese* (specially selected grapes allowed to dry up like raisins before picking), *Ausbruch* (hand-picked dried grapes, the best to be had); *Wachstum* or *Gewächs* means 'growth' and is followed by the name of the vineyard; *Kellerabzug* and *Schloßabzug* mean 'château-bottled' (*v.* MOST, SAFT).

weisen. 'To show'. *Weisen* is an interesting verb because when forming combinations or used in prose or poetry it is highly literary German but when used in speech it is not only colloquial but also sounds crude and uneducated. If a foreigner were to ask *können Sie mir den Weg zu . . . weisen?* a German would assume that he had been taught biblical German or had learnt the language in a village in the back of beyond. *Weis mal her* is a crude alternative to *zeig mal her*, 'Show me' or 'Let me see'; but *mit Fingern auf jemand weisen* is a good alternative to the form with *zeigen* and means 'to point at someone derisively'.

weismachen. *Jemandem etwas weismachen,* 'to make someone believe an untruth'.

weiß. 'White'; *weiße Kohle,* 'hydro-electric power'. A common colloquial expression is *er bringt mich zur Weißglut,* 'he makes me boil with rage'.

weit. 'Far' or 'long' for distances and 'wide' only when referring to open spaces; it also has wide-ranging idiomatic application. *So weit* (often strengthened by adding *ganz gut*) is equivalent to a hesitant 'quite good' but it can also mean 'ready': *Sind Sie so weit?* 'Are you ready?'. *Damit ist es nicht weit her* indicates poor quality or performance as in *mit meinem Deutsch ist es nicht weit her,* 'My German isn't up to much'. The comparative means 'farther' or 'further' but colloquially it can mean 'else', e.g. *War weiter noch jemand da?* 'Was anybody else there?' (this construction is confined to questions or negative statements). *Weiter* can form part of a phrase meaning 'not all that bad' or 'it doesn't really matter': *Das ist nicht weiter schlimm,* 'It's not all that bad'; *Das ist* *weiter kein Unglück,* 'That presents no great problem'. The stress is then always on the verb or noun following *weiter: Er hat nicht weiter geweint,* 'He did not really cry much'; to put the stress on *weiter* gives it the meaning of 'to continue' and makes it a prefix to a separable verb: *Er hat nicht weitergeweint,* 'He did not continue crying'. (Such confusion is impossible with a noun; when meaning 'further' *weiter* takes adjectival endings and is placed directly before the noun: *Es besteht weiter keine Gefahr,* 'There is no real danger'; *Es besteht keine weitere Gefahr,* 'There is no further danger'.) *Ohne weiteres,* 'without further ado' or 'just like that' and *bis auf weiteres* 'for the time being'.

welch.   'Which' or 'what' in questions; in colloquial usage often 'some' or 'any' when the object in question has been mentioned before: *Ich möchte ein paar Krimis, haben Sie welche?* 'I should like some detective stories, have you any?'

Welle (f -n).   'Wave'. Traffic sign often seen in towns *Grüne Welle* (green wave) followed by a figure; the sign means that if you continue to drive at the speed indicated by the figure you will find all the traffic lights 'green' on the next stretch of road.

wer.   'Who' and also 'he who', 'the one who'. In bad colloquial speech it is sometimes used in the sense of 'somebody': *Das ist wer für Sie,* 'There's somebody to see you'; *Ist wer gekommen?* 'Did anybody come?' Although this is extremely common among the uneducated it sounds atrocious and should not be imitated.

-wesen (n).   The ending *-wesen* often denotes the practice of a skill, e.g. *das Bankwesen,* 'banking'.

Wespentaille (f -n).   Wasp-waist.

Westentasche (f -n).   'Waistcoat pocket'; *ich kenne es wie meine Westentasche,* 'I know it like the palm of my hand'.

Wette (f -n).   'Bet'. There are various phrases for the English 'I bet that . . .' expressing near certainty: *ich wette, daß . . .; ich gehe jede Wette ein, daß . . .; was gilt die Wette, daß . . .; wetten, daß . . .;* this last one is used in the form of a question and may precede or follow the statement: *Wetten, daß er kommt?* or *Er kommt, wetten?* 'He's coming, do you want to bet?' The phrase *so haben wir nicht gewettet* is equivalent to 'you'd like that, wouldn't you!'

Wetter (n -).   'Weather' but also 'thunderstorm' or a bad storm with rain and so the verb *wettern* has come to have a figurative meaning 'to shout angrily' or 'to curse and swear'.

Wetterschmerzen (m.pl.).   The headaches and depression that often accompany changes in the weather; *Wetterfühligkeit* describes the susceptibility to these.

wie.   'How' or 'as'; observe the difference between *so wie* (equal stress on both words) and *sowie* (last syllable stressed): *ich schreibe es so, wie er es gesagt hat,* 'I'm writing it just as he said it' and *Ich* *schreibe es, sowie er es gesagt hat,* 'I'll write it as soon as he's said it'. *Wie* is often short for *wie bitte?* 'pardon?' and sometimes it can be a substitute at the end of a sentence for *nicht wahr? Wie* is commonly and incorrectly used instead of *als* following a comparative: *Er ist größer wie* (correct is *als*) *sein Bruder,* 'He is taller than his brother' but this usage should never be imitated. Not quite as bad but still incorrect is the use of *wie* instead of *als* meaning 'when': *Wie ich am Fenster vorbeiging . . .,* 'When I passed the window'. *Wie man's nimmt* is an often heard phrase meaning 'that depends' or 'that's a matter of opinion'.

wieviel. 'How much' and 'how many' but can be spelt in two words and then takes endings: *wie viel* 'how much', *wie viele* 'how many'. Unlike English, *wieviel* may adopt the endings of an ordinal number and as there is no equivalent to 'the how-many-eth' it must be translated by a circumlocution *Der wievielte ist heute* (or *den wievielten haben wir heute*)? 'What day of the month is it today?'; *Der wievielte Kunde ist das?* 'How many customers have come before this one?'

wild. 'Wild' and part of a colloquial consolatory expression: *Es ist ja halb so wild,* 'Come on, it's not as bad as all that'.

Winkel (m -). 'Angle' or 'corner' and in compounds it often indicates 'sharp practices', e.g. *Winkeladvokat,* 'shyster lawyer'; *Winkel-zug,* 'subterfuge' or 'trick'.

wissen. 'To know' a fact because one has read or heard it. The phrase *wer weiß wie* in the middle of a sentence is emphatic and similar in tone to 'ever so': *Er denkt, er sei wer weiß wie schlau,* 'He thinks he's ever so smart'.

Witz (m -e). 'Wit' and 'joke'; *ein verfänglicher Witz* is 'a blue joke'. *Das ist der ganze Witz* is often added to an explanation: 'and that's all there is to it'.

wo. 'Where' and as a substitute for a relative pronoun it is much abused in colloquial speech but it can correctly replace a relative pronoun plus a preposition in sentences referring to place or time, e.g. *Ich war in einem Zimmer, wo* (for *in dem*) *viele Menschen herumsaßen,* 'I was in a room where many people were sitting about'; *Es war zu einer Zeit, wo* (for *zu der*) *ich das nicht wußte,* 'It was at a time when I didn't know this'. It is glaringly incorrect but very common among the uneducated to substitute *wo* for a relative pronoun referring to people or objects, e.g. *Die Leute, wo* (for *die*) *hier leben,* 'The people who live here' and *Der Tisch, wo* (for *den*) *ich gekauft habe,* 'The table that I bought'. The phrases *ach wo, ach woher denn, i wo* are short answers all signifying 'of course not' or 'not at all'.

wohl. 'Well' as in *ich fühle mich nicht wohl,* 'I don't feel well' and in various salutations such as *leben Sie wohl,* a rather formal 'good-bye' though not as old-fashioned as 'farewell'; *Wohl bekomm's,* 'I hope you like it' for food and drink; *Ich wünsche wohl geruht* (*gespeist*) *zu haben,* 'I hope you enjoyed the rest (meal)' and others. The phrase *wohl oder übel* 'like it or not' is common in everyday speech. *Wohl* is, besides, a frequently used expletive expressing probability in a statement and wondering astonishment or doubt in a question, e.g. *Das ist wohl das beste,* 'I suppose that's the best thing'; *Was er wohl hat?* 'I wonder what's wrong with him?' In exclamations *wohl* stresses surprise and disbelief: *Sie sind wohl verrückt!* 'You must be mad!' and in combination with *aber* it translates into 'it is true but . . .', e.g. *Ich habe es wohl gewußt, aber was konnte ich machen?* 'It's true that I knew (it) but what could I do?' In some dialects *wohl* (also pronounced as if spelt *woll*) is used as a question tag equivalent to *nicht wahr.*

Wohlstandsgesellschaft (f -en). Affluent society.

Wolke (f -n). 'Cloud' and a colloquial expression characteristic of Berlin is *das ist 'ne Wolke,* 'That's wonderful'.

wollen. 'To want' or 'wish' and the verb is often omitted, e.g. *Ich will zu Herrn X,* 'I want to see (go to) Mr X'. *Na, dann wollen wir mal* is 'all right, let's get started'. *Wollen* is also used in the sense of 'maintain' as in *er will es nicht gewesen sein,* 'He maintains that it wasn't him' and in officialese it is a euphemism for 'must': *Sie wollen sich bitte um acht Uhr hier einfinden,* 'Kindly be here at eight o'clock'.

womöglich. 'Perhaps'.

Wort (n). 'Word' and has two plurals: *Wörter* when meaning unconnected words or words standing alone as in *sagen Sie mir drei Wörter mit der Endung -keit,* 'Give me three words ending in *-keit'* and *Worte* when 'words' refers to the topic or context of the sentence, e.g. *Er sagte einige Worte über den Zweck der Reise,* 'He said a few words about the purpose of the journey'. The rule is not strictly observed and as *Worte* seems more pleasing to German ears, even educated Germans use it when they ought to use *Wörter.*

Wurst (f ˝-e). 'Sausage'; there are many varieties and the most important are *Blutwurst* (black pudding), *Zervelatwurst* also spelt *Cervelatwurst* (bolony or Bologna), *Mettwurst* (Brunswick), *Schinkenwurst* (ham sausage), *Zungenwurst* (tongue sausage), *Leberwurst* (liver sausage), *Fleischwurst* (meat sausage) and *Dauerwurst* (similar to salami). All have one thing in common, they are not spicy. *Bockwurst,* a pink sausage, is *Fleischwurst* cooked in water and can be obtained from kiosks, stalls, little one-roomed shops and almost everywhere in towns. The hot *Bockwurst* is usually eaten with cold *Kartoffelsalat* and this combination is the German counterpart to our fish and chips. At station kiosks and buffets the *Bockwurst* comes laid across a split roll or *Brötchen* or is served on a little paper plate with a *Brötchen* and a dab of mustard. *Frankfurter Würstchen* and *Wiener Würstchen* are the same type of sausage as *Bockwurst* but smaller and usually served in pairs. *Bratwurst* is a kind of fried *Bockwurst* and both are sometimes offered 'king-size' as *Riesenbockwurst* and *Riesen-bratwurst*. In Cologne the speciality is a whitish sausage of a truly repulsive appearance *Weißwurst*. Many of the cheaper cafés and *Schnellimbisse* (snack-bars) serve a *Currywurst* and this is a fearsome object being a *Bratwurst* slit open and filled with crude curry powder, sprinkled with paprika and drenched in tomato ketchup; the origin of the dish is unknown.

A very commonly used colloquialism is *es ist mir Wurst* or, in its modern form written as pronounced, *es ist mir wurscht*, 'I couldn't care less' and Bismarck coined the word *Wurstigkeit* from this expression when he spoke of *die Stimmung gänzlicher Wurstigkeit*, 'an all-embracing couldn't-care-less attitude'. To say about a person *er will immer eine Extrawurst (gebraten) haben* means that he thinks he's something special and always wants to be given special consideration or concessions. *Es geht um die Wurst* is another colloquialism meaning 'now or never' or 'everything is at stake now'.

Z

Zack. *Auf Zack sein*, 'to be quick', 'smart', 'to always know what's doing'; the word stands for 'quickness' and an order is often accompanied by *zack, zack* which cannot be translated but can, from the sound alone, be well understood by a foreigner; from it *zackig* and *Zackigkeit* have been derived for describing military smartness or smart general appearance.

zahlen. 'To pay' and in most cases interchangeable with *bezahlen*, e.g. *Herr Ober, (be)zahlen, bitte*, 'Waiter, the bill please'; *bargeldlos zahlen* is a bank slogan for 'payment by cheque'; *Lehrgeld zahlen* is 'to learn by one's own mistakes'.

Zahn (m ¨-e). 'Tooth'. *Das war etwas auf einen hohlen Zahn*, 'That was barely enough to fill a hollow tooth' and is one way of saying that it was not enough either to eat or to satisfy some other need. *Zahn* is also a colloquialism for the speed of a vehicle and *der hatte aber einen Zahn drauf* could be rendered as 'he was going like a bat out of hell'. *Den Zahn müssen Sie sich ziehen lassen* means 'you must have that tooth extracted' but it could also mean in figurative language that you must give up an illusion, e.g. *Er denkt, er bekommt eine Gehaltserhöhung, aber den Zahn wird er sich ziehen lassen müssen*, 'He thinks he is going to get a rise but he will be disillusioned'. The phrase *den Zahn habe ich ihm gezogen* could be rendered (if it is not meant literally) by 'I showed him what's what!' And finally, *Zahn* is slang for a girl – a 'bird', found in combinations such as *Goldzahn*, long-term girl friend, *Platinzahn*, very rich girl.

Zange (f -n).   'Pliers' or 'tongs'; newspapers use *in die Zange nehmen* to refer to the interrogation of a suspect by the police.

zappenduster.   (Colloquial) 'pitch dark'; often used figuratively: *Nun ist es aber zappenduster*, 'Now we're really in the soup', 'Now we've had it'.

zehntausend.   'Ten thousand'; *die oberen Zehntausend*, 'high society'.

Zeit (f -en).   'Time', and note the following highly idiomatic expressions: *Wir sind die längste Zeit Freunde gewesen*, 'This is the end of our friendship'; *Das hat Zeit*, 'There's no hurry about it'; *Lassen Sie sich Zeit*, 'Take your time'; *zur Zeit*, 'at the moment'; *zu nachtschlafender Zeit*, 'in the middle of the night'; *Jetzt wird es aber langsam Zeit . . .*, 'It's about time . . .', 'It's getting late . . .'. Observe that the adjective *zeitig* means 'early' whereas *zeitlich* is 'referring to time'; *das Zeitliche segnen* is an ironic term for *sterben* 'to die'.

Zeitlupentempo (n -s).   *In Zeitlupentempo* or *in Zeitlupe* (derived from film-making) mean 'in slow motion' and in everyday speech they can describe a slow person's actions. *Die Lupe* (-n) is a 'magnifying-glass'.

Zeitungsdeutsch (n -).   Contemptuous for the bad German found in popular newspapers.

Zeitungsfritze (m -n).   Colloquial for a 'journalist', 'newspaperman'.

ziehen.   'To pull' or 'draw' and is also used to indicate that 'there is a draught': *es zieht*.

ziemlich.   'Rather'; combined with *so* it is 'approximately', 'just about': *ich bin so ziemlich fertig*, 'I've just about finished'.

zieren, sich.   'To be affected' or in social life 'to stand on ceremony' and thus 'be shy'; *zieren Sie sich nicht* is a phrase used by a host to put a guest at ease or induce him to help himself freely.

Zierflasche (f -n).   'Decorative bottle' in which spirits etc. are often sold so that when empty they may serve as ornaments.

-zig.   (Pronounced as if spelt *zich*) it is equivalent to 'umpteen' or 'an awful lot', e.g. *Es waren -zig Leute da*, 'There were umpteen people there'; it is rather colloquial and hardly ever used in writing.

Zigarre (f -n).   'Cigar'; *eine Zigarre verpaßt bekommen* is 'to be told off' on a specific point and 'to tell somebody off' is *jemandem eine Zigarre verpassen*. The phrases are used mostly in business life, i.e. when a superior reproaches an employee.

zinken.   'To mark cards' (for cheating) and *Zinken* (m -) is the system of signs and chalk-marks left by tramps, hawkers and even travelling salesmen on doorsteps and gate-posts.

Zivilcourage (f -).   The courage to express one's opinion in spite of unpopularity; there is no English equivalent. Note that the pronunciation of '*courage*' is as in French.

Zuckerlecken (n).   Nothing to do with actually 'licking sugar' but used figuratively to indicate that something (a job or a way of life) is not easy: *Die Nachkriegsjahre waren kein Zuckerlecken für uns,* 'We went through quite a lot during the post-war years' or 'The post-war years were no joy ride for us'.

zugreifen.   'To seize' or 'grasp' and *greifen Sie zu* is 'help yourself' at table or 'don't miss this opportunity' in advertising.

zum.   *Es ist zum* (and a verbal noun), 'it's enough to make one . . .', e.g. *Es ist zum Heulen, Verrücktwerden, Aus-der-Haut-Fahren, In-die-Luft-Gehen usw.,* 'It is enough to make one cry, lose one's sanity, blow one's top, burst with anger etc.'

zünftig.   An adjective indicating complete conformity with a group's requirements, e.g. *Eine zünftige Anglerkluft,* 'A proper angler's outfit'.

zurechtmachen.   'To get (something) ready' or 'to prepare (something)' and *sich zurechtmachen* is 'to put on make-up'. 'To get oneself ready' in the ordinary sense, i.e. to put on clothes and make other preparations to go out, is rendered by *sich fertigmachen.*

Zustand (m ¨-e).   'Condition' or 'state'; *das ist doch kein Zustand!* is a frequently heard colloquial complaint 'things really can't go on like this!' and *was sind das für Zustände* is rather similar in meaning to 'what a disgusting state of affairs'; *ich kriege Zustände* means 'I'm near bursting with rage' and is usually followed by a *wenn*-clause: *ich kriege Zustände, wenn das so weitergeht,* 'I'll burst with rage if this goes on'.

Zweiter Bildungsweg (m -e).   Alternative to the *Abitur,* i.e. by occupational certificate and *Gesamthochschule* to equivalence with the university graduate. *Dritter Bildungsweg* is through the *Volksschule* and *Volkshochschule* to the *Abitur.*

zwitschern.   'To twitter' and colloquially *einen zwitschern* is 'to have a drink' from the strange habit that quite a few drinkers have of rubbing the cork against the side of the bottle before drinking; the sound thus produced is described by *zwitschern* and the verb has come to stand for the actual drinking itself.

Special Vocabularies

The use of the abbreviation 'Coll.' indicates that the word or phrase is a colloquialism. 'Off.' indicates that the word is 'Officialese' and used by the pertinent authorities. C.L. denotes a word or phrase used in the fields of commerce and/or finance.

False Friends

There are many German words which have a form similar to some English words; this is not surprising when the common origin of much English and High German is taken into account and the fact that both languages use many words of Latin and Greek derivation. We have listed below 'false friends', some of which are not pronounced as in English but are spelt like an English word with which they might or might not have an affinity, or bear a strong resemblance to an English word when seen in print. German verbs which 'sound' like English verbs probably are connected through a common root with them but modern English and modern German have since moved far apart. Mistranslations are easy: *beraten* does not mean 'to berate' but 'to advise' and *bedecken* does not mean 'to ornament' or 'decorate' or 'bedeck' but only 'to cover'. German verbs the forms of which are like modern English verbs usually have much wider meanings than their English twins, the meanings of which have often become narrow.

German–English	*English–German*
absolvieren, to participate in and complete an examination, test or course of instruction	**absolve**, lossprechen
After (m -), the correct and polite lay term for rectum	**after**, nach
Agonie (f -n), the suffering preceding death	**agony**, Qual (f -en)
Akkord (m -e), musical chord or an agreement with one's creditors; **akkordieren** is to come to terms; **Akkordarbeit** is piece-work	**accord**, gewähren, übereinstimmen (mit); Übereinstimmung (f -en)
Akt (m -e), act (theat.), depiction of the nude in photography, painting and sculpture	**act**, Tat (f -en)

122

German–English	*English–German*
Aktion (f -en), operation, drive, campaign	**action**, Handlung (f -en), Unternehmen (n -)
aktuell, topical, of this moment, timely, up-to-date	**actual**, eigentlich
Allee (f -n), tree-lined avenue	**alley**, Gasse (f -n)
Allüren (f.pl.), conceited, whimsical or eccentric mannerisms and behaviour	**allure**, anlocken, verlocken, anziehen
also, v. GERMAN-ENGLISH	**also**, auch
Ambulanz (f -en), v. BEHAND-LUNG, GERMAN-ENGLISH	**ambulance**, v. BEHANDLUNG, GERMAN-ENGLISH
Ampel (f -n), traffic lights	**ample**, reichlich, geräumig, groß
apart, describes a woman who is attractive or distinguished in an unusual way	**apart**, gesondert; **apart from**, außer
Appell (m -e), roll-call (mil.)	**appeal**, Anziehungskraft (f ¨-e); Berufung (f -en) (law)
Argument (n -e), proof, reasons or grounds for holding opinion	**argument**, Streit (m -ig keiten), Streitfrage (f -n)
Art (f -en), v. GERMAN-ENGLISH	**art**, Kunst (f ¨-e)
Artist (m -en), theatrical performer	**artist**, Künstler (m -)
As (n -se), ace	**as**, wie
	ass, Esel (m -)
Audienz (f -en), official reception or audience	**audience**, Publikum (n -s)
Bagage (f -n), (coll.) rabble	**baggage**, Gepäck (n)
bald, soon; (coll.) almost	**bald**, kahl
bekommen, to receive, to get	**become**, werden
Biskuit (m -e), a special type of dough used for cakes	**biscuit**, Pläzchen (n -), Keks (m -e)
blamieren, v. GERMAN-ENGLISH	**blame**, Tadel (m -), Schuld (f); jemandem die Schuld geben (an)
blank, bright, shiny	**blank**, unbeschrieben, leer
Born (m -e), spring, well (poetic)	**born**, geboren
Bowle (f -n), punch, and punchbowl	**bowl**, Schüssel (f -n)
Brand (m ¨-e), v. GERMAN-ENGLISH	**brand**, Marke (f -n)
brav, good, decent, well-behaved	**brave**, tapfer, mutig
Brief (m -e), letter	**brief**, kurz
Chef (m -s), head of a firm or department, boss	**chef**, Chefkoch (m ¨-e), Küchenchef
Christ (m -en), Christian	**Christ**, Christus

German–English

English–German

Dame (f -n), v. COURTESY

dame (Am.), Weib (n -er) (vulg.)

delikat, v. GERMAN-ENGLISH
Dentist (m -en), v. GERMAN-ENGLISH
deplaciert, v. GERMAN-ENGLISH
desinteressiert, uninterested

delicate, zart, fein
dentist, Zahnarzt (m ¨-e)

displaced, verdrängt, vertrieben
disinterested, unparteiisch, unbefangen
decent, anständig

dezent, unobtrusive, unobtrusively elegant (clothes or decorations), soft (music)
Direktion (f -en), v. GERMAN-ENGLISH
Distanz (f -en), aloofness
engagieren, to hire

direction, Richtung (f -en)

distance, Entfernung (f -en)
engage, einstellen; **engaged** (to be married) verlobt; **engaged** (not free) besetzt

Etikett (n -e), price-tag, label
eventuell, possible, perhaps
exerzieren, to drill (military)
Existenz (f -en), livelihood, living, income
Expertise (f -n), investigation, critical report by expert
Fabrik (f -en), factory
fade, boring, insipid, tasteless
Fall (m ¨-e), v. GERMAN-ENGLISH
famos, fine, first-rate, marvellous
fast, almost, nearly
fatal, annoying, tricky, terrible; **fatale Lage**, predicament
firm, well-versed
fix, quick, smart

etiquette, Etikette (f -n)
eventual, schließlich
exercise, üben
existence, Vorhandensein (n), Bestehen (n)
expertise, Fachwissen (n), Fachkenntnisse (f.pl.)
fabric, Stoff (m -e)
fade, verblassen
fall, Sturz (m ¨-e), Fall
famous, berühmt

fast, schnell
fatal, tödlich

firm, fest; Firma (f -men)
fix, befestigen, in Ordnung bringen; Klemme (f)

Formular (n -e), (printed) form
fort, away, off
Fraktion (f -en), political party, parliamentary group
genial, brilliant, endowed with genius
Gratifikation (f -en), bonus payment
Gymnasium (n -ien), v. GERMAN-ENGLISH
Hall (m -e), sound, resonance
handeln, to act

formula, Formel (f -n)
fort, Festung (f -en)
fraction, Bruchteil (m -e); Bruch (m ¨-e) (math.)
genial, freundlich, heiter

gratification, Freude (f -n), Befriedigung (f -en)
gymnasium, Turnhalle (f -n)

hall, Halle (f -n), Flur (m -e)
handle, handhaben, behandeln

German–English

English–German

hold, graceful, charming, lovely (poetic)

hold, halten, festhalten

human, humane

human, menschlich

Ignorant (m -en), ignoramus

ignorant, ungebildet

irritieren, to distract, disconcert, confuse

irritate, reizen, ärgern

Justiz (f), the administration of justice

justice, Gerechtigkeit (f -en)

Kadaver (m -), carcass, dead body of animal

cadaver, Leiche (f -n)

Kapazität (f -en), capacity, but also authority (person), i.e. 'an authority on . . .'

capacity, Fähigkeit (f -en)

Kaution (f -en), guarantee, bond, bail

caution, Vorsicht (f)

Keks (m -e), biscuit

cakes, Kuchen (m.pl.)

Kittchen (n -), prison (coll.)

kitchen, Küche (f -n)

Klosett (n -e or -s), W.C.

closet (Am.), Wandschrank (m ¨-e)

komisch, strange

comic(al), lustig, spaßig

Konfektion (f), ready-made clothing

confection(ery), Konfekt (n)

Konfession (f -en), religious denomination

confession, Geständnis (n -se), Beichte (f -n)

Konjunktur (f -en), economic situation

conjuncture, Verbindung (f -en); Krise (f -n)

Konkurrenz (f), competition, rivalry (C.L.)

concurrence, Zusammentreffen (n -), Einverständnis (n -se)

konsequent, logical, consistent, rigorous

consequent, folgend

Konsequenz (f -en), can mean consequence but often means rigour or consistency

consequence, Folge (f -n)

konsistent, firm, compact (tech.)

consistent, konsequent, übereinstimmend

Kontrolle (f -n), can be control in the sense of mastery but mostly means checking; **kontrollieren,** check

control, Aufsicht (f), Leitung (f -en), Beherrschung (f -en); überwachen, lenken

Konvent (m -e), convent, but also convention, assembly

convent, Kloster, Frauenkloster (n -)

Konzept (n -e), draft, sketch

concept, Begriff (m -e)

Konzern (m -e), large firm

concern, Sorge (f -n) Anliegen (n -)

korrekt, proper, irreproachable (only in social sense)

correct, richtig

Kost (f), food, board

cost, Kosten (pl.), Preis (m -e); kosten

German–English

English–German

Kritik (f -en), criticism
kultiviert, cultured
kurios, odd, queer (not inqui-
sitive)
Kurs (m -e), can mean course
but also trend, stock exchange
quotation, rate of exchange
(C.L.)

Last (f -en), load, burden
Lektüre (f -n), reading matter,
reading
Lokal (n -e), v. GERMAN-ENGLISH

Lot (n -e), plumb-line

Lump (m -en), rascal, yobo

Lust (f), v. GERMAN-ENGLISH
Marine (f), navy

Mark (f), Mark (money)
Mark (n), marrow
Menu (n -s), complete meal
consisting of various courses
Mine (f -n), refill for ball-points
and propelling pencils
Mist (m), v. GERMAN-ENGLISH
Mode (f -n), fashion
Most (m -e), v. GERMAN-ENGLISH
nämlich, v. GERMAN-ENGLISH
necken, to tease

nobel, generous
Note (f -n), v. GERMAN-ENGLISH
Notiz (f -en), v. GERMAN-ENGLISH

Novelle (f -n), long 'short story'
ordinär, vulgar, low, common
Pamphlet (n -e), narrower in
meaning than English; a skit
or lampoon
Paragraph (m -en), refers only
to a section of a legal or
official document
Partie (f -n), v. GERMAN-ENGLISH
passen, v. GERMAN-ENGLISH

critic, Kritiker (m -)
cultivated, bebaut
curious, neugierig

course, Kurse, Verlauf (m)

curse, Fluch (m ¨-e); fluchen
last, letzt
lecture, Vorlesung (f -en)

local, örtlich, ansässig, einhei-
misch
lot, Los (n -e); (coll.) Menge
(f -n)
lump, Klumpen (m -); (swelling)
Beule (f -n)
lust, Gier (f), Wollust (f)
marine, Meer-, See- (in
compounds)
mark, Zeichen (n -), Mal
(n -e); (school) Note (f -n)
menu, Speisekarte (f -n)

mine, Bergwerk (n -e)

mist, Dunst (m), Nebel (m)
mode, Art und Weise (f)
most, meist
namely, nämlich, zwar
neck, Hals (m ¨-e); schäkern,
schmusen
noble, adlig, edel
note, Notiz (f -en)
notice, Anzeige (f -n);
Kündigung (f -en)
novel, Roman (m -e); neu
ordinary, üblich, gewöhnlich
pamphlet, Broschüre (f -n)

paragraph, Absatz (m ¨-e)

party, Party (f -s or -ies)
pass, vorbeigehen, vorbeifahren,
überholen

German–English

English–German

passieren, to happen
patent, smart, clever

pathetisch, solemn, impressive,
with pathos
Patience (f -n), patience (cards)
Patron (m -e), *v.* GERMAN-
ENGLISH
Patrone (f -n), cartridge
Pension (f -en), *v.* GERMAN-
ENGLISH
Pest (f), plague (not nuisance)
Photograph (m -en), photographer
Photographie (f), both photograph and photography
plump, clumsy, unrefined,
uncouth
positiv, can mean affirmative
but usually good or certain
primitiv, can mean primitive but
usually crude, uneducated,
uncouth
prinzipiell, in or on principle

pro, per
Probe (f -n), trial, test

Prominenz (f), the leading group
in social or political life
Promotion (f -en), attainment of
a doctorate
Prospekt (m -e), prospectus
Protektion (f -en), patronage or
'pull', help from important
people
Provision (f -en), commission,
brokerage (C.L.)

Prozeß (m -(ss)e), law suit, trial

Publikum (n -s), audience,
patrons, customers
Puff (m -e), *v.* GERMAN-ENGLISH

Qualm (m -e), dense smoke

patent, offenbar; **patent leather,**
Lackleder (n -)
pathetic, kläglich, bemitlei-
denswert
patience, Geduld (f)
patron, Gönner (m -), Kunde
(m -n), Gast (m ¨-e)

pension, Ruhegehalt (n ¨-er)

pest, Quälgeist (m ¨-er)
photograph, Photographie (f -n)

photography, Photographie (f)

plump, mollig, drall

positive, bestimmt

primitive, Ur- (in compounds)

principal, hauptsächlich
principle, Grundsatz (m ¨-e)
pro, für
probe, Sondierung (f -en);
sondieren
prominence, Vorsprung (m ¨-e),
Bedeutung (f -en)
promotion, Beförderung (f -en)

prospect, Aussicht (f -en)
protection, Schutz (m)

provision, Vorsorge (f -n);
provisions, Lebensmittel
(n.pl.)
process, Vorgang (m ¨-e);
Verfahren (n -)
public, Allgemeinheit (f),
Öffentlichkeit (f); öffentlich
puff, Hauch (m -e), Windstoß
(m ¨-e), (smoking) Zug
(m ¨-e)
qualm, Übelkeit (f -en); **qualms,**
Gewissensbisse (m.pl.)

German-English

English-German

Rain (m -e), border, strip of grass between fields (poetic)

rank, slim, slender

Rat (m -schläge), advice

Rate (f -n), instalment (hire-purchase)

rationell, expedient

reell, solid, respectable, fair (C.L.)

Rekord (m -e), only used of achievements in sport

rentabel, profitable

Rente (f -n), annuity

Residenz (f -en), only describes dwelling of a prince or great noble (cannot be used in house agents' sense of 'desirable residence')

Ressort (n -s), field of activity or government department

Rest (m -e), remainder

restlos, completely

Rezept (n -e), recipe, also prescription

Rock (m ¨-e), skirt and also man's coat

Roller (m -), scooter

Roman (m -e), novel

Routine (f), routine but more commonly skill or dexterity

rumoren, to make a noise while invisible to the hearers

Salve (f -n), salute of guns

schwindeln, to fib

sensibel, sensitive, having tender feelings, easily moved

Sentenz (f -en), maxim, aphorism

seriös, reliable, trustworthy, honest

Service (n), set of crockery

skurril, mildly ludicrous

Slip (m -s), women's panties

rain, Regen (m); regnen

rank, kraß

rat, Ratte (f -n)

rate, Maß (n -e), Kurs (m -e); **rates and taxes**, Steuer und Abgaben

rational, vernünftig

real, wirklich

record, Bericht (m -e); (gramophone) Schallplatte (f -n)

rentable, mietbar, Miet- (in compounds)

rent, Miete (f -n)

residence, Wohnung (f -en), Wohnsitz (m -e)

resort, Versammlungsort (m -e); Ausweg (m -e); (health) Kurort

rest, Erholung (f), Ausruhen (n)

restless, ruhelos, unruhig

receipt, Quittung (f -en)

rock, Felsen (m -)

roller, Walze (f -n)

Roman, Römer (m -); römisch; romanisch

routine, alltäglicher Gang (m)

rumour, Gerücht (n -e)

salve, Salbe (f -n)

swindle, betrügen

sensible, vernünftig

sentence, Satz (m ¨-e); Urteil (n -e) (law)

serious, ernst

service, Dienst (m -e); Bedienung (f -en)

scurrilous, gemein

slip, (clothing) Unterrock (m ¨-e); Fehltritt (m -e)

German-English

English-German

solide, moderate, respectable

Span (m ¨-e), chip, splinter

sparen, to save

Spektakel (m -), row, unholy din

spenden, to donate

Spur (f -en), trace, clue, track, vestige, spoor

Star (m -e), starling, cataract on the eye, film star (m -s)

stark, strong, severe, stout

Stipendium (n -ien), educational grant or scholarship

Sympathie (f -n), inclination, fondness, liking

sympathisch, nice, likeable

Technik (f -en), technique, also technology

These (f -n), proposition, assertion

Tip (m -s), only hint, advance information

toll, mad, silly, daft

Ton (m ¨-e), v. GERMAN-ENGLISH

Vehikel (n -), derogatory for an old vehicle or one in bad condition

virtuos, masterly, perfect

Visage (f -n), very vulgar slang for face

Visite (f -n), the doctor's tour of his patients in hospital

Warenhaus (n ¨ -er), department store

Zensur (f -en), censoring, also mark in school

Zivil (n), plain (civilian) clothes; in compounds, civilian

solid, fest

span, Spanne (f -n)

spare, übrig haben; verschonen

spectacle, Schauspiel (n -e); spectacles, Brille

spend, (time) verbringen; (money) ausgeben

spur, Sporn (m Sporen)

star, Stern (m -e)

stark, steif, ganz

stipend, Gehalt (n ¨-er)

sympathy, Anteilnahme (f), Mitgefühl (n)

sympathetic, mitfühlend, verständnisvoll

technique, Technik (f -en) Methode (f -n)

thesis, Dissertation (f -en), Doktorarbeit (f -en)

tip, Trinkgeld (n -er)

toll, Zoll (m ¨-e)

ton, Tonne (f -n)

vehicle, Fahrzeug (n -e)

virtuous, tugendhaft

visage, Gesicht (n -er)

visit, Besuch (m -e); besuchen

warehouse, Lager (n -)

censure, Tadel (m -), Verweis (m -e)

civil, gesittet, anständig, höflich

Journalese

Journalese is as much a vice of German as of English newspapers and we have included some of the clichés and over-used phrases found in contemporary journalism. German newspapers tend to fall into three rough categories: the older 'quality' papers, of which *Die Frankfurter Allgemeine* is typical, the newer 'qualities' such as *Die Welt* and the popular press of which *Bild Zeitung* is representative. Each category has a distinctive style; that of the older 'qualities' makes use of high-brow and archaic words and complicated adjectival phrases preceding nouns and almost interminable sentences which meander across columns of type and are difficult even for educated Germans to understand. There is also a plethora of high falutin' clichés in which five or more words serve the purpose of one (journalists are paid by the line); the style can best be described as turgid. The newer 'quality' papers are slightly less stuffy but their style is basically similar save for the addition of many modern idiomatic expressions not all of which are appropriate. There are many self-coined terms such as *Koepenickiade* indicating a clever ruse and derived from the Hauptmann von Koepenick affair. The general turgidity which characterizes these old and new 'qualities' probably stems from the large number of university graduates in modern journalism; they have almost achieved a monopoly of the profession and as learned obscurity is still one of the ambitions of many German intellectuals, the stylistic shortcomings should cause no surprise. The popular press is inelegant in style but almost free of the defects of its betters. It abounds in correctly used idioms and colloquialisms and has a vast vocabulary deriving from sport; it is much looked down upon by the middle classes, who often read *Bild* surreptitiously.

in Anbetracht der Tatsachen, considering
sich widerrechtlich aneignen, to steal
in angetrunkenem Zustand, under the influence of alcohol
ein nationales Anliegen, a matter of national concern
im Anschluß daran, after that
der Auftakt zu, the signal for
die Frage aufwerfen, to raise the question
ins Auge fassen, to consider
der Erwartung Ausdruck geben, daß, to express the hope that
sich übereinstimmend aussprechen für, to support unanimously
auf die lange Bank schieben, to postpone
Bedenken hegen, to be apprehensive

etwas bedingt annehmen, to accept something with reservations
Begleiterscheinungen, side effects
ein begrüßenswerter Abschluß, a commendable conclusion
im Brennpunkt des öffentlichen Interesses, the cynosure of public
   interest
in groben Zügen darlegen, to outline roughly
die derzeitige Lage, the present situation
sich von einer Erklärung distanzieren, to retract a statement
in Ermangelung (gen.), for lack of
eine Einigung erzielen, to come to an agreement
folgenschwer, consequential
ein Freibrief für, a carte blanche for
einen Gesetzentwurf einbringen, to introduce a bill
einen Gesetzentwurf verabschieden, to pass a bill
gewissermaßen, so to say
von solcher Größenordnung, of such importance
ein Gutachten erstellen, to give an expert opinion
ein innerparteiliches Zerwürfnis, quarrels within the party
jüngsten Nachrichten zufolge, according to the latest news
Justizmord, miscarriage of justice
es kam zu Kundgebungen, demonstrations occurred
die Lage hat sich verschärft, (zugespitzt), the situation has worsened
die Lage hat sich entspannt, the situation has become less tense
die Gespräche laufen darauf hinaus, daß, the gist of the discussions
   is that
Machthaber, those in power
in zunehmendem Maße, more
maßgebende Stimmen der Öffentlichkeit, influential organs of public
   opinion
Maßnahmen begrüßen, to welcome measures
Maßnahmen zur Erhaltung des Lebensstandards, measures to
   maintain the standard of living
Meinungsaustausch, exchange of views
linksgerichtete (rechtsgerichtete) Meinungsverkündungen, left-wing
   (right-wing) demonstrations
in Mitleidenschaft ziehen, to affect
mitunter, sometimes
der mutmaßliche Täter, the alleged perpetrator
eine offene Angelegenheit, an unresolved matter
der Plan scheitert an der Tatsache, daß, the plan is doomed because
ein umstrittener Punkt, a disputed point
ans Ruder kommen, to come to power, to achieve a leading position
die Möglichkeiten sondieren, to sound out the possibilities
Stellungnahme, comment
zu Tätlichkeiten (Handgreiflichkeiten) kommen, to come to blows
Tatort, scene of the crime
Übergangsregelung, temporary arrangement
mit Umsicht, prudent(ly)
Unruhen auslösen, to create a disturbance
unsachgemäße Behandlung, irregular (improper) treatment

verantwortlich zeichnen für, to be responsible for
veräußern, to sell
Verhandlungen abschließen, to conclude negotiations
in einer gemeinsamen Verlautbarung, in an announcement prepared
  by the parties concerned
wie verlautet, according to sources
vernichtende Kritik, scathing criticism
vertuschen, to hush up
als bekannt voraussetzen, assuming knowledge of
die Voraussetzungen schaffen für, to create the basis for
unter Vorbehalt, with reservations
vordringlich, important; necessary
das weitere Vorgehen, the future course of action
einer Entscheidung vorgreifen, to act precipitately
den Vorrang geben, to give priority
auf einen Vorschlag eingehen, to take up a proposal; to agree to a
  proposal
einen Vorschlag unterbreiten, to submit a proposal
Vorspiegelung falscher Tatsachen, misrepresentation
den Vorzug geben, to give preference
ein entscheidender Wendepunkt, a decisive turning-point
im Wortlaut wiedergeben, to report verbatim
der Wortlaut des Vortrages, the contents of the speech
zugegen sein, to be present
zumal, particularly as (because)
es kam zu Zusammenstößen zwischen, it reached the stage of (open)
  conflict between; it came to a head-on collision between
das Zustandekommen einer Vereinbarung ergab sich, an agreement
  was reached

Telephoning

German-English

abhängen, to ring off
Amt (n ¨-er), exchange
Amtszeichen (n -), dialling tone
Anruf (m -e), call
anrufen, to call
wieder anrufen, zurückrufen, to call back
Anschluß (m ¨-(ss)e), official term for telephone installation but
    equivalent to 'subscriber'
Apparat (m -e), apparatus, telephone
Auskunft (f ¨-e), information, directory enquiries
besetzt, engaged
Besetztzeichen (n -), engaged signal
Branchenverzeichnis (n -se), classified directory
Durchwählnummer (f -n), the main telephone number of an
    organization or large firm; for the firm's switchboard you dial this
    number plus 1; for extensions (not via the switchboard) you dial
    this basic number plus the extension number
Fernamt (n ¨-er), exchange
Ferngespräch (n -e), call, long-distance call
Fernsprechansagedienst (m -e), information services (weather, time
    etc.)
Fernsprechauftragsdienst (m -e), answering service
Fernsprechbuch (n ¨-er), directory
Fernsprecher (m -), telephone
Freizeichen (n -), dialling tone
Gabel (f -n), cradle
Gebühr (f -en), charge
Gespräch (n -e), call
ein Gespräch anmelden, to book a call
Handapparat (m -e) (off.) receiver
Hörer (m -), receiver
den Hörer abnehmen, to lift the receiver
den Hörer auflegen, to put down the receiver, to hang up
Klingel (f -n), bell
Leitung (f -en), line
Münzfernsprecher (m -), coin-operated telephone
Muschel (f -n), ear-piece, mouthpiece
Nachricht (f -en), message
Nebenapparat (m -e), **Nebenstelle** (f -n) extension
Notruf (m -e), emergency number

133

öffentlicher Fernsprecher (m -), public telephone
Ortsgespräch (n -e), local call
Ortsnetzkennzahl (f -en), STD code
R-Gespräch (n -e), reversed charge
Rufnummer (f -n), telephone number
Selbstwählferndienst (m -e), STD (i.e. the system)
Störung (f -en), breakdown, disturbance, interference
Störungsannahme (f -n), engineers
Teilnehmer (m -), subscriber
Telegrammaufnahme (f -n), telegrams
Telephon (n -e), telephone
Telephonbuch (n ¨-er), directory
Telephonhäuschen (n -), telephone booth
Telephonzelle (f -n), telephone box
verbilligte Gesprächszeiten (f.pl.), cheap rate periods
verbinden (mit), to put through (to), to connect (with)
Verbindung (f -en), connection
Vermittlung(sstelle) (f -en (f -n)), exchange
V-Gespräch (n -e), Gespräch mit Voranmeldung, personal call
Vorwahlzahl (f -en), STD code
wählen, to dial
Wahlscheibe (f -n), dial
Wettervorhersage (f -n), weather forecast
auf Wiederhören, 'good-bye' on the phone
Zeitansage (f -n), speaking clock
Zeitzeichen (n -), time signal

English–German

answering service, Fernsprechansagedienst (m -e)
apparatus, Apparat (m -e)
bell, Klingel (f -n)
to book a call, ein Gespräch anmelden
breakdown, Störung (f -en)
call, Anruf (m -e), Gespräch (n -e)
to call, anrufen
to call back, zurückrufen, wieder anrufen
charge, Gebühr (f -en)
cheap rate periods, verbilligte Gesprächszeiten (f.pl.)
classified directory, Branchenverzeichnis (n -se)
code, Vorwahlzahl (f -en) (coll.); Ortsnetzkennzahl (f -en) (off.)
coin-operated telephone, Münzfernsprecher (m -)
to connect (with), verbinden (mit)
connection, Verbindung (f -en)
cradle, Gabel (f -n)
dial, Wahlscheibe (f -n)
to dial, wählen
dialling tone, Amtszeichen, Freizeichen (n -)
directory, Fernsprechbuch, Telephonbuch (n ¨-er)
directory enquiries, Auskunft (f ¨-e)
ear-piece, Hörer (m -), Muschel (f -n)

emergency number, Notruf (m -e)
engaged, besetzt
engaged signal, Besetztzeichen (n -)
engineers, Störungsannahme (f -n)
exchange (operator), Amt (n ¨-er), Fernamt (n ¨-er), Vermittlung
    (f -en)
extension, Nebenapparat (m -e), Nebenstelle (f -n)
information, Auskunft (f ¨-e), Fernsprechansagedienst (m -e)
to lift the receiver, den Hörer abnehmen
line, Leitung (f -en)
local call, Ortsgespräch (n -e)
long-distance call, Ferngespräch (n -e)
message, Nachricht (f -en)
mouthpiece, Muschel (f -n)
personal call, V-Gespräch (n -e), Gespräch mit Voranmeldung
public telephone, öffentlicher Fernsprecher (m -)
to put down (replace) the receiver, den Hörer auflegen
to put through (to), verbinden (mit)
receiver, Hörer (m -) (coll.), Handapparat (m -e) (off.)
reversed charge, R-Gespräch (n -e)
to ring off, abhängen
speaking clock, Zeitansage (f -n)
subscriber, (Fernsprech)Teilnehmer (m -), Anschluß
    (m ¨-(ss)e)
subscriber trunk dialling, Selbstwählferndienst (m -e)
subscriber trunk dialling code, Ortsnetzkennzahl, Vorwahlzahl
    (f -en)
telegrams, Telegrammaufnahme (f -n)
telephone, Telephon (n -e), Fernsprecher (m -); telephonieren
telephone booth, Telephonhäuschen (n -)
telephone box, Telephonzelle (f -n)
telephone number, Rufnummer, Telephonnummer (f -n)
time signal, Zeitzeichen (n -)
weather forecast, Wettervorhersage (f -n)

Standard phrases
am Apparat, speaking
bitte bleiben Sie am Apparat, please hold the line
ich bemühe mich, I'm trying to connect you
kein Anschluß unter dieser Nummer, no subscriber at this number
die Rufnummer hat sich geändert, the number has been changed
erfragen Sie die neue Rufnummer bei der Auskunft, obtain new
    number from directory enquiries
**dieser Anschluß ist vorübergehend nicht erreichbar (gestört,
    gesperrt),** this number is temporarily unobtainable
der Anschluß ist noch nicht in Betrieb, the number is not yet in use
der Anschluß antwortet nicht, the number doesn't answer
möchten Sie die Anmeldung streichen? would you like to cancel the
    call?
bitte streichen Sie die Anmeldung, please cancel the call

einen Moment, ich verbinde, a moment please, I'm putting you
   through
bitte melden Sie sich, go ahead please
sprechen Sie noch? are you still speaking?
wir sind unterbrochen worden, we've been cut off
wem gehört der Anschluß? what is the name of the subscriber?
Sie werden aus . . . verlangt, there's a call for you from . . .
ich möchte ein Gespräch nach . . . anmelden, I should like to make a
   call to . . .
können Sie mich mit Herrn X verbinden? can you put me through to
   Mr X?
ist Herr X zu sprechen? is Mr X there?
ich möchte Herrn X sprechen, I should like to speak to Mr X
können Sie etwas lauter sprechen? could you speak up please?
bitte sprechen Sie nicht so nahe an der Muschel, please don't speak
   so closely to the mouthpiece
ich kann Sie nicht verstehen, I can't understand you
bitte legen Sie auf, ich rufe wieder an, please replace the receiver, I'll
   call you back
bitte geben Sie mir . . . (town) Nummer . . . mit Gebühren, please
   give me . . . and tell me the cost when I've finished
ist dort. . . ? is that . . . ?
ich habe mich (Sie haben sich) in der Nummer geirrt;
   Entschuldigung, falsch verbunden, sorry, wrong number
Sie können diese Nummer selbst wählen, you can dial this number
   yourself
wer spricht dort, bitte? who is speaking?

Note:

N-Gespräch: a call to a post-office, by which the latter is requested
   to convey a message to a non-subscriber; the charge depends on
   the distance from post-office to recipient of the message.
XP-Gespräch: a call to a post-office requesting the latter to ask a
   non-subscriber to come to a given public telephone at a given time
   to receive a call.

Food and Dishes

This vocabulary mainly contains the names of dishes for which no adequate translation exists, or of dishes peculiar to Germany, or names which if literally translated would cause confusion in the mind of the reader; it is not exhaustive.

das Apfelmus, stewed apples
die Apfeltasche, pastry filled with stewed apples
der Aspik, fish or meat jelly
der Auflauf, soufflé
der Aufschnitt, cold cuts, cold meats
der Aufstrich, anything that can be spread on bread (generic name)
das Backobst, dried fruit or stewed dried fruit
das Bauchfleisch, English-type bacon
das Bauernfrühstück, lunch or supper (never breakfast) of fried egg, potatoes, meat or sausage and bacon
das Beefsteak Tartar, raw minced meat served with a raw egg and spices
das belegte Brot (Brötchen), slice of bread (roll) with cheese, ham or sausage
der Berliner (Berliner Pfannkuchen), doughnut, typical of Fasching
der Bienenstich, layer cream cake with almonds
die Biersuppe, sweet soup of beer, milk and egg
der Bismarckhering, pickled filleted herring
der Blätterteig, puff pastry (generic name)
blau, boiled or cooked (fish)
die Boulette (der Bratklops, die Frikadelle), fried meatball
der Braten, roast (joint)
der Brathering, pickled fried herring
die Brause (mit Geschmack), fizzy fruit drink
die Brause ohne Geschmack, mineral water
das Brötchen (die Semmel, der Weck), roll
der Brühreis, boiled rice
der Brunnen, mineral water (regional name)
der Bückling, smoked herring
die Dauerwurst, salami-type sausage
das deutsche (Hamburger) Beefsteak, hamburger
das Dörrfleisch, smoked or air-dried bacon
verlorene Eier, poached eggs in sweet-sour mustard sauce
Eier im Glas, very soft-boiled eggs with their shells removed and served in a glass

137

Rührei, scrambled egg

Setzei, fried egg

Solei, hard-boiled egg preserved in brine

Spiegelei, fried egg

der Eierkuchen, egg pancake

der Einback (Reihenweck), sweetish soft white roll

eingekocht (eingemacht, eingeweckt), preserved (fruit)

eingelegt, preserved in vinegar or brine

die Einlage, extras in soups (e.g. egg, meat, dumplings, chopped sausage etc.)

der Eintopf, 'all-in-one-dish', i.e. a thick soup of vegetables, potatoes and meat

das Eisbein (die Schweinshaxe), pig's trotter (boiled)

der Erdapfel (Austria), potato

die Fleischbrühe (Kraftbrühe), broth

der Fleischsalat, chopped sausage and pickled cucumber in mayonnaise

die Frühlingssuppe, mixed early vegetables soup

das Gebäck, pastry (generic name)

gedämpft (geschmort), stewed

das Gehackte (Gewiegte), minced meat

gekocht (gesotten), boiled, cooked

gepökelt, salted (meat)

geräuchert, smoked

das Geselchte (Austria), smoked pork

gespickt, larded

die Götterspeise, fruit jelly (dessert)

der Hackbraten, roasted minced meat loaf

der Hackepeter, raw minced meat with onions and spices (to spread on bread)

der Haferschleim, (for stomach upsets) similar to porridge (but much thinner and boiled for so long that it is more like a soup or mush)

das Hähnchen, grilled chicken; other regional names are: *Backhendl, Brathähnchen, Brathendl, Putt vom Grill* and *Gugli* (Switzerland) but *ein halber Hahn* is a Düsseldorf speciality: German cheese with onions and vinegar

der Handkäse mit Musik, German cheese with onions and vinegar (regional name)

der falsche Hase, *Hackbraten* (q.v.)

Hausmacher-, home-made (in compounds)

holländische Sauce, white sauce

das Hörnchen, croissant

das Huhn, chicken, but with adjectives it is often a regional name for a minestrone-type soup, e.g. *buntes Huhn, Westfälisches Blindhuhn* etc.

die Jause (Austria), afternoon coffee

das Kaiserfleisch (Austria), roast ribs of salt pork

der Kaiserschmarren (Austria), sweet pancake (broken into small pieces while being baked)

die Kalbshaxe, leg of calf (upper leg, whereas *Schweinshaxe* is the lower leg)

der Kalbsnierenbraten, breast of calf (stuffed with kidneys)

die kalte Ente, mixture of white wine, champagne and lemon juice

die kalte Küche, cold dishes

die Kaltschale, iced fruit soup

Bratkartoffeln, Röstkartoffeln, fried potatoes (i.e. first boiled and then fried; 'home-fried' (Am.))

Dampfkartoffeln, Salzkartoffeln, boiled potatoes

Kartoffelbrei, Kartoffelpüree, Kartoffelschnee, Quetschkartoffeln, mashed potatoes

Pellkartoffeln, potatoes boiled in their jackets (served with fish and peeled directly before eating)

Schwenkkartoffeln, small new potatoes in butter and with herbs

der Kartoffelkloß, potato dumpling

der Kartoffelpuffer (Reibekuchen), potato fritter

die Käsetorte, der Käsekuchen, (cream) cheese cake

das Kasseler (der Kasseler Rippenspeer), smoked ribs of salt pork

die Kieler Sprotten, sprats

das -klein (Enten-, Gänse- etc.), giblets (fowl)

das Kompott, stewed fruit

die Konfitüre, jam (but better quality than *Marmelade*)

die Königsberger Klopse, boiled meatballs in sweet-sour sauce

die Königin Pastete, veal stew in pastry

das Kraut, common abbreviation for *das Sauerkraut*

der Kreppel, doughnut (*v.* BERLINER)

das Labskaus, a hash (peculiar to Hamburg) made from minced meat or corned beef, herring, mashed potatoes and chopped gherkins with an egg on top

der Lebkuchen, ginger bread (cakes and biscuits)

das Leipziger Allerlei, mixed vegetables

die Limonade, fizzy fruit drink

mariniert, pickled (fish)

die Marmelade, jam

der Matjeshering, tender young raw, salted, filleted herring (seasonal, and considered a delicacy)

die Mettwurst, soft, fatty, salami-type sausage

der Mohnkuchen, poppy seed cake

der Mostrich (Senf), mustard

die Nachspeise, sweet (dessert) (generic name)

naturell, plain, i.e. not breadcrumbed (fried meat)

die Nockerln (Austria) (*Wiener* or *Salzburger Nockerln*), small, sweet dumplings

die Palatschinken (Austria), pancakes

paniert, breadcrumbed or in batter (fried meat)

der Pfannkuchen, pancake, either egg or potato

die Pilze, mushrooms (generic name); popular types: **Champignons, Pfifferlinge** and **Steinpilze**

das Plundergebäck, small sugar-powdered pastry baked in oil

der Pudding, blancmange

der Quark (Weißkäse), crude cream cheese
das Ragout fin, veal stew
der Rahm, cream (of milk) (regional name)
die Remouladensauce, mayonnaise sauce with herbs and spices
die Restaurationsschnitte, heavily garnished *belegtes Brot* (q.v.)
das Rippchen, boiled pork chop
der Rollmops, pickled rolled-up herring filled with onions and pickled cucumber
der Rostbraten, rib of beef roasted with onions
der Rotkohl, das Rotkraut, red cabbage
die Roulade, slice of meat rolled and filled with bacon, onions and spices
russische Eier, egg mayonnaise
die Sahne, cream (of milk)
der Salat, salad
grüner Salat, Kopfsalat, lettuce
gemischter Salat, mixed salad
russischer Salat, vegetable salad with chopped egg and mayonnaise
der Sauerbraten, braised beef soaked for a few days in a vinegar solution before being served
der Schaschlik (Nierenspieß), kebab
die Schillerlocke, either: roll of puff pastry filled with whipped cream; or: strip of smoked haddock
die Schlagsahne (der Schlagrahm, der Schlagobers), whipped cream
das Schmalz, lard, dripping
der Schmorbraten, braised meat
die Schonkost, special dietetic food easy to digest (generic name)
die Schwalbennester, rolled calf fillet filled with a hard-boiled egg and cut in half before serving
die Schwedenplatte, selection of cold fish
die Selter, der Sprudel, mineral water
die Spätzle (Swabia), home-made type of noodles
der Speck, smoked bacon fat
der Stollen (Christstollen), bread-like cake with raisins (eaten mostly at Christmas)
der stramme Max, ham and fried egg on bread
der Strudel (Austria), thin dough rolled and filled with fruit, mince meat but also with cheese, vegetables or meat
das Stückchen (Teilchen), fancy pastry (generic name)
die Sülze, jellied pig's or calf's head
das Sülzkotlett, jellied pork chop
die Vanillesauce, custard
das Weinkraut, another name for *Sauerkraut*
das Wiener Schnitzel, escalope in egg and breadcrumbs
der Windbeutel, puff pastry bun filled with whipped cream

Travelling

German–English

Abfahrt (f -en), departure
Abteil (n -e), compartment
an Bord gehen, to go aboard
an Land gehen, to go ashore
Ankunft (f ¨-e), arrival
Anschluß (m ¨-(ss)e), connection
Anschlußstation (f -en), connecting station
aufgeben, to register (luggage)
Auskunft (f ¨-e), information
aussteigen, to alight, to get out
Bahnbus (m -se), railway bus (coach)
Bahnhofsmission (f -en), travellers' aid office
Bahnsteig (m -e), platform
Bahnsteigkarte (f -n), platform ticket
Bahnübergang (m ¨-e), level-crossing
Bezirkskarte (f -n), 1,000 Km touring ticket
buchen, to book
Bummelzug (m ¨-e), (coll.), stopping train
Bus (m -se), bus, coach
Dienstabteil (n -e), personnel compartment
Durchgangsreisender (m -den), passenger changing train
D-Zug (m ¨-e), express
Eckplatz (m ¨-e), corner seat
Eiltriebwagen (m -), express autorail train
Eilzug (m ¨-e), fast train
einfach, single
einsteigen, to board, to get on (in)
Elektrische (f -n), tram
erreichen, to catch (train etc.)
Fahrausweis (m -e), (off.), ticket

Fahrgast (m ¨-e), passenger (train and bus)
Fahrkarte (f -n), ticket
Fahrplan (m ¨-e) time-table (wall)
Fahrschein (m -e), ticket
Fahrt (f -en), trip
in Fahrtrichtung (f -en), facing the engine
FD-Zug (m ¨-e), long-distance express
Fensterplatz (m ¨-e), window seat
Flug (m ¨-e), flight
Fluggast (m ¨-) passenger (aeroplane)
Flughafen (m ¨-), **Flugplatz** (m ¨-e), airport
Flugzeug (n -e), aeroplane
Gang (m ¨-e), corridor
in Gegenfahrtrichtung (f -en), back to the engine
Gepäckannahme (f -n), left-luggage (in)
Gepäckaufbewahrung (f -en), left-luggage office
Gepäckausgabe (f -n), left-luggage (out)
Gepäcknetz (n -e), luggage rack
Gepäckschalter (m -), luggage (forwarding) office
Gepäckschein (m -e), luggage receipt
Gepäckträger (m -), porter,
Gleis (n -e), track, (coll.) platform
Hafen (m ¨-), port
Haltestelle (f -n), stop
Hauptbahnhof (m ¨-e), main station
Hinfahrt (f -en), **Hinreise** (f -n), outward journey

141

Hin- und Rückfahrt (f -en), round trip
hin und zurück, return
Kabine (f -n), **Kajüte** (f -n), cabin
Kraftpost (f), post-office passenger bus service
Kursbuch (n ¨-er), time-table (book)
Kurswagen (m -), through carriage
Landungskarte (f -n), landing ticket
Landungssteg (m -e), gangway
Liegestuhl (m ¨-e), deck-chair
Liegewagen (m -), couchette carriage
lösen, to buy (ticket)
luftkrank, air-sick
Luftloch (n ¨-er), air pocket
Maschine (f -n), aeroplane
Monatskarte (f -n), monthly season ticket
nachlösen, to pay for additional travel
Netzkarte (f -n), 7,000 Km touring ticket
Nichtraucher (m -), non-smoker
nicht übertragbar, not transferable
Notbremse (f -n), emergency brake
Notsitz (m -e), additional seat (when train is full)
O-Bus (m -se), trolley bus
Passagier (m -e), passenger (ship and aeroplane)
Paß- und Zollkontrolle (f -n), passport and customs examination
Personenzug (m ¨-e), stopping train
Platzkarte (f -n), seat reservation receipt
Raucher (m -), smoker
Reise (f -n), journey
reservieren, to reserve
Rettungsboot (n -e), life-boat
Rettungsring (m -e), life-belt

Rückfahrkarte (f -n), return ticket
Rückfahrt (f -en), **Rückreise** (f -n), return journey
Schaffner (m -), ticket collector, guard, conductor
Schalter (m -), counter, ticket office
Schiff (n -e), boat
Schlafwagen (m -), sleeping car
Schließfach (n ¨-er), luggage locker
Schnellzug (m ¨-e), fast train
Schranke (f -n), barrier (level crossing)
Schwimmweste (f -n), life-jacket
seekrank, sea-sick
Seereise (f -n), voyage
Sichtkarte (Streifenkarte, Knipskarte) (f -n), forms of season ticket (trams and buses)
Sitzplatz für Schwerbeschädigte (Kriegsversehrte) mit amtlichem Ausweis, seat reserved for the disabled
Sonderzug (m ¨-e), excursion train
Sonntagsrückfahrkarte (f -n), weekend return ticket
Speisewagen (m -), dining-car
Sperre (f -n), barrier (station)
Straßenbahn (f -en), tram
Triebwagen (m -), autorail train
U-Bahn (f -en), underground railway
Überfahrt (f -en), (sea) passage
überfällig, overdue
Überfracht (f -en), **Übergewicht** (n -e), excess luggage (weight)
Überführung (f -en), viaduct, fly-over
umsteigen, to change
Umsteigerkarte (f -n), bus ticket permitting holder to transfer routes
Unterbrechung (f -en), break of journey
Unterführung (f -en), subway, underpass

verfahren, sich, to lose one's way (travelling)
verirren, sich, to lose one's way (walking)
verpassen, versäumen, to miss (train etc.)
versichern, to insure
Verspätung haben, to be late (trains)
Wartesaal (m ¨-e), waiting room
Wochenkarte (f -n), weekly (season) ticket

English–German

aeroplane, Flugzeug (n -e), Maschine (f -n)
air pocket, Luftloch (n ¨-er)
airport, Flugplatz (m ¨-e), Flughafen (m ¨-)
air-sick, luftkrank
alight, aussteigen
arrival, Ankunft (f ¨-e)
autorail train, Triebwagen (m -)
back to the engine, in Gegenfahrtrichtung (f -en)
barrier, Schranke (f -n) (level crossing); Sperre (f -n) (station)
board, einsteigen
boat, Schiff (n -e)
book, buchen
break of journey, Unterbrechung (f -en)
bus, Bus (m -se)
buy (ticket), lösen
cabin, Kabine (f -n), Kajüte (f -n)
catch (train etc.), erreichen
change, umsteigen
coach, Bus (m -se)
compartment, Abteil (n -e)
conductor, Schaffner (m -)
connecting station, Anschlußstation (f -en)
connection, Anschluß (m ¨-(ss)e)
corner seat, Eckplatz (m ¨-e)
corridor, Gang (m ¨-e)
couchette carriage, Liegewagen (m -)

Zahlgrenze (f -n), fare stage
Zahlmeister (m -), purser
Zollbeamte (adj. noun), customs officer
zollpflichtig, dutiable
Zug (m ¨-e), train
Zuschlag (m ¨-e), supplement
zuschlagfrei, not liable to supplement
zuschlagpflichtig, supplement payable

counter, Schalter (m -)
customs officer, Zollbeamte (adj. noun)
deck-chair, Liegestuhl (m ¨-e)
departure, Abfahrt (f -en)
dining car, Speisewagen (m -)
dutiable, zollpflichtig
emergency brake, Notbremse (f -n)
excess luggage (excess weight), Überfracht (f -en) (Übergewicht (n -e)
excursion train, Sonderzug (m ¨-e)
express, D-Zug (m ¨-e)
express autorail train, Eiltriebwagen (m -)
facing the engine, in Fahrtrichtung (f -en)
fare stage, Zahlgrenze (f -n)
fast train, Eilzug (m ¨-e)
gang-way, Landungssteg (m -e)
get off (out) aussteigen
get on (in) einsteigen
go aboard, an Bord gehen
go ashore, an Land gehen
guard, Schaffner (m -)
information, Auskunft (f ¨-e)
insure, versichern
journey, Reise (f -n)
landing ticket, Landungskarte (f -n)
be late (trains), Verspätung haben

left luggage (in), Gepäckannahme (f -n)
left luggage (out), Gepäckausgabe (f -n)
left luggage office, Gepäckaufbewahrung (f -en)
level crossing, Bahnübergang (m ¨-e)
life-belt, Rettungsring (m -e)
life-boat, Rettungsboot (n -e)
life-jacket, Schwimmweste (f -n)
long-distance express, FD-Zug (m ¨-e), IC, TEE
lose one's way (travelling), sich verfahren
lose one's way (walking), sich verirren
luggage (forwarding) office, Gepäckschalter (m -)
luggage locker, Schließfach (n ¨-er)
luggage receipt, Gepäckschein (m -e)
main station, Hauptbahnhof (m ¨-e)
miss (train etc.), verpassen, versäumen
monthly season ticket, Monatskarte (f -n)
non-smoker, Nichtraucher (m -)
not transferable, nicht übertragbar
outward journey, Hinfahrt (f -en), Hinreise (f -n)
overdue, überfällig
(sea) passage, Überfahrt (f -en)
passenger, Fahrgast (m ¨-e) (bus and train), Fluggast (m ¨-e) (aeroplane), Passagier (m -e) (aeroplane and ship)
passport and customs examination, Paß- und Zollkontrolle (f -n)
personnel compartment, Dienstabteil (n -e)
platform, Bahnsteig (m -e)
platform ticket, Bahnsteigkarte (f -n)
port, Hafen (m ¨-)

porter, Gepäckträger (m -)
post-office passenger bus service, Kraftpost (f)
purser, Zahlmeister (m -)
railway bus, Bahnbus (m -se)
register (luggage), aufgeben
reserve, reservieren
return, hin und zurück
return journey, Rückfahrt (f -en), Rückreise (f -n)
return ticket, Rückfahrkarte (f -n)
round trip, Hin- und Rückfahrt (f -en)
sea-sick, seekrank
season ticket (bus and tram), Knipskarte, Sichtkarte, Streifenkarte (f -n)
seat reservation receipt, Platzkarte (f -n)
single, einfach
sleeping car, Schlafwagen (m -)
smoker, Raucher (m -)
stop, Haltestelle (f -n)
stopping train, Bummelzug (m ¨-e) (coll.), Personenzug (m ¨-e)
subway, Unterführung (f -en)
supplement, Zuschlag (m ¨-e)
supplement payable, zuschlagpflichtig
supplement not payable, zuschlagfrei
through carriage, Kurswagen (m -)
ticket, Fahrschein (m -e), Fahrkarte (f -n), Fahrausweis (m -e) (off.)
ticket collector, Schaffner (m -)
ticket office, Schalter (m -)
time-table, Fahrplan (m ¨-e) (wall), Kursbuch (n ¨-er) (book)
track, Gleis (n -e)
train, Zug (m ¨-e)
tram, Elektrische (f -n), Straßenbahn (f -en)
travellers' aid office, Bahnhofsmission (f -en)
trip, Fahrt (f -en)

trolley bus, O-Bus (m -se)
underground railway, U-Bahn
(f -en)
underpass, Unterführung (f -en)
viaduct, Überführung (f -en)
voyage, Seereise (f -n)
waiting room, Wartesaal (m ¨-e)

weekend return ticket, Sonntagsrückfahrkarte (f -n)
weekly ticket, Wochenkarte
(f -n)
window seat, Fensterplatz
(m ¨-e)

Useful phrases

Sitz hochklappbar für Traglasten, collapsible seat to accommodate
extra luggage
noch jemand zugestiegen? has anyone got in since last ticket check?
noch jemand ohne Fahrschein? anybody without a ticket?
einmal erster (zweiter) hin und zurück, one first-class (second-class)
return ticket
Auf- und Abspringen während der Fahrt verboten (untersagt), getting
on and getting off forbidden when bus (train etc.) in motion
der Zug hat Einfahrt auf Gleis . . . , the train is arriving at platform
. . .
kann die Fahrkarte verlängert werden? can the ticket validity be
extended?
bitte das Fahrgeld abgezählt bereit halten! please have the exact fare
ready
können Sie einen Moment auf mein Gepäck aufpassen? could you keep
an eye on my luggage for a moment?
wann habe ich Anschluß nach . . . ? when is there a connection for (to)
. . . ?
hat der Zug Verspätung? is the train late?
hat der Zug Aufenthalt in . . . ? does the train wait in the station at
. . . ?
ich habe nichts zu verzollen, I have nothing to declare.

Motoring

German–English

abblenden, to dip (lights)
Abblendlicht (n -er), low beam
Abschleppdienst (m -e), towing service
Abschleppseil (n -e), tow-rope
Abschleppwagen (m -), breakdown lorry
abschmieren, to grease, lubricate
Ampel (f -n), traffic lights
anhalten, to stop
per Anhalter fahren, to hitchhike
anlassen, to start (trans.)
Anlasser (m -), starter
anspringen, to start (intrans.)
Aufbau (m -ten), body
aufladen, to charge (battery)
aufpumpen, to pump
Auspuff (m -e), exhaust
Auspufftopf (m ˝-e), silencer
ausschalten, to switch off
Auto (n -s), car
Batterie (f -n), battery
Beifahrer (m -), front passenger, co-driver
Beleuchtung (f -en), lighting
Benzin (n), petrol, (Am.) gas
Blinker (m -), **Blinkleuchte** (f -n), **Blinklicht** (n -er), (direction) indicator light
Bremsbelag (m ˝-e), brake lining
Bremse (f -n), brake
Bremsflüssigkeit (f -en), brake fluid
Bremslicht (n -er), stop (brake) light
Bremsweg (m -e), braking distance
Einbahnstraße (f -n), one-way street
einfahren, to run in (new car)

einordnen, sich, to move into the correct traffic lane
einschalten, to switch on
Entfroster (m -), defroster, defrosting spray
entkohlen, to decarbonize
Ersatz-, (in compounds) spare, replacement
ersoffen, (coll.) flooded (carburettor)
fahren, to drive
Fahrer (m -), driver
Fahrpraxis (f), driving experience
Fahrprüfung (f -en), driving test
Fahrschule (f -n), driving school
Federung (f -en), springs, spring suspension
Fehlzündung (f -en), backfiring
Felge (f -n), rim (wheel)
Fensterkurbel (f -n), window winder
Fernlicht (n -er), high beam
Flitzer (m -), (coll.) small sports car
Frostschutzmittel (n -), antifreeze
Führerschein (m -e), driving-licence
funktionieren, to work
Fußbremse (f -n), foot brake
Gang (m ˝-e), gear
Gangschaltung (f -en), transmission
Gas geben, to accelerate
Gas wegnehmen, to decelerate
Gaspedal (n -e), accelerator
Gefahr (f -en), danger
Gefälle (n -), descent, gradient
Gemisch (n -e), mixture

146

Gepäckbrücke (f -n), Gepäck-
halter (m -), luggage rack
Geschwindigkeitsbegrenzung
(f -en), speed limit
Getriebe (n -), transmission
Griff (m -e), handle
Haftpflichtversicherung (f -en),
third-party insurance
Handbremse (f -n), handbrake
Handschuhfach (n ¨-er), glove
compartment
Haube (f -n), bonnet
Hebel (m -), lever
Heck (n -s), rear of car
Heckscheibe (f -n), rear window
Heizung (f -en), heater, heating
system
Hupe (f -n), horn, klaxon
Insasse (m -n) passenger,
occupant
Karosserie (f -n), body
Kaskoversicherung (f -en),
general insurance
Katzenauge (n -n), rear
reflector, cat's eye
Kennzeichen (n -), registration
Kilometerstand (m ¨-e), mileage
Kilometerzähler (m -), mileage
indicator, milometer
klappern, to rattle
klemmen, to jam
Kofferbrücke (f -n), Koffer-
halter (m -), luggage rack
Kofferraum (m ¨-e), boot
Kombiwagen (m -), minibus;
estate car (station wagon)
Kotflügel (m -), wing, mudguard
Kraftstoff (m), fuel
Kraftwagen (m -), (off.), car
Kraftwagenführer (m -) (off.),
driver
Kriechspur (f -en), slow lane on
Autobahn
Kühler (m -), radiator
Kupplung (f -en), clutch
Lack (m -e), Lackierung (f -en),
paintwork
Lastkraftwagen (m -), (off.),

Lastwagen (m -), LKW (m -s),
(coll.), lorry
Lauffläche (f -n), tread (tyre)
Leerlauf (m ¨-e), neutral
(position), idle
Leerlaufeinstellung (f -en),
idling speed
Lenkrad (n ¨-er), steering-wheel
Lichtmaschine (f -n), generator,
dynamo
Luftdruck (m -e), air pressure
Luftklappe (f -n), choke
Luftschlauch (m ¨-e), (inner)
tube (tyre)
Mangel (m ¨-), defect
Mantel (m ¨-), tyre casing
Motor (m -en), engine
Motorrad (n ¨-er), motor-bike
(Motor)roller (m -), (motor-)
scooter
Mühle (f -n) (coll.) old car
Mund S Reifen (Matsch- und
Schneereifen), special tyres
for slush and snow
Münztank (m -s), automatic
(coin-operated) petrol station
nachstellen, to re-adjust
Nebellampe (f -n), fog light
Nuckelpinne (f -n) (coll.),
small and slow car
Nummernschild (n -er), number
plate
Öl (n), oil
Ölablaßschraube (f -n), oil drain
plug
Ölmeßstab (m ¨-e), oil dipstick
Ölstandsanzeiger (m -), oil gauge
Ölwechsel (m -), oil change
Panne (f -n), breakdown
parken, to park
Parkleuchte (f -n), parking-
(side) light
Parklücke (f -n), parking-space
Parkplatz (m ¨-e), parking-place
Park-Uhr (f -en), parking-meter
Personenkraftwagen (m -), (off.)
Personenwagen (m -), PKW
(m -s) (coll.), four-seater,
saloon (sedan)
Platten (m -) (coll.), Plattfuß

(m ¨-e) (coll.), 'flat', puncture
polieren, to polish
Polsterung (f -en), upholstery
Probefahrt (f -en), trial run
Profil (n -e) (coll.), tread (tyre)
prüfen, to examine
Querrinne (f -n), traffic sign indicating drainage gully crossing the road or uneven surface
Rad (n ¨-er), wheel
Radkappe (f -n), hub cap
Radwechsel (m -), changing of a wheel
Reifen (m), tyre
Reparaturwerkstatt (f ¨-en), repair shop
reparieren, to repair
Reservekanister (m -), petrol can
Reserverad (n ¨-er), spare wheel
Richtungsanzeiger (m -), direction indicator
Rückenlehne (f -n), seat back
Rücklicht (n -er), rear light
Rückspiegel (m -), rear view mirror
Rückwärtsgang (m ¨-e), reverse (gear)
mit Saxomat (m -en), clutchless
schalten, to shift (change) gears
Schalter (m -), switch
Schalthebel (m -), gear lever
Scheibenwischer (m -), windscreen wiper
Scheibenwischerblatt (n ¨-er), windscreen wiper blade
Scheinwerfer (m -), headlight
schlauchlos, tubeless
schleudern, to skid
Schlitten (m -) (coll.), large car
Schlußlicht (n -er), rear light
Schmierdienst (m -e), lubrication service
Schutzblech (n -e), mudguard
Schwimmer (m -), carburettor float
Sicherheitsgurt (m -e), safety belt
Sicherung (f -en), fuse

Sitz (m -e), seat
Sonnenblende (f -n), sunscreen, visor
Sonnendach (n ¨-er), sliding-roof
Standlicht (n -er), parking-light
Starterklappe (f -n), choke
Steigung (f -en), incline, gradient
steuern, to steer
Steuer(rad) (n ¨-er), steering-wheel
Störung (f -en), malfunctioning
Stoßdämpfer (m -), shock absorber
Stoßstange (f -n), bumper
stottern (coll.), to cough (engine)
Strafmandat (n -e), (coll.), **gebührenpflichtige Ver-warnung** (f -en) (off.), 'ticket'
Straßenfloh (m ¨-e) (coll.), small car, 'mini'
Straßenkreuzer (m -) (coll.), large car
Straßenkreuzung (f -en), cross-roads, crossing
Straßenlage (f -n), road-holding
Strom (m), current (electric)
Tachometer (m -), **Tacho** (m -s) (coll.), speedometer
Tankstelle (f -n), petrol station
überholen, to overhaul; to overtake
Umleitung (f -en), diversion
Unfall (m ¨-e), accident
Unfallhilfsstelle (f -n), **Unfall-station** (f -en), first-aid post
Ventil (n -e), valve
Verbrauch (m), consumption
Verdeck (n -e), roof
Vergaser (m -), carburettor
verkehrstüchtig,* roadworthy
Verkehrszeichen (n -), traffic sign
Verschleiß (m), wear and tear
Verteiler (m -), distributor
Vorfahrt (f -en), right of way
Wagen (m -), car

Wagenheber (m -), jack
Wagenpapiere (n.pl.), log book
Wagenpflege (f -n), maintenance
  service
Wartung (f), maintenance
Wegweiser (m -), road sign
wenden, to turn
Werkstatt (f ¨-en), garage
  (repairing)
Werkzeug (n -e), tool
(Wind)schutzscheibe (f -n),
windscreen
ziehen, to accelerate (intrans.)
Zubringerstraße (f -n), access
  road leading to the Autobahn
Zündschlüssel (m -), ignition key
Zündung (f -en), ignition
Zündzeitpunkt (m -e), ignition
  timing
Zusammenstoß (m ¨-e), collision
Zwischengas geben, to double-
  declutch

* Cars have to be examined for roadworthiness every two years and
this is done by the local branch of the *Technischer Über-
wachungsverein* (colloquially called *TÜV*), an official organization
with a branch in every licensing district. The certificate of roadworthiness is in the form of a disc affixed to the rear numberplate of
the car; the disc indicates when the next examination is due.

English–German

accelerate, Gas geben, beschleu-
  nigen; ziehen (intrans.)
accelerator, Gaspedal (n -e)
access road (leading to the
  Autobahn) Zubringerstraße
  (f -n)
accident, Unfall (m ¨-e)
air pressure, Luftdruck (m -e)
anti-freeze, Frostschutzmittel
  (n -)
back-firing, Fehlzündung (f -en)
battery, Batterie (f -n)
body, Aufbau (m -ten), Karosserie (f -n)
bonnet, Haube (f -n)
boot, Kofferraum (m ¨-e)
brake, Bremse (f -n)
brake fluid, Bremsflüssigkeit
  (f -en)
brake fluid supply tank,
  Nachfüllbehälter für Bremsflüssigkeit
brake lining, Bremsbelag (m ¨-e)
braking distance, Bremsweg
  (m -e)
breakdown, Panne (f -n)
breakdown lorry, Abschleppwagen (m -)
bumper, Stoßstange (f -n)
cable, Kabel (n -)
car, Auto (n -s), Wagen (m -),
  Kraftwagen (m -) (off.)
carburettor, Vergaser (m -)
carburettor float, Schwimmer
  (m -)
casing (tyre), Mantel (m ¨-)
changing of a wheel, Rad-
  wechsel (m -)
charge (battery), aufladen
choke, Luftklappe (f -n),
  Starterklappe
claxon, Hupe (f -n)
clutch, Kupplung (f -en)
clutchless, mit Saxomat (m -en)
co-driver, Beifahrer (m -)
collision, Zusammenstoß (m ¨-e)

consumption, Verbrauch (m)
cough (engine), stottern
crossing, cross-roads, Straßenkreuzung (f -en)
current (electric), Strom (m)
danger, Gefahr (f -en)
decarbonize, entkohlen
decelerate, Gas wegnehmen
defect, Mangel (m ¨-)
defroster, defrosting spray, Entfroster (m -)
descent, Gefälle (n -)
dip (lights), abblenden
direction indicator light, Blinker (m -), Blinkleuchte (f -n), Blinklicht (n -er), Richtungsanzeiger (m -)
distributor, Verteiler (m -)
diversion, Umleitung (f -en)
double-declutch, Zwischengas geben
drive, fahren
driver, Fahrer (m -), Kraftwagenführer (m -) (off.)
driving experience, Fahrpraxis (f)
driving licence, Führerschein (m -e)
driving school, Fahrschule (f -n)
driving test, Fahrprüfung (f -en)
dynamo, Lichtmaschine (f -en)
engine, Motor (m -en)
examine, prüfen
exhaust, Auspuff (m -e)
first-aid post, Unfallhilfsstelle (f -n), Unfallstation (f -en)
flat, Platten (m) (coll.), Plattfuß (m ¨-e) (coll.)
flooded (carburettor), ersoffen (coll.)
fog light, Nebellampe (f -n)
foot brake, Fußbremse (f -n)
fourseater, Personenkraftwagen (m -) (off.), Personenwagen, PKW (m -s) (coll.)
front passenger, Beifahrer (m -)
fuel, Kraftstoff (m)
fuse, Sicherung (f -en)
garage (repairing), Werkstatt (f ¨-en)

gas (Am.), Benzin (n)
gear, Gang (m ¨-e)
gear lever, Schalthebel (m -)
general insurance, Kaskoversicherung (f -en)
generator, Lichtmaschine (f -n)
glove compartment, Handschuhfach (n ¨-er)
gradient (descent), Gefälle (n -)
gradient (incline), Steigung (f -en)
grease, abschmieren
hand brake, Handbremse (f -n)
handle, Griff (m -e)
headlight, Scheinwerfer (m -)
heater, heating system, Heizung (f -en)
high beam, Fernlicht (n -er)
hitch-hike, per Anhalter fahren
horn, Hupe (f -n)
hub cap, Radkappe (f -n)
idle, Leerlauf (m ¨-e)
idling speed, Leerlaufeinstellung (f -en)
ignition, Zündung (f -en)
ignition key, Zündschlüssel (m -)
ignition timing, Zündzeitpunkt (m -e)
incline, Steigung (f -en)
instrument panel, Armaturenbrett (n -er)
jack, Wagenheber (m -)
jam, klemmen
joint, Scharnier (n -e)
level-crossing, Bahnübergang (m ¨-e)
lever, Hebel (m -)
lighting, Beleuchtung (f -en)
log book, Wagenpapiere (n.pl.)
lorry, Lastkraftwagen (m -) (off.), Lastwagen (m -), Laster (m -) (coll.), LKW (m -s) (coll.)
low beam, Abblendlicht (n -er)
lubricate, abschmieren
lubrication service, Schmierdienst (m -e)
luggage rack, Gepäckbrücke (f -n), Gepäckhalter (m -),

Kofferbrücke (f -n),
Kofferhalter (m -)
maintenance, Wartung (f)
maintenance service, Wagenpflege (f -n)
malfunctioning, Störung (f -en)
mileage, Kilometerstand (m ¨-)
mileage indicator, milometer,
Kilometerzähler (m -)
mixture, Gemisch (n -e)
motor-bike, Motorrad (n ¨-er)
(motor-)scooter, (Motor)roller
(m -)
mudguard, Kotflügel (m -),
Schutzblech (n -e)
neutral (position), Leerlauf (m
¨-c)
number plate, Nummernschild
(n -er)
occupant, Insasse (m -n)
oil, Öl (n)
oil change, Ölwechsel (m -)
oil dipstick Ölmeßstab (m ¨-e)
oil drain plug, Ölablaßschraube
(f -n)
oil gauge, Ölstandsanzeiger (m -)
one-way street, Einbahnstraße
(f -n)
overhaul, überholen
overtake, überholen
paintwork, Lack (m -e),
Lackierung (f -en)
park, parken
parking-light, Standlicht (n -er)
parking (side) light, Parkleuchte
(f -n)
parking-meter, Park-Uhr (f -en)
parking-place, Parkplatz (m ¨-e)
parking-space, Parklücke (f -n)
passenger, Insasse (m -n)
petrol, Benzin (n)
petrol can, Reservekanister
(m -)
petrol station, Tankstelle (f -n)
polish, polieren
puncture, Platten (m -) (coll.),
Plattfuß (m ¨-e) (coll.)
radiator, Kühler (m -)
rattle, klappern
re-adjust, nachstellen

rear (of car), Heck (n -s)
rear light, Rücklicht (n -er),
Schlußlicht (n -er)
rear reflector, Katzenauge (n -n)
rear view mirror, Rückspiegel
(m -)
rear window, Heckscheibe (f -n),
Rückfenster (n -)
registration, Kennzeichen (n -)
repair, reparieren
repair shop, Reparaturwerkstatt
(f ¨-en)
replacement, Ersatz- (in compounds)
reverse (gear), Rückwärtsgang
(m ¨-e)
right of way, Vorfahrt (f -en)
rim (wheel), Felge (f -n)
road-holding, Straßenlage (f -n)
road sign, Wegweiser (m -)
roadworthy, verkehrstüchtig
roof, Verdeck (n -e)
run in (new car), einfahren
safety belt, Sicherheitsgurt
(m -e)
saloon (sedan), Personenkraftwagen (m -) (off.),
Personenwagen, PKW
(m -s) (coll.)
seat, Sitz (m -e)
seat back, Rückenlehne (f -n)
seat runner, Gleitschiene (f -n)
set, einstellen
shift (change) gears, schalten
shock absorber, Stoßdämpfer
(m -)
silencer, Auspufftopf (m ¨-e)
skid, schleudern
sliding-roof, Schiebedach
(n ¨-er), Sonnendach
spare, Ersatz- (in compounds)
spare wheel, Reserverad (n ¨-er)
speed limit, Geschwindigkeitsbegrenzung (f -en)
speedometer, Tachometer (m -),
Tacho (m -s) (coll.)
springs, spring suspension,
Federung (f -en)
start (trans.), anlassen
start (intrans.), anspringen

starter, Anlasser (m -)
steer, steuern
steering-wheel, Lenkrad (n ¨-er),
 Steuerrad
stop, anhalten
stop (brake) light, Bremslicht
 (n -er), Stopplicht
sun-screen, Sonnenblende (f -n)
switch, Schalter (m -)
switch off (on), ausschalten
 (einschalten)
ticket, Strafmandat (n -e) (coll.),
 gebührenpflichtige Verwar-
 nung (f -en) (off.)
tool, Werkzeug (n -e)
towing-service, Abschleppdienst
 (m -e)
tow-rope, Abschleppseil (n -e)
traffic lights, Ampel (f -n)
traffic sign, Verkehrszeichen
 (n -)
transmission, Gangschaltung
 (f -en), Getriebe (n -)
transmission case, Getriebe-
 kasten (m ¨-)

tread (tyre), Lauffläche (f -n),
 Profil (n -e) (coll.)
trial run, Probefahrt (f -en)
tube (inner), Luftschlauch
 (m ¨-e)
tubeless, schlauchlos
turn, wenden
tyre, Reifen (m -)
upholstery, Polsterung (f -en)
valve, Ventil (n -e)
visor, Sonnenblende (f -n)
wear and tear, Verschleiß (m)
wheel, Rad (n ¨-er)
window winder, Fensterkurbel
 (f -n)
windscreen, (Wind)schutz-
 scheibe (f -n)
wing, Kotflügel (m -),
 Schutzblech (n -e)
wiper, Scheibenwischer (m -)
wiper blade, Scheibenwischerblatt (n ¨-er)
work, funktionieren
wrench, Schraubenschlüssel
 (m -)

Animal Comparisons and Analogies

German seems richer than English in the variety and number of terms, phrases, comparisons and analogies referring to animals and for this reason the inclusion of a special German–English vocabulary of the commonest of these seemed desirable. In most cases we have not translated by an English equivalent (as such rarely exist) but by an explanation; it is hard to see what purpose is achieved by translating *Backfisch* by 'flapper' but when there is a good equivalent we have given it, e.g. the Germans buy a cat in a sack and the English buy a pig in a poke. Nearly all English animal phrases such as crow's feet (*Krähenfüßchen*) and the lion's share (*Löwenanteil*) can be safely translated into German and for this reason we have omitted most of them; our main concern has been to deal with terms such as *dackeln*, a verb describing the wobbly toddling of infants by comparing it with the odd locomotion of the *Dackel* (dachshund).

Aal (m -e). 'Eel'; *sich aalen,* 'to lounge about' (particularly sunbathing on the beach).

Affe (m -n). 'Ape', 'monkey'; name for a flat, fur-covered rucksack; *ich denke, mich laust der Affe,* 'well, I'll be . . .'; *mit affenartiger Geschwindigkeit,* incredibly quickly; *affig,* silly, gigglish, affected; *die Affenschaukeln,* looped pigtails; *das Affentheater,* exaggerated fuss; *mit (einem) Affenzahn,* 'like a bat out of hell'; *der Lackaffe,* fop; *Maulaffen feilhalten,* to gawp; *nachäffen,* to mimic.

Bär (m -en). 'Bear'; in compounds 'very', e.g. *einen Bärenhunger haben,* to be extremely hungry, *bärenstark,* 'very strong', etc.; *jemandem einen Bären aufbinden,* to tell somebody a lie; *einen Bärendienst erweisen,* to render a disservice; *auf der Bärenhaut liegen,* to laze about; *bärbeißig,* scowling; *der Bärendreck,* liquorice (regional name); *der Seebär,* 'old sea-dog'.

Biest (n -er). 'Beast' but the equivalent of 'beast' when used figuratively is *die Bestie*; *kleines Biest,* smart little rascal (girl); *großes Biest,* any large and bulky object; *Biester,* annoying insects.

Bock (m ¨-e). 'Ram'; *einen Bock schießen,* to commit a blunder; *den Bock zum Gärtner machen,* choose the wrong person for the job; *jemand ins Bockshorn jagen,* to intimidate or bluff a person; *bockig, bockbeinig,* stubborn.

153

Büffel (m -). 'Buffalo'; *die Büffelei*, cramming, swotting; *büffeln*, to cram, to swot.

Bulle (m -n). 'Bull'; very strong and big person; colloquial for policeman, 'cop', 'bull' (Am.); *die Bullenhitze*, hot as a furnace, sweltering heat.

Dachs (m -e). 'Badger'; *junger Dachs*, inexperienced youngster; *Frechdachs*, cheeky young fellow.

Dackel (m -). 'Dachshund', 'German sausage dog'; *Dackelbeine*, bow-legs; *Dackelfalten*, furrowed brow; *Dackeln*, waddling gait.

Drohne (f -n). 'Drone'; *das Drohnendasein*, a life of Riley (ease).

Elefant (m -en). 'Elephant'; *wie ein Elefant im Porzellanladen*, 'like a bull in a china-shop'; *aus einer Mücke einen Elefanten machen*, 'to make a mountain out of a mole-hill'; *das Elefantenbaby, das Elefantenküken*, fat young girl.

Ente (f -n). 'Duck'; *lahme Ente*, slow and unimaginative person; *Zeitungsente*, false statement in a newspaper, canard; *häßliches Entlein*, nick-name for the Citroën 2CV.

Esel (m -). 'Donkey'; silly fool; *die Eselei*, 'asininity'; *die Eselsbrücke*, mnemonic; *Eselsohren haben*, 'to be dog-eared (book)'; *Packesel*, 'beast of burden'.

Fisch (m -e). 'Fish'; *das sind kleine Fische für ihn*, that's easy for him; *munter wie ein Fisch im Wasser*, healthy and lively; *der Fisch will schwimmen*, indicates the opinion that one shouldn't eat fish without wine; *das ist weder Fisch noch Fleisch*, 'that's neither fish, nor flesh, nor good red herring'; *der Backfisch*, awkward, self-conscious teenage girl (supposedly derived from English: a fish too small to eat and thus thrown back into the sea); *Goldfisch*, teenage girl of rich parents; *das Backfischaquarium* (n), ironic for a girls' grammar school or girls' boarding-school.

Fliege (f -n). 'Fly' (insect); bow-tie; *keiner Fliege etwas zuleide tun*, to be completely harmless; *zwei Fliegen mit einer Klappe schlagen*, 'to kill two birds with one stone'; *der Fliegenfürst*, euphemism for the devil ('Lord of the Flies').

Floh (m ¨-e). 'Flea'; *Flöhe*, lolly (money); *die Flöhe husten hören*, 'to think oneself the cat's whiskers'.

Frosch (m ¨-e). 'Frog'; term of endearment to children; *sei kein Frosch*, don't be a spoil-sport; *Knallfrosch*, jumping cracker; *Nacktfrosch*, naked child; *Wetterfrosch*, the weather man.

Fuchs (m ¨-e). 'Fox'; sly person; sorrel horse; *wo sich Fuchs und Hase gute Nacht sagen*, literally 'where fox and hare say good night to one another' describes an isolated and remote place; *es fuchst mich*, not 'it foxes me' but 'it nettles me'; *der Fuchsschwanz*, hand-saw; *fuchsteufelswild*, furiously angry; *der Pfennigfuchser*, pinch-penny.

Gans (f ⁻-e). 'Goose'; silly woman; *im Gänsemarsch,* Indian file; *das Gänseblümchen,* daisy; *die Gänsefüßchen,* 'little geese feet' colloquial and schoolboy name for 'inverted commas'; *die Gänsehaut,* 'goose pimples', 'goose flesh'; *der Gänsewein,* water (ironic); *jemand wie eine Weihnachtsgans ausnehmen,* to rook a person.

Hahn (m ⁻-e). 'Cock'; 'tap (water, gas etc.)'; *er ist Hahn im Korb,* similar to 'he's the cock of the walk'; *es kräht kein Hahn danach,* nobody is in the least bit interested; *der Streithahn,* quarrelsome person.

Hammel (m -). 'Ram'; stupid person; *jemandem die Hammelbeine langziehen,* to tell somebody off; *der Hammelsprung,* parliamentary division (vote); *der Neidhammel,* envious person.

Hase (m -n). 'Hare'; *ach, da liegt der Hase im Pfeffer,* 'so that's the fly in the ointment'; *wissen, wie der Hase läuft,* to know how a situation will develop; *mein Name ist Hase,* said by a person claiming to know nothing about the topic under discussion; *ein alter Hase,* an experienced man; *das Hasenbrot,* uneaten sandwich; *der Hasenfuß,* coward; *die Hasenscharte,* 'hare-lip'; *der Angsthase,* coward; *der Skihase,* woman on skis.

Hecht (m -e). 'Pike'; fug in a room from smoking; *es zieht wie Hechtsuppe,* there is a terrible draught; *ein toller Hecht,* (in admiration) a fun-loving lively young man, similar to 'the life and soul of the party'; *hechten,* to dive head-first; *der Hechtsprung,* dive.

Heimchen (n -). 'Cricket'; *wie ein Heimchen essen,* to eat sparingly.

Huhn (n ⁻-er). Generic name for 'chicken' of all types, sizes and both sexes; also for the grown female (in preference to *Henne*); *ein Hühnchen mit jemandem zu rupfen haben,* 'to have a bone to pick with someone'; *da lachen ja die Hühner,* 'that would make a dog laugh'; *ein blindes Huhn findet auch mal ein Korn,* expresses the opinion that even someone stupid can do what is right by chance; *mit den Hühnern zu Bett gehen (aufstehen),* to go to bed (get up) very early; *ein verrücktes Huhn,* a 'nut-case'; *das Hühnerauge,* corn.

Hund (m -e). 'Dog'; in compounds 'very (bad)', e.g. *hundekalt, hundemüde,* extremely cold, tired, *das Hundewetter,* very bad weather; *ein armer Hund,* 'poor devil' (but without an adjective it is very offensive 'scoundrel', 'bastard'); *kalt wie eine Hundeschnauze,* said of a person with no feeling; *auf den Hund kommen,* to go from bad to worse; *vor die Hunde gehen,* 'to go to the dogs'; *mit allen Hunden gehetzt sein,* to know every trick of the trade; *bekannt wie ein bunter Hund,* well-known by sight; *das ist ein dicker Hund,* indicates that something is incredible; *hundsmiserabel,* extremely bad; *verhunzen* (derived from *verhundsen*), to worsen something, spoil or make a mess of it; *der Windhund* (greyhound), 'windbag'.

Käfer (m -). 'Beetle'; usual name for the *Volkswagen*; *ein süßer Käfer*, sweet girl.

Kater (m -). 'Tom-cat'; *einen Kater haben verkatert sein*, to have a hangover (the textbook word *Katzenjammer* is rarely used except figuratively); *der Katerbummel* and *das Katerfrühstück* are hangover remedies, a 'brisk' walk to a *Gasthaus*, and a breakfast of beer and pickled herring.

Katze (f -n). 'Cat' in generic sense and also 'tabby-cat'; while the Englishman may be persuaded 'to buy a pig in a poke' the German buys a cat in a sack, *eine Katze im Sack kaufen*, but both nationalities 'let the cat out of the bag', *die Katze aus dem Sack lassen*; *wie die Katze um den heißen Brei gehen*, 'to beat about the bush'; *alles ist für die Katz*, when things turn out badly, 'all was in vain'; *katzig* not 'catty' but 'snappish'; *die Katzenmusik*, discordant music; *ein Katzensprung*, a very short distance away; *die Katzenwäsche*, inadequate wash or 'cat's lick'; *die Schmeichelkatze*, ingratiating woman.

Kauz (m ¨-e). 'Screech-owl' whose cry, according to German superstition, foretells death; odd and solitary person often brusque and unpleasant in manner (to differentiate between the two, the bird is usually referred to as *Käuzchen*); *kauzig*, odd.

Kröte (f -n). 'Toad'; unpleasant woman; *ein paar Kröten*, a few pence; *krötig*, unpleasant.

Kuckuck (m -e). 'Cuckoo'; in exclamations a euphemism for 'devil' or 'hell', e.g. *scher dich zum Kuckuck*, is equivalent to go to hell, but less coarse; when property is seized by a court for non-payment of debts or fines a seal bearing the German eagle is affixed to the article and the noble bird is disrespectfully referred to as the cuckoo: *da klebt der Kuckuck dran*.

Kuh (f ¨-e). 'Cow'; stupid girl or woman; *das geht auf keine Kuhhaut*, an indescribable quantity; *der Kuhhandel*, corrupt practices in the achievement of a desired aim.

Küken (n -). 'Chicken'; inexperienced young girl.

Laus (f ¨-e). 'Louse'; *ihm ist eine Laus über die Leber gelaufen*, he is peeved; *lausig*, 'lousy'.

Marder (m -). 'Marten'; thief who breaks into and steals from cars (*Automarder*) or automatic vending machines (*Automatenmarder*) etc.

Maus (f ¨-e). 'Mouse'; *weiße Mäuse sehen*, to have hallucinations, but *weiße Mäuse* is also the nick-name for 'traffic police' because of their white coats; *mausen*, to pinch (steal); *sich mausig machen*, to be unpleasant about something; *mucksmäuschenstill*, very silent.

Mops (m ¨-e). 'Pug dog'; small fat person; *mopsen* is 'to pinch (steal)' but also 'to annoy'; *sich mopsen*, 'to be bored' and 'to be annoyed'; *mopsfidel,* very gay, chirruping with joy; *Rollmops,* rolled pickled herring.

Motte (f -n). 'Moth'; *du kriegst die Motten,* 'well, I'll be . . .' (always in the familiar form as one is addressing oneself).

Ochse (m -n). 'Ox'; *ochsen,* to swot.

Pferd (n -e). 'Horse'; *mit ihm kann man Pferde stehlen,* he is a good sport; *der Pferdefuß,* snag; *der Pferdeschwanz,* 'pony tail (hair)'; *Steckenpferd,* hobby horse and hobby.

Polyp (m -en). 'Polyp'; policeman.

Pudel (m -). 'Poodle'; *des Pudels Kern,* the heart of the matter; *wie ein begossener Pudel abziehen,* to depart dejectedly and frustratedly; *die Pudelmütze,* long tasselled woollen cap; *pudelwohl,* (to feel) very well.

Rabe (m -n). 'Raven'; *ein weißer Rabe,* a rare bird; *die Rabeneltern* (*der Rabenvater, die Rabenmutter*), unloving and cruel parents; *kohlrabenschwarz,* 'raven black'.

Rappe (m -n). 'Black horse'; *auf Schusters Rappen,* on foot, 'Shanks's pony'.

Ratte (f -n). 'Rat'; in established compounds 'enthusiast', e.g. *Wasserratte,* keen swimmer, *Leseratte* or *Bücherratte,* bookworm (but self-coined compounds may be offensive or incomprehensible); *ein Rattenschwanz von,* a chain of . . ., a sequence of . . . (unpleasant things); *die Rattenschwänzchen,* small pigtails; *Balettratte,* young ballet dancer (girl); *Landratte,* 'landlubber'.

Roß (n -(ss)e or ¨-er). 'Horse' (poet.); *Riesenroß,* very stupid person (but inoffensive); *Stahlroß,* bicycle (ironic).

Sau (f ¨-e). 'Sow'; extremely dirty person (very offensive); in compounds and stock phrases it is inoffensive but coarse and means very (bad), e.g. *unter aller Sau,* very bad in quality or execution; *wie eine gesengte Sau fahren,* to drive like a maniac.

Schaf (n -e). 'Sheep'; *sein Schäfchen ins trockene bringen,* to make one's pile; *Schäfchen,* little clouds; *der Schafskopf,* silly person (inoffensive); *die Schäferstunde,* amorous hour.

Schimmel (m -). 'White horse'; *Amtsschimmel,* red tape.

Schlange (f -n). 'Snake'; queue; *Schlange stehen,* to queue; *Brillenschlange,* cobra, (unpleasant) girl with glasses.

Schnecke (f -n). 'Snail'; *jemand zur Schnecke machen,* to cut a person down to size; *Schnecken,* type of hair style, type of fancy pastry; *das Schneckentempo,* very slow, 'at a snail's pace'.

Schwan (m ¨-e). 'Swan'; *mein lieber Schwan,* an exclamation emphasizing the gravity of an unpleasant fact; *mir schwant nichts Gutes,* I foresee disaster.

Schwein (n -e). 'Pig'; dirty person (very offensive); *Schwein haben,* to be lucky; *die Schweinsöhrchen,* type of fancy pastry; *Glücksschwein,* lucky pig (charm); *Sparschwein,* 'piggy bank'; *das Ferkel* (piglet), 'mucky duck'.

Spatz (m -en). 'Sparrow'; term of endearment for children; *wie ein Rohrspatz schimpfen,* to scold or grumble vociferously; *die Spatzen pfeifen es schon von allen Dächern,* refers to a secret now known to everybody (even the sparrows); *Dreckspatz,* dirty child.

Storch (m ̈-e). 'Stork'; *wie ein Storch im Salat,* describes a clumsy pedant; *nun brat mir einer 'nen Storch,* an exclamation of surprise.

Taube (f -n). 'Pigeon'; *hier geht es zu wie in einem Taubenschlag* is said about a very busy place with a lot of coming and going.

Tier (n -e). 'Animal'; *ein hohes Tier,* a V.I.P., bigwig; *tierischer Ernst,* deadly serious(ness); *Trampeltier,* 'clumsy clot (clod)'.

Unke (f -n). Type of toad; *unken,* to foretell evil or disaster.

Vogel (m ̈-). 'Bird'; the English have 'bats in the belfry' or 'bees in the bonnet' while the German *hat einen Vogel,* and the idea that birds might be nesting in the heads of those who are a bit odd provides the idiomatic *bei dem piept's* (*piepsen* is the sound that young birds make); both statements are often accompanied by pointing at one's forehead: *jemandem einen Vogel zeigen* (a punishable offence); *den Vogel abschießen,* to be the best of the lot; *Lockvogel,* decoy; *Spaßvogel,* joker.

Wanze (f -n). 'Bug'; colloquial for a concealed microphone.

Wespe (f -n). 'Wasp'; colloquial for a female member of the detective branch of the civil police; *die Wespentaille,* very slim waist.

Wolf (m ̈-e). 'Wolf'; *Fleischwolf,* meat mincer.

Wurm (m ̈-er). 'Worm'; *da sitzt der Wurm drin,* there is something rotten about it; *jemandem die Würmer aus der Nase ziehen,* to extract information; *armes Würmchen,* poor little thing; *es wurmt mich* indicates gnawing anger.

Zicklein (n -). 'Kid'; *die Zicke,* stupid and unpleasant girl; *Zicken machen,* 'to play the goat'.

Ziege (f -n). 'Goat'; stupid and unpleasant woman; *der Ziegenpeter,* mumps.

Courtesy

The Germans are a formal people, much more so than the English, but although standard polite phrases are commonly used this does not mean that they are insincere or hypocritical.

Perhaps the greatest difficulty for English speakers is the rules governing the familiar form of address *du* and the polite form *Sie* (the verbs are *duzen* 'to address with *du*' and *siezen* 'to address with *Sie*'). You *duzen* intimate friends, members of the family, children and animals. Children are addressed by *Sie* on all official occasions after reaching sixteen. Sometimes quite intimate friends who are on first-name terms use *Sie*. A complicated protocol governs the change from *Sie* to *du*; the change has to be offered by the older or more important or superior in rank or the lady so it is wisest for the foreigner to await a cue rather than commit a social blunder by taking the first step. Very often this strict formality is not found at work; among colleagues of more or less equal rank *du* is the sign of group acceptance and to insist on using *Sie* could create hostility. Friends who use *du* are often called *Duzfreunde* or *Duzbrüder* and the ritual change to the familiar form of address is *Duzbrüderschaft trinken*. In those areas where *Fasching* is celebrated there is a convention whereby all persons at a *Fasching* party, even complete strangers, address one another with *du* irrespective of rank or intimacy but when the party is over there must be a return to whatever mode of address is normal.

If you do not know a man's name you can address him as *mein Herr* (rather like the English 'sir' between equals) and you can call after him this way too. Unfortunately nothing similar exists for a lady; *Dame* 'lady' is only used as a direct address by waiters and shop assistants (*bitte, die Dame?* 'yes, madam?') and should be avoided. If you do not know a woman's name it is best to avoid any direct address as the courteous *gnädige Frau* and *gnädiges Fräulein* can easily seem overdone. While *Fräulein* is the correct way to call a waitress, salesgirl or telephone operator it should never be used without a name in any other cases as the American and British troops have used it in a manner that makes it inadvisable to imitate. Do not forget that *Herr* does not eliminate other titles and so Dr Braun ought to be addressed as *Herr Doktor Braun* or *Herr Doktor* but never as just *Docktor Braun,* which is very impolite. The habit of addressing a doctor's wife as *Frau Doktor* is fast dying but women possessing a doctorate should be addressed as *Frau* (or *Fräulein*) *Doktor*. Remember that single women of middle age and over are usually, out of politeness, addressed as *Frau . . . .*

The Germans have no equivalent to the English 'how do you do?—how do you do?' pattern and the nearest is *wie geht es Ihnen?* to which a proper reply and return must be given *danke, und Ihnen?* A more formal version is *wie befinden Sie sich?; wie geht's?* should be confined to intimate friends.

Danke can create problems. It is the correct response to *bitte* (please) and a limited conversation can arise from their exchange. It is polite to accompany the doing of a kindly act with *bitte* and the recipient replies with *danke,* but *danke* can also be the answer to a question: *Möchten Sie noch etwas Kaffee?* 'Would you like some more coffee?' *Danke* 'no thanks' or 'yes please' according to the intonation: raised voice on *-ke* for 'yes' lowered for 'no' but to avoid confusion you can use *ja bitte* or *ja danke* for 'yes' and *nein danke* or *danke, nein* for 'no'. *Danke* can also be a dismissal for servants etc. but can be offensive if said too curtly. *Danke schön* and *bitte schön* are mostly used by sales staff and waiters and to be emphatic it is better to say *vielen Dank* 'many thanks'.

When you have not understood something you say *bitte?* or *wie bitte?* 'pardon' or *was?* 'what?' which is preferred by the working classes.

There is an elaborate protocol governing the way to refer to a husband or wife; always refer to your own as *meine Frau* or *mein Mann* and keep to the same pattern when inquiring about the spouse of a friend. If you are speaking to a person who is not a close friend but about your equal in rank and age the forms *Ihr Gatte* and *Ihre Gattin* should be used. If the person addressed is higher in rank or older the very formal *Ihr Herr Gemahl, Ihre Frau Gemahlin* are advisable, and such a person's parents or children should be referred to as *Ihr Herr Vater, Ihre Frau Mutter* and *Ihr Fräulein Tochter* etc.

When introducing someone the formula is *darf ich Ihnen Herrn . . . vorstellen?* or *darf ich Sie mit Herrn . . . bekannt machen?* and those introduced murmur *angenehm* or *sehr erfreut* ('pleased to meet you') in reply.

Writing letters always poses the problem of address. Formal business letters are not difficult though: 'Dear Sir', 'Dear Sirs', 'Dear Madam' are *Sehr geehrter Herr* (with or without a name), *Sehr geehrte Herren, Sehr geehrte gnädige Frau* or *Sehr verehrte gnädige Frau* (without a name) and *Sehr geehrte* (or *verehrte*) *Frau . . .* followed by an exclamation mark or comma; after a comma, the letter begins without a capital. When using *Sehr geehrter Herr* it is usual to add *Doktor, Professor* or any other title the person has. For such formal letters the close would be *Hochachtungsvoll* (equivalent to 'yours faithfully') and the signature. For less formal letters the *Sehr geehrter . . .* pattern is retained but the close can be *Mit freundlichen Grüßen* equivalent to 'yours sincerely'. Intimate letters have the same possibility of variation as in English and can be commenced with *Liebe(r)* 'Dear' and close with such phrases as *Mit herzlichen Grüßen, Mit allen guten Wünschen* 'yours cordially', 'with every good wish'.

On entering a shop, office, hairdresser's or railway carriage Germans always murmur *guten Tag* and *auf Wiedersehn* or *auf Wiederschauen* on leaving. Among friends *bis auf bald, bis morgen* 'see you soon', 'see you tomorrow' are frequently heard; *grüß dich* is 'hello' among very intimate friends. *Tschüß* (also *Tschö* and *Tschau*) is an informal 'good-bye' much affected by young people as is *Servus* (mainly used in Austria), which is also common among workers.

English–German

Cross-Reference Index

This index is designed as a guide to the use of the main section and not to provide German translations of English. Here you will find an indication after each English word which will lead you to the commentary, explanation and examples of the various and associated German equivalents. Do not take the German word blindly as an appropriate translation of the English preceding it as in all but a very few cases the German is far from being a translation; this cross-reference index is like a railway timetable: it indicates the train but you cannot travel in it.

A

abortionist, Engelmacher
about, an, um, ungefähr
absent, fehlen
absolute, ausmachen
accept, sagen
by accident, ungefähr
according(ly), entsprechend
of no account, Sache
achieve, leisten, Kanone
acquaintance, bekannt; kennenlernen
acquit, frei
additional, nachträglich
adhesive tape, Tesafilm
in advance, voraus
to advance, fortkommen, vorschießen
advantageous, dankbar
advertisement, Annonce, Reklame
affair, Geschichte, Sache
affected, etepetete, zieren
affluent, Wohlstandsgesellschaft
afford, leisten
after, ab, hintereinander
all, also, schließlich
again, noch
ages, lang
agitator, Scharfmacher
agree, meinen
(food), bekommen
agreed, ausmachen

air-conditioner, Klimaanlager
allow, erlauben, lassen
all right, ja, meinetwegen, recht, schön
for money, Kasse
almost, direkt
alone, für, mutterseelenallein
altogether, hoch
always, alle, immer, laufen
ambulance, Behandlung
amiss, krumm
among, unter
ample, reichlich
amuse, Unterhalt
angle, Winkel
angry, Rage, geladen
announcement, bekannt
annoy, reizen
anti-government satire, Flüsterwitz
antiquated, überholen
anti-social, sozialschwach
anything but, anders, **else,** dürfen
apologize, verzeihen
appointment, bestellen, Verabredung
apprentice(ship), Lehre, Stift
approach, hinkommen
approve, billig
approximately, ungefähr
April fool, April
apt, sitzen
arm-wrestle, hakeln
around, rund

burst, platzen
bustle, treiben
busybody, Hans
butter up, gebauchpinselt,
  Honig

C

calamity, Landplage
calculate, ausrechnen
call, heißen
cancel, entwerten, Essig,
  platzen, Rückgang, sagen
capable, imstande
mark cards, zinken
play cards, dreschen
care for, machen
  less, egal, Wurst
careful, aufpassen, ohne,
  schwer
careless, leicht, verschludern
car insurance,
  Vollkaskoversicherung
car park, parken
carton, Stange
turn a cartwheel, radschlagen
case, Fall
cash register, Kasse
cast (drama), besetzt
stand on ceremony, zieren
certain(ly), bestimmt
certify, prüfen
chaff, frotzeln
chairman, Moderator
change, verändern
  (money), rausbekommen,
  rausgeben
little chap, Knirps
chaperone, Anstand
characteristic, Note
charge, Last
charming, reizen
charwoman, Putzfrau
chatter, leid
  -box, Quasselstrippe
cheap, aussehen, billig
cheating, Schmu
check, nachsehen, prüfen
cheek, Stirn, glatt, frech
cheerful, heiter
cheers (toast), prost
chemist, Dienst, Drogerie
chic, flott

chicanery, Schikane
childish, Kind
child-like, Kind
chubby, mollig
cigarette, Kippe, Sarg
cinema, Lichtspiele, Kintopp
citizen's action, Bürgerinitiative
clash, Accrochage
clear, einleuchten, klar, rein
cleavage, offenherzig
clever, klug, schlau
clinic, Krankenhaus
clip-joint, Nepplokal
close-up (cinema), Aufnahme
clown, Hans
no clue, Ahnung
coal-miner, Kumpel
coffee-bar, Eisdiele
coffin, Sarg
college, Kolleg
come down on, Minna
  in handy, gebrauchen
  off it, ach, machen
  to an end, alle
  to blows, Hand
Common Market, EWG
common sense, gesund
  in — with, gemein
commuter traffic, Pendlerverkehr
company, Aktie
complaint, Anstand, Reklame
conceited, einbilden
concerning, Betreff
condone, nachsehen
confused, irr
congratulations, Glück
connection, Anschluß
consignment, Partie
consultant, Arzt
consulting hours, Sprechstunde
consume, verzehren
contestable, revisibel
continually, laufen
continue, fort
continuously, Tour
control oneself, Maß
convey, ausrichten, bestellen
conviction, Überführung
cope with, fertig, Rand,
  schaffen
corner, Winkel
corpulent, stark

correct, stimmen
correspondence course,
   Fernstudium
cost, kommen, kosten
costume (trad.), Tracht
cosy, mollig
count on, verspitzen
counterfoil, aufheben
countryside, Land
courage, Zivilcourage
course, Kurs
   of —, ach, freilich
crack, springen, Sprung
crazy, rein, toll
crescent, Bogen
crew-cut, Stift
criticism, fressen
crooked, krumm, schief
cross-eyed, Silberblick
as the crow flies, Luftlinie
cry, Wasser
cuddle, schmusen
off the cuff, Stegreif
cultivate someone, halten
culture, Niveau
cunning, Raffinesse
currently, laufen
customer, Patron
cut, Schnitt
   of gem, Schliff
   off, abschneiden
cute, goldig

D

daft, meschugge, toll
damage, Blechschaden
dandruff, Schuppe
dangerous driver, Geisterfahrer
dare say, meinen
dash of . . . , Schuß
dead drunk, sternhagelvoll
debt, Schuld
   collecting agency, Inkassobüro
debunk, Unterhosen
deceive, aufsitzen, Dunst,
   täuschen
decline, husten
definite, bestimmt
deliberately, extra
delicate, delikat
delightful, reizen

demonstrate, vormachen
denial, Gegendarstellung
department store, Kaufhaus
depressed, niedergeschlagen
deterioration, verschludern
dialect, Mundart
diaphanous, duftig
die, verschieden, Zeit
diet, Nulldiät
different, anders, verschieden
difficult, delikat, fallen, schwer
difficulties, Schneider
digs (lodgings), Bude
dim, Mattscheibe
din, Krach
dirty, dreckig, Gammler
disappeared, weg
disappoint(ed), nachsehen
discretion, diskret
disgusting, Zustand
dishwater, Plürre
disillusioned, Zahn
disinterested, interessieren
dislike, fressen, stehen, stoßen
distinguish, ausmachen
distracted, Gedanke
distress, Not
diverge, Art
diverted, Gedanke
divorced, Leute
dizzy, toll
doctor, Arzt
dodge, kneifen
domestic science, Frikadellenakademie, Puddingabitur
don, Akademiker
donate, spenden, stiftengehen
done for, aufgeschmissen, erledigen, futsch, verraten
doss house, Penne
double-faced, fuffzig
doubtful, problematisch
downright, ausmachen
draw dole, stempeln
dress up, Putzfrau
drink, lumpen
drinking, süffig
   hours, Polizei
   place, Lokal
drive, fahren, fort
   silly, meschugge, weich
drop off (sleep), Nickerchen
drug store, Drogerie

drunk, blau, duhn, intus
dubious, problematisch
dull, Muffel
duration, Dauer
during, übermorgen

E

ear, Löffel, Ohr
earnings, Brot
easy, fallen, leicht
eat, drücken, fressen, stärken,
   verzehren
ecological, Umweltschutz
education, zweiter
egg-head, lehren
   whisk, Schneebesen
electric current, Strom
electric shock, Schlag
emergency, Not, Behandlung
employee, anstellen, Leute
empty stomach, Magen
empty talk, schmusen
enclosure, Anlage
endure, bieten
enjoy, bekommen, wohl
enough, erst, lang, langen,
   reichen, zum
enquire, erkundigen
entertain, Unterhalt
enthusiasm, Hand
entry, Fahrt
equal, egal, gleich
err, irren
error, Irrtum
escapade, Seitensprung
escape velocity, Fluchtgeschwindigkeit
eternal, leid
etiquette, Ton
evening, Nacht
every, alle
evident, klar
not exactly, gerade
examine, prüfen
exceedingly, ungemein
excellent, Bilderbuch; **(of wine)**
   süffig
except, auf, außer
excessive, Heide
exchange, Umtausch
excite, reizen, spannen
excitement (nervous), Rage

excursion, Tour
excuse, verzeihen
exorbitant, Pfeffer
extract (tooth), Zahn
extremely, Maß, ungemein
extrovert(ed), kontaktarm

F

fag, Kippe
fair, englische Art
fall apart, Leim
   for, Leim
falling off, Rückgang
far, weit
   go too far, Bogen, Kirche,
     Maß, reichen
   from, lang
fast colours, echt
fasting, Heilfasten
fault, Schuld
favour, gefällig
feature, Note
fed up, bedienen, Hals, langen,
   leid
feed, Futter
feel, fühlen, Gefühl, Lust
female (animal), Mann
few, letzt, mal
fifty-fifty, halb
file cover, Leitzordner
film (trashy), Heimatschnulze
find, auftreiben
   fault, Kritik
   room for, unterbringen
finished, erledigen, fertig,
   vorbel
fire, Brand, Feuer
firm, Aktie
first-aid, erst
   shot, Anhieb
fishy, spanisch
fit, passen
fix, in a, Patsche
flat, Apartment
flatly, rundweg
flattered, gebauchpinselt
fleece, ausnehmen
fleeting, flüchtig
flipper, Flosse
flop (failure), daneben
flustered, fisselig
fly-over, Überführung

follow, nachsehen
fool, halt, Hans, Heini
  to fool, drankriegen
foot, on, laufen
football pool, Toto
forbid, verbieten
foremost, vorerst
forged banknote, Blüte
forget, lassen, verschwitzen
forthcoming, nah
fortitude, fassen
foundation garments, Mieder
French leave, drücken
fresh (impudent), frech
friend, bekannt
friendly, freundlich
from, ab, lang
front, Aushängeschild
fruit (bad), faul
  juice, Most
fun, machen
  fair, Jahrmarkt, Kirmes
funny, gelungen, Lust
furious, geladen
furnish, einrichten
fuss, aufheben, Theater,
  Umstand
fussy, pingelig
future, Morgen

G

gadget, Schikane
game, Partie
gang, Band
gaping, sperrangelweit
gaudy, Fahne, Knall
generous, spenden
genial, freundlich
gentlemanly, dämlich
get, bekommen, besorgen,
  kommen, kriegen
  by, auskommen
  hold of, auftreiben
  on, auskommen
  ready, machen
  rid of, ausbooten, los, Mann
  started, machen
get-up (outfit), aufziehen
ghost (TV), Geisterbild
  writer, Neger
gibberish, Kohlen
giddy, toll

gift, Drachenfutter
gin, klar
girl, Ding, Zahn
give a hand, packen
  a piece of one's mind,
  Bescheid
  up, aufgeben, einpacken, nah
glance round, umgucken
glass, Stein
  of . . . , Schoppen
glue, Leim, Alleskleber
go, fahren, fort, gehen
  ahead and . . . , mal
  bad, vergammeln
  down well, ankommen
  like clockwork, klappen
  to hell, Pfeffer
  too far, Bogen, Kirche, Maß,
  reichen
  in one go, Schlag
gobble, Futter
go-getter, drauf
goings on, treiben
gold(en), goldig
gone, durch, vorbei, Teufel,
  weg
good, grün, gut
  appetite, Mahlzeit
  at, FF, Kanone
  -bye, wohl
  fortune, Glück
  heavens!, ach, fressen
  natured, freundlich
  old . . . , Tante Emma
  selling line, Schlager
goose pimples, bekommen
gossip, Kaffeekränzchen,
  Tratsch
government building, Beamtensilo
grab, packen
grasp, fassen, zugreifen
grass widow(er), grün,
  Strohwitwer
gratis, Nulltarif
gratuitous, umsonst
great at, groß
greatness, Format
greet, begrüßen
greeting, Gruß
grinding, Schliff
gripe, Maul

grounds (reasons), verwaltungstechnisch
grown-up, groß
guess, tippen
guide, führen
guilty, Schuld
guitar, Bettlerharfe

H

habit, Sitte
hackneyed, Kamelle
hairdrier, Föhn
half, halb
  a mind, Lust
hall, Flur
ham actor, Schmiere
hand, Hand, Flosse
  in, aufgeben
  over, übergeben
handkerchief (paper), Tempotaschentuch
handle, umspringen
handy, gebrauchen
hang (fit, clothes), sitzen
  get the hang of, weghaben
hapless, ausmachen
happen, geschehen, kommen, vorkommen
happy, freuen, Glück
hard times, Zuckerlecken
hardly, schwer
have in mind, Auge
head waiter, Ober
headache, bekommen, Wetterschmerzen
health (foods), Reformhaus
  resort, Kurort
heart beat, Herzschlag
  failure, Herzschlag
heat-resistant glass, Jenaer Glas
help, leisten, packen
  oneself, zugreifen
helpful, gefällig
hen party, Kaffeekränzchen
here, her
hesitation, her
hiding (good), dreschen
high, hoch
  (drunk), intus
  society, zehntausend
  spot, Clou
  time, Eisenbahn

hinge on, abhängen
hippy, Gammler
hit, Knüller, Schlager, treffen
  the sack, Klappe
hold, halten
  brief for, Schutz
  one's own, Mann
homely cooking, Mittagstisch
homosexual, schwül
honeymoon, Flitterwochen
hooligan, halb
hope for, verspitzen
hopeless case, Hopfen
horror film, Gruselfilm
hospital, Krankenhaus
hospitality, Aufnahme
host, Schwarm
hostess, Gesellschafterin, Sandlerin
hour, Lektion, Stunde
howl, heulen
human being, Mensch
humbug, vormachen
hunger, Hunger, Kohldampf
hurry, Eile, immer, machen

I

ice-cream parlour, Eisdiele
idea, Ahnung, Einfall, Gedanke
  (big), Einfall
identity papers, Ausweis
ignore, links, übergehen
ill, Nase
  at ease, fühlen
illegal, krumm, schief, schwarz
imbecile, dämlich
immediately, stehen
immersion heater, Tauchsieder
important, haben
impossible, Ding
imprisonment, Knast
improve, machen, verballhornen
impudent, frech
in, drin
inclusive, Endpreis
indeed, freilich
indifferent, egal
infatuated, verknallt, Schwarm
infected, schlimm
information, Bescheid, beschlagen

infuriate, Palme
infuriating, an, -wesen
ingratiate, Kind
inhuman, Mensch
in-patient, Behandlung
insane, irr
insatiable, Hals
insert, einwerfen, praktizieren
inside out, links
intend, meinen
intensive care, Intensivstation
intention, Absicht
interest, interessieren
interrogation, Zange
intimate, Intimsphäre
introvert(ed), kontaktarm
investment, Anlage
invitation, liebenswürdig
irritate, reizen
isolated, Flur
itch, jucken

J

Jack Robinson, ruck-zuck
jilt, sitzen
jittery, fisselig
job, leisten
joke, Jux, machen, Witz
josh, frotzeln
journalist, Schmock
juice, Saft
jump, springen, Sprung
  at, reißen
  for joy, Decke
just, gerade, wie

K

keep, aufheben, halten, leisten
  an eye on, Auge
  up to date, laufen
key (key-word etc.), Stich
kick up a row, Krach
kill, umlegen
kind, freundlich, liebenswürdig
  of, Art, irgend
knock down, ausknocken
know, Ahnung, bekannt,
  kennen, wissen
know-all, Naseweis
knowledge, Kenntnis

L

ladder, Laufmasche
ladylike, dämlich
laid up, Nase
last penny, Heller
  straw, hoch
  time, mal
  train or bus, Lumpensammler
late developer, Spätentwickler
later, drauf
lavatory, Örtchen, W.C.
lay-about, Rumtreiber
lead (metal), Blei
leather shorts, Krachledernen
leave in the lurch, sitzen,
  verlassen
  off, lassen
lecture, Kolleg
leg, Bien, Haxe
leisure wear, Räuberzivil
lend, pumpen
lenient, nachsehen
lesson, Lehre, Lektion, Stunde
let, lassen, los
letter, Brief, Buchstabe
  box, Briefkasten
level crossing, Überführung
licence (driving), Ausweis
  plate, Nummernschild
lie, liegen
  (untruth), Kohlen
  down, umlegen
lift, aufziehen, aufheben
light (digestible), bekommen
light-shunning, Licht
limit, hoch
limousine, Straßenkreuzer
lining, Futter
listen, hören, Löffel
literal(ly), Buchstabe
live (grand style), Fuß
livelihood, Unterhalt
liven up, unsicher
living, auskommen
load, Last
loan, Anschaffungsdarlehen,
  Kleinkredit
lollipop, Dauerlutscher
long shot, fehlen
  time, lang
look, aussehen, Geltung,
  gucken, Note

after, kümmern
at, ansehen
for (up), nachsehen, suchen
forward to, freuen
good (right), Geltung
round, dienen
loose, los
lorry driver, Rasthaus
lose, fortkommen
way, irren, verfranzen
weight, abspecken
loss, Schlag
at a loss, Bescheid, fallen
lost, fortkommen, futsch, kommen, Teufel, verschüttgehen,
wegkommen
lost property office, Fundbüro
lot, ziemlich, -zig
(of money), Kasse, Stange
lots and lots, rauh
love, be in, verknallt
affair, Verhältnis
lover, Lebensgefährte
luck, Hals, Glück
lucky, Glück, gut, Hans
luscious, duftig

M

mad, meschugge, toll
made to order, Maß
magnifying-glass, Zeitlupentempo
main event, Clou
mains, Leitung
maintain, Unterhalt
make difference, machen
do with, auskommen
ends meet, Decke
fool of, blamieren, drankriegen
fun of, aufziehen, Lust
fuss, anstellen
head or tail of, klug, schlau
mistake, irren, Mist
off, Staub
up, zurechtmachen
up to, machen
male (animal), Mann
malingerer, faul
maltreat, traktieren
manage, auskommen, hinkriegen, packen, schaffen

management, Direktion,
Leitung
manner (way), Art
manners, Anstand, Kinderstube, Knigge, Schliff
map, Karte
margin, Rand
marks, Note
marry well, Partie
master clock, Normaluhr
matching (not), egal
mate, Kumpel
maternity clothes, Umstand
matron, Schwester
matter, ausmachen, Fall,
machen, Sache
meal, Mahlzeit
(cold), kalt
mean, heißen, meinen
(ungenerous), kleinlich,
popelig, schorel
(vicious), gemein
to, Absicht
meet, begegnen, treffen
mental hospital, Klaps
mention, Rand, Ursache
menu, Magenfahrplan
mere(ly), bloß, ledig
mess, Dreck, heiter
microphone, Abhörgerät
middle of the night, Zeit
mildly, gelinde
milk bar, Eisdiele
mind, ausmachen, Jacke,
machen
(beware), stoßen
out of one's mind, Trost
misappropriate, vergreifen
misbehave, daneben, Rolle
miscalculate, irren
misgiving, Ahnung
mishap, Panne
mislaid, weg
mislay, fortkommen, verschludern
to miss, vermissen, zugreifen
be mistaken, irren, täuschen
misted over, beschlagen
mock, veräppeln
molest, Last
at the moment, Zeit
for the moment, vorerst
mono-rail, Alwegbahn

more, noch
morning, früh, Morgen
slow motion, Zeitlupentempo
motor bike, Feuerstuhl
move over, up, rücken
much (very), doll
mug, Stein
mystery, schleierhaft

N

naked (stark), splitterfasernackt
name, heißen
nap, Nickerchen
narrow-minded, kleinlich
nation, Leute
near-miss, gefährliche
to neck, schmusen
neglect, übergehen
nerve, Nerv
neurosis, Aktualneurose
never mind, machen
new admission, Neuzugang
new-fangled, neumodisch
news, Kamelle, neu
newspapers, Generalanzeige-
  presse
next, acht, anders, nah
next door, Tür
nice, recht, schön
night-cap, Schlafmütze
no matter, egal
non-iron, bügelarm
non-proliferation, Atomsperrvertrag
nonsense, Kohlen, Quatsch,
  schmusen
nosh, naschen
note, Kenntnis, Note, Notiz
noteworthy, merkwürdig
nothing doing, Essig, Pustekuchen
notice, Notiz
notion, Ahnung, Einfall
novel, Roman
novelette (trashy), Groschenroman
novelty, neu
now or never, Wurst
nudge, anstoßen, Puff
nuisance, Landplage
numbers game, Lotto
nurse, Diakonisse, Schwester

O

objection, Reklame
obliging, gefällig
obscene literature, Schund
obstetrician, Arzt
occasional table, Beistelltisch
occur, Einfall
odds and ends, Klamotten
off (bad), Stich
off-chance, Geratewohl, Glück
off-day, schief
offend, krumm, Leberwurst,
  nah, stoßen
officialese, Kanzleideutsch
oil shortage, Ölverknappung
old, Eisen, oll
on, drauf, laufen
  the spot, Ort
  the move, Achse
once, einmal, mal
only, los, nur
onwards, ab
open-handed, spenden
operator, smooth, dick
opinion, meinen
oppressive, schwül
order, bestellen, heißen
ordinary, gewöhnlich
orphan, Waisenknabe
other day, neu
out, auswärts, her
  of, außer
  of order, außer
  of place, deplaciert
out-distance, abhängen
outlive, überleben
out-of-date, überholen, überleben
out-patient, Behandlung
outward, auswärts
over-eating, Edelfreßwelle,
  Mord
overhear, überhören
overlook, nachsehen, übersehen
over-stimulation,
  Reizüberflutung
overtake, überholen
owe, Schuld

P

pack, packen
  up, einpacken

pub, kneippen
public, öffentlich
  opinion, Meinung
  telephone, öffentlich
puerile, Kind
pull off a job, Ding
  someone's leg, aufziehen,
    Schippe, veräppeln
pullover, Pulli
pump, pumpen
  (for information), fühlen
punch-up, Hand
purchase, Kauf
purge, entschlacken
on purpose, Absicht, extra,
  ungefähr
push, drücken, Puff, stoßen
  around, umspringen
pusher, Schieber
pussy-footing, leise
put, stecken, stellen

Q

quality, good, dankbar, Format
quarrel, Krach
questionable, problematisch
questionnaire, Bogen
queue, anstellen, Reihe
quick, fix, flott, Zack
  on the uptake, kapieren
quickly, heute
be quiet, irr
quilt, Decke
quite, einigermaßen

R

race, Art
racketeer, Schieber
rag, Lappen
rag-and-bone man, Lumpensammler
rage, Rage, weiß, Wetter,
  Zustand
random, Geratewohl
rather, reichlich
ready, fertig, fix,
  zurechtmachen
real, direkt
realize, klar
really, ach, Gott, meinen, so

reason, Ursache
reasonable, hören
rebellious, aufmüpfig
receptionist, Sprechstunde
recession, antizyklische
reckless, leicht
reckon, tippen
recording, Band
refinements, Raffinesse
refreshment, stärken
register, eintragen
regular, Stamm
rehearsal, Probe
rely on, verlassen
remarkable, merkwürdig
remember, lassen, merken
render, fassen
beyond repair, Eimer
repay, vergelten
reproach, Zigarre
reputation, Rufmord
residence permit, Aufenthaltsgenehmigung
restore, sanieren
retarded, Spätzündung
rethink, umdenken
rewarding, lohnen
ribbon, Band
rid, los, Mann
right, machen, recht, stimmen
  the right people, Beziehung
ring (bell), ausschellen, Glocke
risk, Kragen
road hog, Landstraßenschreck
off one's rocker, Knall
roll, Brot, Rolle, Semmel
room and board, Pension,
  Station
rough, Puff, rauh
round the bend, Klaps
rubbish, Quatsch, Schund,
  Sperrmüll
rugged, rauh
ruined, Eimer, Teufel
run, laufen
  across (meet), begegnen
running, hintereinander
rush hour, Hauptverkehrszeit
rush-hour traffic, Berufsverkehr

S

sack (someone), schassen

talk, Quatsch, Rede
  big, Spucke
be talked into, breit
tall story, Latein
tangled, filzen
tape recorder, Band
taste, kosten, schmecken
tavern, kneippen
teach, lehren, Lektion
tease, Pflaume
telegenic, telegen
telephone, Quasselstrippe
television, Pantoffelkino
  screen, Mattscheibe
  success, Straßenfeger
tell, heißen, sagen
  (recognize), ansehen
tense, spannen
tenterhooks, Kohlen
test, Probe, Warentest
thank, vergelten
thankful, dankbar
that's that, Traum
theatre, Theater
thief, Ganove
thingumibob, Ding
thirst, Brand, Hunger
three-piece, Klubgarnitur
thriller, Krimi
through (finished), Laufpaß
thrust, Stich
on tick, pumpen
ticket inspector, Probemann
ticking off, Gardine
tidy, ordentlich
tie, Band
time, mal, Zeit
  do time, Knast
  in time, recht
times, mal
tip, Tip, Trinkgeld
tipsy, beschwipst
tiro, Waisenknabe
toast (drink), anstoßen
toehold, Fuß
toilet bag, Kulturbeutel
Tom, Dick and Harry, Hinz
to-morrow, früh, Morgen
  -night, Nacht
tommyrot, Mist
topic, Thema
towards, her
town plan, Karte

tracing service, Suchdienst
trade union, Gewerkschaft
tramp, Penne, tippeln, Stadtstreicher, Trampel
transference, Überführung
translate, fassen
transport, Überführung
trash(y), Kitsch, Schnulze
treat, traktieren, umspringen
treatment, Behandlung
tremendously, unheimlich
trick, Kunst, Winkel
tried, prüfen
trimmings, dran
trip (to country), grün
tripe, Quatsch
triviality, Dreck
trollop, Schickse
trotter, Haxe
trouble, Last, Not, Teufel,
  Umstand
the honest truth, ungelogen
try, kosten, Probe
tube, Röhre
tune, Ohrwurm
turn, Reihe
  in, klappen
  out, Geratewohl
twaddle, Quatsch
twitter, zwitschern
type, tippen
typical, Buch, echt
typist, tippen

U

umbrella, Knirps
umpteen, -zig
uncanny, unheimlich
uncertain, problematisch,
  unsicher
underpants, Unterhosen
underpass, Überführung
understand, Bahnhof, kapieren,
  kennen, fressen, Vers
undo, Rückgang
undress, frei
unfairness, Schmu
unheard of, unerhört
unilateral, Alleingang
uninterested, interessieren
unique, einmal
university, Gesamthochschule

unquestioning, unbedingt
unsaleable article, Ladenhüter
untidy, verschludern
untruth, weismachen
unusual, ausgefallen
up, what is, los
upside down, stellen
slow on the uptake, Spät-
  zündung
used up, alle

V

vagabond, tippeln
vain attempt, Wasser
value added tax,
  Mehrwertsteuer
various, verschieden
very, ach
  same, noch
viaduct, Überführung
vice squad, Sitte
vicinity, nah
village, Ort
violate, vergreifen
voice, Stimme
volume, Band
voluntarily, Stück
vomit, übergeben
voter, Stimme
vulgar, gewöhnlich

W

waiter, Ober
walk, laufen
wangle, Lotse
ward, Station
  sister, Schwester
warm, mollig
washable, lavabel
wasp-waist, Wespentaille
watch out, aufpassen
way, Art
  lose the way, irren, verfranzen
wedding (shotgun), Mußehe
week, acht

weight-reducing, Appetitzügler
welcome, Bahnhof, begrüßen
well, also, halt, wohl
  done (meat), durch
  -fed, Futter
Western (story), Groschenroman
wet-blanket, Leberwurst
what, für, was, welch
whatever, was
whatsitsname, Ding
when, wann, wie
wherever, immer, wohl
wicked, gemein
wind (warm), Föhn
wind up, aufziehen
wine, Glühwein, Wein
wit, Witz
wits' end, Latein
women's libber, Emanze
wonder, nur, spannen
wonderful, dämlich, einmal,
  Wolke
wood, touch, unberufen
work, klappen, machen,
  schaffen
working-order, Schuß
worn-out, oll
worry, Gedanke, kümmern, Lot
worse, Bein
wrap up, einpacken
wretched, hausen
writing materials, Kolleg
wrong, be, irren, Irrtum,
  täuschen
wrong, go, Ahnung, daneben,
  schief
wrong track, be on the, Holz
wrong with, fehlen

Y

yarn, Latein
year (of birth, production),
  Jahrgang
yes, doch, Eisen
yobbo, halb
young, grün